One Miracle at a Time

··

Getting Help for a Child with a Disability

IRVING R. DICKMAN
with Dr. Sol Gordon

··

A FIRESIDE BOOK
Published by Simon & Schuster
New York London Toronto Sydney
Tokyo Singapore

FIRESIDE
Simon & Schuster Building
Rockefeller Center
1230 Avenue of the Americas
New York, New York 10020

Library of Congress Cataloging-in-Publication Data
Dickman, Irving R.
One miracle at a time : getting help for a child with a disability/
Irving R. Dickman with Sol Gordon. — 1st Fireside rev. ed.
p. cm.
"A Fireside book."
Includes index.
1. Handicapped children — United States.   2. Handicapped children —
United States — Family relationships.   3. Parents of handicapped
children — United States.   4. Handicapped children — United States —
Information services — Directories.   I. Gordon, Sol, date —
II. Title.   III. Title: 1 miracle at a time.
HV888.5.D54   1993
649'.151 — dc20   92-34040
CIP

ISBN 0-671-78934-1

To my wife

and all the other parents

and caregivers

Contents

Foreword

I think that in my head I've been working on this book for over twenty-five years: ever since I went looking for a book like it and couldn't find it, when my wife and I were a couple of stunned and bewildered parents without any information on where to look for help for *our* son.

What actually got me to write it—with my friend Dr. Sol Gordon (whose special expertise in the area of sexuality education is offered in Chapter 14)—was when, in the course of researching another writing project, my discussions made me realize that despite all the excellent books now available on coping with disabilities many parents are *still* looking for the same book we couldn't find, "a book about how things *are,* not how they're supposed to be," as the mother of a child with brain damage put it.

To make it that kind of book, we set out to find those who are the experts on "how things are"—parents who have "been there"—to ask them to share their experiences and the lessons they have learned with other parents (and also with grandparents, siblings, friends of parents, and professionals concerned about children with disabilities, but primarily with parents).

Hundreds of mothers and fathers agreed to participate, including some who were reluctant to have their names used (and we respected their wishes). Many did so because they felt that they were already part of a de facto parent support group: "There have always been people here for me, and I feel a very strong commitment to other parents," the mother of a baby with spina bifida said; and the mother of two young men with visual impairments added that "I am anxious to share with others the experiences we have dealt with. I feel that along with other parents we have learned much—and the learning should be shared, to make the path easier and quicker for others who must make the journey."

Such experiences shaped this book: what is not quoted directly is nevertheless almost wholly based on what parents said. Reading and hearing their comments were a revelation and an education: Every parent is an expert on some aspect of getting help for a child who has a disability, and often on more than one aspect. For that reason, their collective experience provides a matchless view of the realities with which families have to deal, the way they feel, the way they succeeded in finding help: what works and what doesn't. It is our regret that we were unable to quote all their comments, but we thank all who assisted us, and we hope we have done justice to their contributions.

We want also to acknowledge with gratitude the aid of the many parent and disability groups* and concerned individuals, professionals as well as parents, who helped to circulate our questionnaire and provided us with additional materials. But special thanks for special help is owed to the National Down Syndrome Congress (and Diane M. Crutcher and Emily Kingsley); National Information Center for Handicapped Children and Youth (and Patty McGill Smith); New Jersey Self-Help Clearinghouse (and Edward J. Madara and Abbie Meese); March of Dimes Birth Defects Foundation (and Dick Leavitt); PACER, the Parent Advocacy Coalition for Educational Rights (and Paula F. Goldberg); Parentele (and Pat Koerber); The Association for Persons with Severe Handicaps, TASH (and Liz Lindley and Elli Dumont); United Cerebral Palsy Associations (and Rachel Warren, Ernie Weinreich and Rosemary Addarich); and Westchester Self-Help Clearinghouse Project Time Out (and Dr. Leslie Borck and Barbara MacInnes).

Something we had not anticipated when we began our work

*See Appendix B and Appendix C.

was the astonishing number of parents who expressed their gratitude to us for undertaking the book. "We should be thanking *you* for the opportunity to express our feelings and opinions," the divorced mother of a child with Down syndrome wrote. "If you are surprised at the volume of responses, possibly it is because many of us have not been treated as though our opinion had value. If you see pain in that statement, believe it!"

Parents insist again and again that that kind of pain does not *have* to be: It is not simply part of the package. As a mother named Marge Mann testifies, much of the "time and tears and energy" her son cost her were not the inevitable and inescapable consequences of her having borne a child with a disability; rather they were necessary to overcome the man- and system-made hurdles to get the help he needed.

That so many families agreed to describe their own painful experiences speaks of the desire to help other parents avoid at least some of the unnecessary agonies, because it is parents, who have themselves faced and overcome those obstacles, who understand most clearly why parents *must* persist. Like Marge Mann, they have no choice: "I have to speak for him," she says, "because he cannot speak for himself."

Irving R. Dickman
1985

The eight years since *Miracle* first appeared have brought some vitally needed benefits for children and young people with disabilities. Notable have been successful legislative efforts to plug the loopholes in PL 94-142 and increase its scope, through mandated services for three-to-five-year-olds, through outreach to newborns, and through reinforced transition programs for young graduates and school-leavers. A start has been made toward the full inclusion of children with severe and multiple disabilities in regular classes in neighborhood schools as a step toward eventual inclusion in the community at large. Added impetus is being given to such acceptance by assistive communication technology, only recently beginning to demonstrate its potential as an educational tool and social equalizer for children with cognitive as well as physical disabilities.

Yet many parents describe the same problems in the nineties as others faced in the seventies and eighties. One need has, in fact, increased: As medicine and science are increasingly able to keep alive newborns with formerly fatal birth defects, their parents often face incredible financial burdens because of an inadequate health care system. "I feel like my baby got caught in a machine," one anguished mother cries out, "and I've gotten no help from the system."

Clearly the speed of change is increasing, thanks not only to PL 94-142 but also to the growing awareness of parents and the increasing empowerment of the child-disability movement. That manifests itself in the new material that has been added to this edition of *Miracle*. I am grateful to the many parents and parent advocates who agreed to speak to me; but special thanks are owed to such parent leaders and agents of change as Patricia Smith, now head of the National Parent Network on Disabilities and NPND's Administrative Assistant, Sandy Trujillo; Marge and Paula Goldberg, Co-Directors, and the staff and parents of PACER in Minneapolis; Florene Poyadue, CEO, and the people at Parents Helping Parents in San Jose, California; and Diana Cuthbertson, Executive Director of SPAN, New Jersey's Statewide Parent Advocacy Network. I hope I have done justice to their contributions. I owe thanks also to Jane Coleman, Director of Nursing Education, Children's Specialized Hospital, Mountainside, N.J.; and Lillian Tepper, RN, for their help in clarifying much of the medical terminology in the newer material; and not least to Sheridan Hay, my editor, for her invariable patience and her many valuable comments and suggestions.

I.R.D.
1993

1
....

"Tell Parents to Believe in Miracles"
"Vegetables" and Decisions

That day in April seemed to Susan and Tim Hamilton the end of their world. Having lost a six-year-old daughter two years earlier in an auto accident, and then a premature baby a year later after only twelve hours, they learned on that traumatic April day that their son Jody had been born with spina bifida, a severe spinal column defect.

Jody was rushed by ambulance from their small Georgia town to an Atlanta children's hospital. There he was examined by two neurosurgeons, a urologist, and an orthopedist. "We were told Jody would be a vegetable, that he was deaf and blind. The neurosurgeons strongly recommended that we not treat him, that it would be better to allow him to die."

The boy would not live long in any case, the specialists indicated, and the Hamiltons were so stunned by the prognosis that they immediately agreed to place him into a Georgia retardation center. "Following so soon after our travail, we felt that we could not bring him home and watch him die."

But somehow the baby kept surviving, and even though the Hamiltons felt unable to care for him at home because of all their family tragedies, after a time they did begin to bring him home on weekends. "It was a time of serious mental and emotional trauma for all the members of the family," Susan Hamilton recalls. "We finally began to realize that we were trying hard not to love Jody, because we were still so frightened that he would die. But when Jody was eighteen months old, we realized that we did love him dearly and felt strong enough to take the chance and bring him home permanently."

There would still be times when the Hamiltons were again frightened that Jody would die, but by the time he was four he was scooting around in a new red wheelchair: "He talks to everyone he meets, and his brown eyes and red hair make him a very appealing little fellow." And when he was six, he was already going to a regular public school, where he was mainstreamed for reading and other subjects. The "vegetable" was enjoying swimming and horseback riding by then, and according to his mother, the biggest problem was trying to keep him in the house.

"As I look back to the dark days at the time of his birth," Susan Hamilton says now, "I am angry. No one told us he could be so like other children. Nobody said we didn't need M.D. degrees to care for him. No one told us that he could even pick up his head, or smile, or recognize his family.

"I would tell all new parents of children with permanent disabilities not to give up hope: at birth, no one can say what a child will or will not be able to be or to do." Yet clearly it was those "dark days" and the chilling predictions that make the present so rewarding: "When a child that you were told was deaf, blind, and profoundly retarded looks up and says 'Mama,' you have witnessed a miracle."

Sitting up, scooting around, talking, saying "Mama": To others these might seem like very small miracles indeed. But to parents of children with severe disabilities, each such achievement brings a special joy that other parents experience much less often, if ever. With other youngsters, these events just happen. With children who have special needs, each accomplishment is a milestone to be celebrated. And nearly always parents—with others—have helped to make it happen.

In 1984 Terrie Pearman, living in a small Florida community, was still not ready to believe in miracles, perhaps because her daughter, who has multiple disabilities, was only two.

But, defying all the pessimistic predictions, this is what had already happened to Kelly:

When she was born, she was barely living. The doctors showed doubt that she would survive the first week of life; but after a month in the intensive care unit, she came home. She has several disabilities, including cerebral palsy. She has been diagnosed as totally deaf, she has a seizure disorder and is microcephalic.

At six months, we took her back for a follow-up visit with a neurologist. She stated that Kelly would never be able to sit, roll over, walk, or amount to a "full individual." Her advice was nothing other than "take your baby home." I totally disregarded her. We have started Kelly on extensive therapy and gone further with her hearing (she is getting hearing aids). Through extensive physical therapy Kelly can track objects and hold a rattle.

We are doing all we can for her; we try not to miss any avenue of help. We grow to love her more each day. I find it hard to believe at this point, but Kelly will be starting preschool when she is three.

By 1992, Kelly, now ten, was in a special class for children with severe and multiple disabilities in a regular school. When her parents went to enroll her in 1986, they were fortunate to get in at the beginning of a pilot program the public school system was then initiating. Kelly was one of the initial group of five youngsters selected ("because of her personality," Terrie Pearman adds). The program has since been expanded to several classes in a number of schools.

Kelly is still nonverbal, and has had several surgeries over the years. But, says her mother,

With the way the school has worked with her, she can now help to feed herself. That may seem like a small thing, but about three years ago my husband and I realized that we shouldn't set too high expectations for her, but be pleased with what we have. Kelly has taught us what really matters: She is a happy kid, and she has taught us patience.

Not a Child, But a "Vegetable"

Almost always progress like this has gone against the odds, achieved, not infrequently, after the mother has been told that what she is cradling in her arms or cuddling in her lap is not a child, but a "vegetable." It is a word that has a long-standing history as a shorthand buzz word for a lot of lengthy medical explanations.

In Wisconsin, more than twenty years ago, Ethel Clough recalls,

> I was told that my daughter had Down syndrome when she was two days old. The pediatrician who came to see me told me to "sign on the dotted line, and you'll never have to see her again. She'll be nothing but a vegetable; she'll never walk or talk, ride a bike, or swing on a swing. Please sign here." But the doctor who delivered Mary disagreed and said he thought I'd be sorry if I did that . . . and I *knew* the doctor was right. Mary was in school at age three. During her school years she was mainstreamed, and it worked very well for her. She was accepted, and she graduated at age twenty-one. She is now working in a child care training program in the same nursery school where she started at age three. She can read, write, and do simple math, and I believe she could do more.

After twenty years, all the details are still clear. They are to every parent. It is the one moment no parent to whom it has ever happened ever forgets.

Finding Out

There never is a good way to find out that a child has a birth defect. But some of the bad ways are considerably worse than others: the pediatrician who came to the mother's hospital room and, from the doorway, no closer, blurted out that her daughter was a "mongoloid"; the mimeographed form from the hospital, with an insert in the middle, signed by the physician: "Your daughter has brain damage"; the telephone call, an anonymous voice from the hospital, saying that the baby was found to have mental retardation; the hospital bill with the diagnosis of cerebral palsy— up to then the parents had had no inkling that anything was wrong.

Among the many tales, though, Linda Lampman's story is something special. The Lampmans lived in a small Pennsylvania town. When their daughter Amanda began to have seizures at two months old, they took her to a Philadelphia hospital. She spent four days there going through a battery of tests. During all that time, no one in the hospital gave the parents any indication of what they were hunting for, or of what might be wrong.

On Thanksgiving Day we were still waiting to hear. No doctor came, and I had promised to come home for dinner, so we started to leave. In the lobby, the doctor came up to us and said: "I'm glad I ran into you. We have the results of the tests. Your daughter has severe brain damage and will never do anything more than she is doing now. Have a good Thanksgiving and we will talk more tomorrow."

I think I went into shock, for all I said was "Goodbye, see you tomorrow" and left with my husband. Later I fell totally apart. The next morning when I went back I overheard the same doctor telling the resident, "If *it* were mine, I'd put *it* away." With that, I totally freaked out. I physically attacked the doctor and had to be sedated.

Prescription: "Put Baby Away"

It is rare to find a pediatrician or a physician so unthinking as to call a baby born with a disability "it," but the advice to "put the baby away" may seem to parents just as dehumanizing. Until not too long ago, infants with Down syndrome in particular were treated as "throwaway babies." "Advice given by the doctor: Go home and leave the baby in the hospital. They would place the baby with the state."

The mother of Mindie Crutcher, another baby with Down syndrome, was warned not to become "attached" to the little "vegetable."

But the word is by no means reserved for Down syndrome: There's Mary Ann Benka, who has cerebral palsy: "She may be a vegetable—best to put her in an institution," the doctor tossed off over his shoulder as he walked out and left the stunned parents in the room. It was a word once applied almost universally to babies having spina bifida, like Jody Hamilton, provided they even survived. Occasionally there were, and are, some small variations: When Jason Kingsley was born with Down syndrome, his parents were told there would be very little to distinguish between their son and "mashed potatoes." The kindly obstretician also suggested a way to make it easy on themselves: "Put him away and tell your friends he died."

The "diagnosis" and the "prescription" are not confined to newborns and infants. Wendy Lindley was six when she had multiple surgery following the discovery of a tumor on her neck. After the operation, same prognosis: "vegetable"; same suggestion: "Put her away."

Who can blame parents who were persuaded that "putting the baby away" was best not only for the "vegetable" but for the whole family; if people who should know called it "the right thing to do"; if it was so easy: just sign the piece of paper and the hospital would take care of the rest?

Most physicians in this situation would insist they were only being realistic. But to a great many parents, the advice comes across only as callousness, a failure to relate to parents as people, a lack of humanity or heart. It is so shocking to parents that it may in fact throw a shadow, conscious or unconscious, on all of their subsequent dealings with professionals.

Compassion Misdirected

Yet very often the "realistic" advice is given not out of heartlessness, but out of too much heart, too much humanity. Barbara North's doctor cried when he told her that her son Adam had had a stroke while he was still in the womb, between the third and sixth months of pregnancy. In a way, that was even worse because it made the pessimistic prognosis and prescription that much harder to take:

> He really shot us to the bottom. We realized later that he had done this so we would be happy if Adam ever learned *anything*. After the doctor gave us the news, he wanted to know what we wanted to do with Adam. He said if we just wanted to walk away and leave him, he would make the arrangements. But Adam was our first-born; he was very much wanted and

loved. So he said, "Take him home and love him. That's about all you can do."

That doctor might rate high marks on his humanity and compassion, but not necessarily on his crystal-gazing. Adam began going to a special preschool when he was two and a half. In many ways he is now at his right age level. "He has proved the doctors wrong," Barbara North says, very simply.

It often appears that the physician's primary compassion and concern are reserved not for the child so much as for the others in the family, parents and siblings. When Jonathan Struble was born blind, with Down syndrome and a defective heart, no one at the hospital, except the doctor, had any advice for his mother: "Vegetable—institutionalize." Otherwise, he said, the baby would destroy the family.

Jeanne Struble is a determined mother, the prime mover in a parent support group in northern New Jersey, and a redoubtable human being. Her answer was pithy and to the point: "I told him that if the baby would destroy my family, then I didn't think much of what I had raised."

"Don't Decide"

The recommendation to institutionalize infants who have Down syndrome in particular is not made automatically nearly so often as it once was. But Elizabeth Villani, a Yonkers, New York, mother who had to deal with that advice when her son was born and has since become a dedicated parent activist, advises new parents to hold off: "No decision about institutionalization should be made right away. It takes time to adjust to the shock and to absorb information about what it is like to have a retarded/handicapped child."

Many physicians nowadays are advising parents to try it: take the baby home, see how it works out. The decision to institutionalize can always be made at a later time. But in the case of her son Joseph, born with more than one problem, Ms. Villani was warned that she might be faced with another decision that was not postponable: "I was told that should he also need an operation on his intestinal tract, we could withhold permission

for the operation and he would die, and that perhaps that would
be for the best."

This is yet another aspect of what seems to be the same negative philosophy, and again it comes across to parents as extreme
insensitivity, if not inhumanity. That is especially true of the
"kindly" advice that for the infant with a severe physical impairment, "the best thing" might be to "let the baby die," even if it
was not usually posed that bluntly.

Surgery or Death

Parents, especially those whose babies were born with spina bifida,
were quite often told they had a choice: immediate surgery or the
baby's death, probably within a few days or weeks. On the one
hand, surgery and the baby's survival offered a frightening prognosis for the infant's future. On the other, the alternative was
often made to sound so easy: all the parents had to do was to do
nothing. Mrs. Henry Uszal was told it was "immediate surgery or
death" for her son.

> But I had had natural childbirth, had held my baby, and knew
> I was his mother. Regardless of what was wrong, I had a little
> boy whom I had held in my arms. What a sad thing if your
> own mother is the first one to turn her back. I had a son and
> I wanted to take him home with me. Our love for him out-
> weighed every other factor. If God had wanted him, he would
> have taken him during the surgery.

Of the many parents faced with that choice, there is no way
to tell for sure how many, what percentage, did "let it happen."
But certainly many did not, including a group of parents getting
help for their babies with spina bifida through Children's Specialized Hospital in Mountainside, New Jersey—Mrs. Uszal was
one—who had all been given the same option by physicians. Like
George and Liba Nudell:

> Our first reactions were shock and disbelief. We were so ex-
> cited about seeing the baby, and nursing the baby, that there
> was an immediate letdown. After all the emotional investment,

there was the fear that he wouldn't survive. And if he did survive, what would he be like?

I remember we were numb at first, cried a lot. The neurosurgeon told us that there was surgery which could be performed on spina bifida babies, but that if the brain had never developed, he warned us that he himself wasn't of the philosophy that you should save a baby without much of a brain. If there wasn't enough brain cortex, he personally wouldn't do the surgery, but would refer us to someone else.

They had to take Elazar in a box to another hospital for the CAT [computerized axial tomography] scan, and not having him with us, we wondered if we really had a baby. While we were waiting for the results of the CAT scan—it took some time—we had a chance to think and talk, and we decided we were going to have that surgery anyway, even if the baby had no brain.

"Baby Doe"

Whatever the choice, such dilemmas are always harrowing for the parents. They happened often enough—paradoxically, because of the successes achieved by science and technology and medicine in keeping at-risk babies alive—to lead eventually to the "Baby Doe" controversies of the early 1980s.

As early as 1979, the Spina Bifida Association of America had expressed the sentiments of many parent and advocacy organizations when it declared that it "actively encourages the early evaluation and medical/surgical treatment of every infant born with spina bifida."

In the public controversies that erupted after the first Baby Doe case in 1982 and the second in 1983, the focus was entirely on the operating table and the intensive care ward. In both cases, the parents had made their own agonized decisions not to have surgery performed, even though more than twenty families offered to adopt the first Baby Doe. But particularly in the second Baby Doe case, involving a Long Island baby born with spina bifida, the parents' personal anguish was intensified and overwhelmed in a "case" and a "cause" involving physicians; attorneys; federal and state governments; "right-to-life" organizations; parent, disability, and advocacy groups; and both state and federal courts, which, they said afterward, turned it into a "nightmare."

At one point the federal government even proposed "hotlines" in every hospital, as well as "Baby Doe squads" mobilized to respond to complaints, from anyone, that surgery or other life-saving procedures were being denied to newborn babies with severe impairments (the court threw the proposal out). The legislation that was eventually worked out in 1984 by Congress and nearly all the groups that had concerned themselves with the case, including parent and disability organizations, defined the withholding of treatment as "child abuse," and provided that such treatment is compulsory unless the infant is comatose, or, in the physicians' opinion (and that of a review committee), treatment would merely prolong the infant's dying, and would be inhumane.

Only the American Medical Association continued to object, on the ground that the law did not adequately consider the "quality of life" of babies born with a severe physical disability. Parents who had "been there" were also deeply concerned about that issue, but from a somewhat different point of view, an aspect of the baby's quality of life that the legislation had left not only unresolved but unmentioned: What happens afterward? What of the baby's—and parents'—life, *after* the hospital? (For more on this, see Chapter 10.)

"One Day at a Time"

Even if "society" were to shoulder its full financial obligation, were to accept baby saving as a continuing years-long responsibility instead of a one-shot affair by guaranteeing babies and families the care and financial assistance they require, that action would ease only the economic strain, not the psychological strain. Parents of a child with special needs will still have to cope, day after day, and to the best of their ability, with this new fact of life.

There are times when it seems to parents, especially to mothers, to be the only fact of life. It's sometimes even more consuming when the disability is mental rather than physical. On the evidence, for example, autism is one of the most perplexing and exhausting disorders for parents to struggle with.

When the Ramseys were looking for a psychologist to help them cope with their son's autism, a number of them said, in view of what the parents were going through every day, that they could not understand how the parents were taking it so well. "Parents have a hard fight from the minute they find out what is wrong with their child," Eugenia Ramsey says now. It may take time before they can come to face the problem squarely, she adds, "ready to stand and fight: to do the best they can for the child that was entrusted to their care. Whoever can, should help them to find a way to accept it, piece by piece."

"It can really be taken only one day at a time, from the first time you realize that your child is different," adds Jeanne Struble, the New Jersey mother who was once advised to institutionalize her son Jonathan, who had multiple disabilities, because he would always be a "vegetable." Now a teenager, he is attending the local high school, doing well, "and most important, he loves it and is happy." Today he represents another of those "miracles" that weren't supposed to happen, miracles that are really the sum total of many small miracles over time.

Why Parents Won't Give Up

Miracles, like Jody Hamilton and Mary Clough, are the reason parents won't give up. So is Jason Kingsley, who went from being "mashed potatoes" to handling public school in stride and appearing as an actor with his mother on "All My Children," a soap opera; came to be known to youngsters all over the country for his appearances on "Sesame Street"; and was the "star" of an hour-long segment of "The Fall Guy" in late 1984.

Another is Mary Ann Benka, who was deemed another "vegetable" because of her cerebral palsy, another to be "put into an institution." From her mother, Doris:

At fifteen months she entered a rehabilitation program, and I drove a thousand miles a month to take her to this school. At six she entered special education. . . . I received opposition in school because I felt Mary Ann could learn more. There were many sleepless nights, much crying, etc., but I *believed* in what I wanted for her, and I got it.

Today Mary Ann is working with computers in her school work. She also has an equipment room at home with duplicate computer, electric typewriter, calculator, adding machine, etc.

She uses a head pointer. Last week in school was the first time she raised her hand to say her dream was to walk.*

At thirteen she is a regular teenager—she has her laughter, tears, problems, etc., just like everyone else. I'm glad we kept our baby and brought her up to be the beautiful young lady she is today.

Another is Ginny Duncan's daughter, now nine, and diagnosed as having cerebral palsy with ataxic tendencies—a lack of muscular control—at eight months. The mother's comments are terse, almost telegraphic:

> The child disrupted our family life for two years . . . cried about fifteen hours each day . . . Mother in mourning. . . .
>
> We were advised not to search for help, such as therapy, etc., that she was brain-damaged and would only progress on her own. . . . Institutionalizing was suggested at three months, again at eight months. We rejected the idea because she was our child. . . .
>
> We set up an exercise program ourselves. We discovered she was bright and very vocal. . . . At age three, she was evaluated and placed in preschool classes. . . . Now [she is] attending regular classes. . . .

Along with the sense of accomplishment that comes through Ginny Duncan's comments is a note of realism: "I would tell parents to believe in miracles," she says, "but to take life one day at a time."

And one miracle at a time.

---

*For more on assistive technology, see Chapter 13.

2

....

"That Was Precious
Lost Time"
Getting a Diagnosis

There may be no agony for parents comparable to the shock of
learning within minutes or days of a baby's birth that this new
human being will be forever disabled, unless it is the months or
years of gnawing anxiety suffered from *not* knowing.

For Margaret Angrisano, the torture began immediately:

> Anna was ten days overdue, breech birth. She spent the first
> days of her life in intensive care. At that time I was told by
> doctors and nurses that I wasn't to be concerned; all was well;
> my child would be just fine.
>
> All during her first year I questioned numerous doctors as
> to why she had no balance, why she constantly choked at breast
> and bottle, why her milestones were so delayed, and why she
> was constantly falling back on her head. I was continually told
> not to worry: "She's just fine."

When Anna was sixteen months old, Margaret, still anxious and
spurred on by her mother's recommendation, made an appointment for the baby with a neurologist. The electroencephalogram
(EEG) and the CAT scan revealed that Anna had myoclonic epi-

lepsy, spastic/rigid cerebral palsy, and mental retardation. So much
for "She's just fine."

Nancy S., now living in Austria, recognizes that the physicians
may have been trying to spare her by holding back the "bad news."
But her overriding concern is what the delay meant to her son:

> We learned of the problem beginning at eight months, when
> our son couldn't sit up without support. A doctor suggested
> we have him looked at. In the beginning, they told us only
> that it was reflexes that must be helped to go away; they never
> mentioned "brain injury" or cerebral palsy. Not until he was
> twelve months old did we realize what the problem really was.
>
> I know that they wanted to protect us from shock and
> depression, but what happened was that I didn't take the ex-
> ercises seriously enough in the period from eight to twelve
> months, and that was precious lost time—better a hard, short
> shock and then get on with the work.

Knowing = Getting Help

It is better to *know,* even if it is a shock, so you can *do.* Only when
the problem is clear can the hunt, the long and difficult hunt for
suitable programs, begin. Timmy's parents, an Air Force family,
felt the same kind of frustration, though in their case, fortunately,
it lasted only a short time.

> When he was a month and a half old, we started noticing
> problems with his eyes and that he didn't react to his sur-
> roundings. We had him at the doctor's at the Air Force Base
> off and on for five months without anyone coming out and
> telling us what was wrong with our son. We were told during
> this time that Timmy might have allergies, that he had colic,
> but no one ever said he had brain damage. My husband and
> I knew there was something seriously wrong with him and
> could tell the doctors were not telling us everything.
>
> When Timmy was six months old we were transferred to
> a base in Arizona. The pediatrician saw us (and Timmy) as
> soon as we were settled in. He asked us if we would like to
> know what was wrong with Tim (first time anyone had asked
> us if we would like to know and if we could handle it). We

told him that we wanted to know what Tim's problems were, no matter how bad, because once we knew what was wrong with him we could get help for him. That was our main concern.

It turned out that Tim had microcephaly (an abnormally small head) and cerebral palsy, as well as mental retardation.

When the doctor told us, he couldn't believe how well we accepted the diagnosis. All I can say is that it was such a relief to have someone finally just come out and say what we had feared for so long! We felt that now we could move ahead and do the best we could for Timmy.

There is no way of knowing, but if that first doctor balked at spelling out the nature of Timmy's disabilities out of real concern for the parents and how well they would take it, he may have been underestimating how tough parents can be when they have to be. Like other parents, this couple was concerned for their child: they "took it" when they had to. (For more on early intervention programs, see Chapter 11.)

As for Timmy's parents, so it was for Karen May, whose son Sean was born with a severe form of cerebral palsy. The suspicion that something was wrong came early.

At that time, her chief worry was knowing and not knowing. Now, in retrospect, Karen May, like other parents who had the same difficulty (whether for months or for years), regrets the might-have-beens, the help not given.

When I brought my baby home, after the normal four-day stay in the hospital when he was born, I remember looking at this perfect baby they had told me I had, and I knew then that something was wrong.

I found out four years later that the nurses on the maternity floor knew, and they were angry that the doctors were not more honest with me. If only I could have known from the beginning, I could have stopped a lot of problems with Sean. I would have understood him more, and why he was not responding as my first boy had.

To Leslie Giovanniello, that kind of professional reluctance makes no sense. Fortunately, she didn't let it paralyze her. She acted.

His first pediatrician was aware that James had Down syndrome but for some unfathomable reason did not inform us. I was, however, very much concerned about his progress. When I voiced my concerns this doctor would tell me not to be upset—"third children are always lazy!"

When James turned six months old, my husband and I decided to change pediatricians. The second doctor was an angel in disguise. She spotted the problem immediately. . . . The reason I called her an angel was that she finally put an end to the unknown. The not knowing exactly what was wrong was driving me crazy.

For the Child's Sake

The only circumstance under which parents find it possible to sanction the behavior of a physician who deliberately holds back diagnostic information is when it is done for the *child's* sake. When Pat Duffin's doctor told her finally that her baby had Down syndrome, he said that he had

> suspected this at birth; but he told us he had wanted us to bring this child home, and learn to love him and know him as a person before we were told, so that we could make the right decision about how we would want to raise this child. My doctor was not of our faith, but a very religious man, and he told me he had prayed that he would be able to help my husband and me to accept this child. I so appreciated this doctor for his love and concern for our whole family.

Lynette and Doug Soape also came to respect and admire their son's physician, a doctor who chose to wait for the "right moment" to break the news. Eric, who was also born with Down syndrome, was five months old before his parents learned that he had a disability.

> Our doctor chose not to tell us at birth for several reasons, but mainly his philosophy that parent and child need to go through a bonding process before they are unloaded on about the possible—or definite—handicap. He prefers to wait until the parents ask, "Is there a problem?" Then parents who sus-

pect something already have an easier time accepting it, when they're told, "Yes, there is a problem." When we finally did ask why Eric still couldn't hold his head up, our doctor had the chromosome test run, just to confirm the diagnosis. This delay might not be acceptable to everyone, but we are glad our doctor handled the information this way.

"Acceptable" as such motives may be, there are many less acceptable reasons why the parents "knowing" is sometimes delayed.

Other Reasons for a Withheld or Delayed Diagnosis

A doctor may withhold or delay diagnosis because of the normal reluctance to be the bearer of bad news or concern for the family. But parents suggest that some physicians may also be reluctant to become involved in anything except well-baby medicine and do not want to become "entangled," even to the extent of making the diagnosis. Some other reasons that parents cite:

Some Disabling Conditions Are Not Immediately Apparent: If the impairment is mild, problems such as vision or hearing defects, cerebral palsy, and other physical disabilities may go unnoticed at first. And most mental handicaps are understandably "invisible" at birth. Time was when a great many problems, much easier to spot now, remained undiagnosed for months or even years. Take Paula Clearfield, who has a mild physical disability, as well as epilepsy, and also has mental retardation. Yet, says her mother, Elaine,

> there was no indication in the hospital after Paula's birth, and years later, when I mentioned Paula's disabilities to my obstetrician, he was shocked. He had had no idea that Paula was physically or mentally handicapped. He searched the hospital records for a clue to the situation, but there was nothing to indicate she was injured in the birth process.

That was more than twenty years ago. Today, with diagnostic techniques and equipment improving constantly, if the new parents feel any uneasiness about the wellness of the new baby, the apparently "normal" baby, there is no reason not to request the same kind of thorough assessment given routinely by most hospitals today (and required in some states) to "at-risk" newborns. Babies who are "at risk" include, of course, premature infants; but other factors might be a difficult pregnancy or birth, the family's genetic history, or the mother's age (over thirty-five), weight (especially for underweight teenagers), or her general health. Especially if there are lingering questions, some hospitals also schedule regular follow-up clinic visits, so they can monitor the baby's progress.

Some Disabling Conditions Do Not Develop or Emerge Until Later: The list is quite extensive, but here are some examples: Only 30 percent of all epilepsies are detected before the child is five. Autism may not become obvious until the youngster is a year old, and even then it may be the most difficult of the "invisible handicaps" to diagnose with certainty. And many specific learning disabilities are not even suspected until the child enters preschool, kindergarten, or even first grade.

Parents Are Uneasy but Do Nothing: No parent wants to borrow trouble. Most, especially first-time parents, take for granted that any problem the baby has will be spotted by the pediatrician or at the clinic during the regular checkup: Who wants to be labeled an "anxious mother" like Debbie Veasie, whose son was born with spastic diplegia and borderline mental retardation?:

> We were, as parents, very slow to learn Jamie's problems. I guess the signs were there, but we kept attributing them to his being a premature baby and therefore figured he just needed extra time to adjust and catch up. He was probably two before we realized his problems were not going to be outgrown with age.

It can be someone else—a grandmother, another relative, a friend, a neighbor—who first suspects the disability, but usually it is the mother.

Little by little she begins to notice some disturbing patterns: a baby who doesn't localize to sounds, who doesn't follow objects with his eyes and head; or the child whose arm and hand movements seem somehow different, if not "wrong," or who is unable to sit up or to remain sitting without falling over. It is not necessary for a parent to be an expert on disabilities: if the child seems to behave differently than the others in the family did at the same age ("he was reacting differently to my singing voice than my daughter had as an infant"); if (especially with first babies) the child doesn't look or respond or move the way friends' and neighbors' children do ("her speech wasn't as advanced as that of her friends"), then it is worth following up. The parents still reluctant to "bother the doctor" over "foolish" fears can write to one of the disability organizations, nearly all of which have free literature listing "warning signs" worth checking out. (See Appendix B.)

Parents Are Uneasy but Physicians Do Nothing: They tell the pediatrician or clinician about their suspicions, and the professional either ignores their observations or fails to interpret the symptoms properly. Nothing emerges more clearly in parents' stories than the surprising number of instances in which they were told by a physician that they were being "overanxious," that what they were observing was "normal," or that the child would "outgrow it."

- ◆ Item: A little boy whose left midbrain had never developed fully. *I noted when my son was about six months old that he didn't use his left arm, hand, or fingers. When I told his doctor, he said, "Don't worry about it."*
- ◆ Item: A New Jersey boy who was still not toilet-trained at age five and a half. When the mother asked the doctor why, she was told, "You're unduly concerned; he'll grow out of it." The delay proved later to be the result of a learning disability.
- ◆ Item: A three-month-old with mild cerebral palsy. After a cursory ten-minute examination, the doctor told the mother he was "either spoiled or retarded."
- ◆ Item: Brian Struckhoff, who was also eventually diagnosed by a neurologist as having cerebral palsy, a possibility other physicians had apparently not suspected. From the day Brian was born, Connie Struckhoff says, *we had problems: He cried constantly, wouldn't eat properly, and was just all-around crabby. We were told over and over by several doctors that Brian just had colic; we should be patient. But I knew what colic was; I have three older children, one of whom did have colic.*

I tried to tell the doctors there was something else wrong; they ignored me or treated me like an overanxious mother! This is one thing that really bothered me: we were with Brian twenty-four hours a day, and yet the doctors would not believe us when we told them Brian did not act "normally."

- ◆ Item: A Minnesota couple who were disturbed by the failure of their son's speech and language to develop by the time he was eighteen months old but were never able to get the diagnosis (profound hearing loss plus a learning disability) until he was four. Doctors kept saying either that there was nothing wrong or that the boy was retarded.

- ◆ Item: The Missouri grandmother who adopted her grandson two weeks after he was born. *His doctor at his birth and up to three months said there wasn't anything wrong with him except that he had a temper. At three months I saw that he never used his right hand and asked the doctor about that also. He said, "Don't worry about it; he will grow out of it." One night, at three A.M., my baby was tossing and turning and his whole body was thrashing around. We didn't know what was happening. We took him to the hospital, and the doctor, instead of treating the baby, said, "I don't see anything wrong with him. Are you sure it's not just child abuse?"*

I got so angry. I never learned a damned thing from him, and I was mad. In the morning I called the public health nurse, who has been a friend for some time now. She said to forget what the doctor had said. It was a seizure.

Eventually, the little boy was also diagnosed as having cerebral palsy.

Even when they have finally been given a proper diagnosis, parents may feel reluctant to challenge the physician's unwillingness or failure to make sense of the symptoms they themselves noticed and reported, because of the respect, almost bordering on reverence, that most new parents, floundering in a sea of unknowns, have for the doctor's knowledge and expertise. When you're desperate to know what to do, whom can you trust if you can't trust your doctor?

Getting a correct diagnosis often takes longer when you have only questions and suspicions. Cindy M., the Indiana mother of a youngster with developmental delay, needed three years to take action to resolve her doubts.

The signs were there, now that I look back on it. The pediatrician would see us for five minutes each month and never hinted there was anything wrong. John cried so, and he wasn't cuddly. There would be screaming in the car, screaming when the doorbell rang. . . . Still the pediatrician told me nothing was wrong.

By the time he was age three, I knew he was in deep trouble. The hardest thing I ever had to do in my life was walk through the doors of the regional infant development center. I was admitting that my child had a problem, a serious problem. I was terrified, and so alone. After days of testing, John was admitted, as a child with developmental delay.

But calling her child's problem a "developmental delay" was still not what Cindy had been hoping for. It was still too vague: "Most parents have a diagnosis or a 'label.' I am still without." She is far from alone in wanting a label. When the family doctor refused to specify her son's disability, Paula Johnson was relieved to hear from the physical therapist that it was probably cerebral palsy: "Perhaps the doctor was trying to avoid labels, but there was some comfort in knowing what we were dealing with."

Yet not all parents want labels. Perhaps there are others like Cindy M., who, deep inside, do not altogether want to resolve their doubts, to confirm their fears. Often, though, parents' primary objection to labeling is that it stigmatizes the child. One couple resisted when their daughter, who couldn't speak, was termed "mentally retarded"; they felt her speechlessness stemmed from the little girl's cerebral palsy. They fought the label because they felt—not without considerable justice, as many parents have found out—that "labeling tends to make preconceived ideas a reality by teachers and others working with the child. There is a tendency not to expect any progress beyond a certain point." You tend to get, as a great many research experiments have confirmed, what you expect to get. It is called a "self-fulfilling prophecy."

Another mother felt that such labels do "tremendous psychological damage" to everyone in the family, because they "affect the quantity and quality of services provided by the various professionals to the family as a whole." Yet the preponderance of parent sentiment seems to be with the mother who felt that "it is important to get an evaluation/diagnosis, even though it is hard to hear the 'label' and/or handicap that is placed on your child's condition." "If I knew people who suspected something was wrong with their child," another mother adds, "I would encourage them to push for answers," if only because "limbo is *hell*."

With children who have learning disabilities, another mother notes, there is still another good reason for getting a "label": "No one would believe the relief my children found by knowing the *reason* they couldn't remember the months of the year in order, or the sequence of numbers."

Getting the Diagnosis: Step by Step

Suppose parents suspect, or half-suspect, that their child has a disability, or merely a problem of some kind that isn't going away. A list of "warning signs" and symptoms provided by the relevant disability organization only heightens the apprehensions, and a visit to the local library for additional reading material or information doesn't do much to allay them. (It is still worth checking out what the library has: one mother first diagnosed her daughter's rare syndrome, Prader-Willi syndrome, by reading a magazine article. Columbia Presbyterian Hospital in New York confirmed the diagnosis three months later.)

If the family physician or pediatrician continues to *assure* the parents that nothing is wrong but still fails to *reassure* them, they *can* rely on time and chance to make things clear. And sometimes that does happen, without their doing anything more. The state nurse who came to the house on a routine visit took one look at a little girl who was being treated for "low thyroid" and told her mother she had cerebral palsy. Another family found out about their daughter's cerebral palsy from the physical therapist "after two or three months of our family doctor's denying it."

There is no reason, though, to remain in doubt. These days it is not at all uncommon for any patient, in the case of recommended surgery or serious illness, to ask for a second opinion. There is no reason that parents should hesitate to do the same thing—to obtain a second, confirming diagnosis or a different one. Getting answers that make sense early enough may have a critical bearing on the child's future; that ought to be good enough reason for parents to *persist*. (And they might just as well learn persistence early on: it is likely to be central to anything they ever hope to accomplish in helping the youngster.)

Knocking at the Right Door

Parents who have been walking around for months or even years with questions are sometimes astounded at the speed with which they get answers, though not always happy ones, when they finally knock on the right door. One Tennessee couple's pediatrician grudgingly agreed that what their daughter had "could be" cerebral palsy; a pediatric neurologist confirmed the diagnosis without hesitation. A pediatrician confirmed another little girl's cerebral palsy "in a matter of minutes" after the family doctor had been unable to do so. The hospital where a baby was born blind, and where he spent a total of three months on two separate occasions, never alerted the parents to any problem, with no reason given. When the baby was six months old, he was admitted to a different hospital, and the attending pediatrician there detected the disability immediately.

Getting a Referral

The first step to seeking a diagnosis is to persuade the family doctor, pediatrician, or clinic to refer the child to a specialist or to a diagnostic group. That is pretty much routine these days, and usually parents run into no more than mild objections, if any, when they make the request.

But every so often parents do run into resistance. Three pediatricians kept telling Eugenia Ramsey to be patient and that her three-year-old son would talk eventually, though they admitted that they didn't quite know why he wasn't talking already. They dragged their feet about referring the little boy to the evaluation center for a better diagnosis, but Ms. Ramsey persisted. Her mother's instinct was correct: the boy was eventually found to have autism.

Her pediatrician told another mother only that her baby might need some therapy, of an unspecified nature. She kept asking him about "this therapy" until he finally gave her the name of the local rehabilitation center. The parents immediately called for an appointment, the center did an evaluation, and they were referred to an orthopedic surgeon. Diagnosis: cerebral palsy.

There is, of course, no reason why parents *must* wait—or plead—for a referral. Parents can always refer themselves, as Sharon Livingston did, when the pediatrician's answers didn't satisfy her.

> Our son's pediatrician told us he was normal and told me that I should learn to handle him better, be firmer, so that he would behave. He told us not to worry about his talking, that he would begin talking when he was ready.
>
> We finally learned Jon's diagnosis when he was two years old. We had taken him to our local mental health clinic to see a child psychologist, because we felt there was definitely something wrong. We were fortunate that the psychologist we saw at the clinic was familiar with autism. His diagnosis of Jon's problem was not difficult—Jon had all the symptoms of classic autism.

Best Choice:
Diagnostic Clinic or Team

What complicates the search for most parents is that since they are not sure what the child's problem is, or whether there *is* a problem to be concerned about, they can't be sure what kind of specialist to look for without a lot of wasted motion. As the parents' comments indicate, usually the best approach is to look not for that "right" specialist, but for a multifaceted evaluation by a team, whether at a pediatric group or a clinic of some sort, preferably one located in a university or a teaching hospital.

The more difficult the diagnosis, in fact, and the longer the parents have been asking questions without getting satisfactory answers, the more likely it is that only the team approach will produce those answers. When his parents suspected that one-year-old Matthew might have cerebral palsy, his parents took him to a CP clinic. The team that evaluated him there, and confirmed that he did have cerebral palsy, with significant involvement in both arms and legs, consisted of a pediatrician, a children's education specialist, a physical therapist, an occupational therapist, a speech therapist/pathologist, and an orthopedic surgeon. For other types of disabilities, the evaluation team may include a psychologist, psychiatrist, opthalmologist, audiologist, and other specialists called in by the diagnostic center.

When Cost Is a Problem

One factor that may deter some families from seeking a diagnosis is cost. There may be a free or low-cost diagnostic center available at not too great a distance, either through government bodies, disability agencies, or—and it is worth checking—local chapters of national civic and fraternal groups. Families with financial problems may also be able to take their youngsters to one of the periodic Medicaid screenings, which are in fact the only source of health care for millions of children from needy families.

Parents who don't know where to begin might check first with their local health department. This may turn out to be the answer in more ways than one. Some states—Maryland is one—have diagnostic and advisory teams that travel periodically to local health departments to provide health screenings. (See Chapter 10 for more on Early Periodic Screening, Diagnosis, and Treatment [EPSDT] Programs.)

There are also regional diagnostic centers operated by some states (like California), where the cost may be quite reasonable. Other possible community resources worth checking for diagnostic services include the local hospital, an early childhood agency, a health agency, the local medical association, or the United Way (one of the groups that it supports financially may have diagnostic screening available).

Understanding the Diagnosis

Parents who have dealt with diagnostic centers warn of one possible problem: you think you have the diagnosis, but you don't. The diagnosis is made, but the report is couched in language so technical as to be almost totally useless to the parents: written by doctors for doctors, like businesses in which computers speak only to computers in computerese.

As they become more experienced in the special language of their child's disability, parents may get some idea of what a phrase like *neurological motor deficiency* means in English. But when a very famous private Midwest clinic used that phrase about their son, an Iowa couple only had more questions. Even the professionals they checked with were stumped.

> When I asked the doctor if our son had cerebral palsy, he said, "I wouldn't call it that." This was confusing to us, because we didn't know what the medical term meant. Our therapist and the people at the area education agency were also unsure about the term.
>
> When the physical therapist working with Ben finally told us that what he had *was* cerebral palsy, it was like a slap in the face. But it helped us, because finally we could read about it in the medical books and get material to help us work with Ben.

It wasn't the abstract satisfaction of knowing, and understanding the label. It was that now, *finally,* the parents could begin to "work with Ben" and *for* him. Now they knew; now they could help—or find the right kind of help. Families should insist on having the diagnosis explained in language they understand, even if it is other than English—for the child's sake.

It is impossible to be sure whether any of the professionals whom Ben's parents asked deliberately chose not to explain the diagnostic terminology. But obstetricians, pediatricians, and physicians who believe they are doing parents a kindness by keeping the bad news from them as long as possible might really be kinder to give first priority to the effect that delay will have on the child's progress, regardless of how negative the child's prospects may seem to be.

3

"So I Turned Myself On"
How to Get On with It

There is a mother in Burlington, Iowa, with two little girls, born a year apart. On September 3, 1983 (the dates always stick) the older child was diagnosed as having infantile autism. Once the parents had that diagnosis, they became painfully aware that the younger daughter was also manifesting autistic behavior, and even more than the older. The possibility of having two little girls with disabilities was a nightmare.

On December 16, 1983, the nightmare became a reality for Barbara V.: the younger child was also diagnosed as having autism.

> That day it was like God said to me: "OK. Your life so far has been fair. Now just take this, and see what you can do with it." But I felt like, Don't do this to them. Just do something to me instead.

When parents learn that a child has a disability, the lucky ones may be those who go into shock immediately. Temporarily, a blanketing numbness can be preferable to the flood of feelings that overwhelms most mothers and fathers. Some parents remember wishing for a cave, a hole to crawl into, a place to escape to, until the nightmare was over. Others recall wanting to sleep and sleep, as some actually do, with or without sedation.

Name any harrowing, denying, rejecting, self-punishing, self-destroying feeling. Some parents can testify to feeling it and feeling alone with the feeling: To a certain extent suffering, like joy, can be shared, but there is always some part that is personal and individual and not sharable, however much a spouse or other family members are suffering as well.

Nearly everyone goes through such a period of grief; in many respects it clearly resembles mourning for a child who died. Not everyone shows grief to the same degree or in the same way; mothers often become furious at spouses who seem to be taking the situation calmly. But it is less common—less acceptable—for men to grieve openly: unusual quiet may be grief, too.

Every Kind of Feeling Is "Normal"

If "normal" is what most or many of any group do, then it is normal and acceptable for mothers to cry, or sometimes not only to cry, but to shout, scream, curse. And that may be the best way, perhaps the only way, to handle the situation: to get feelings out into the open, get purged of them, get on with the routine of living again.

If anything, self-pity is even more normal: few couples get through this time without asking, Why did it have to happen to us? This is coupled with unbearable pity for the child: Why did it have to be my beautiful little girl?

There are no answers, even for parents who choose or feel compelled to put those questions to God. In *When Bad Things Happen to Good People,* Rabbi Harold Kushner reasons that God has nothing to do with what happens every day in the real world, that He does not control good and evil on a daily basis. God is everpresent as a source of inspiration, comfort, and faith; in Kushner's view, disabled children are in no way an expression of God's will.

That is something worth remembering, for those parents who find themselves guilt-ridden, obsessed with the idea that the "damaged" baby is in some way God's punishment, visited on them for something they did wrong. That kind of guilt is normal, too; in a situation like this, it isn't hard for normal human beings to find *something* to feel guilty about: something done wrong, something not done. Something during pregnancy, something in the genes: Why did I take the chance?

And then parents feel guilty about the way they feel: the superguilt about not being able to love the baby, or about hating the baby, or even wanting or hoping for the baby to die. Maybe this is not a feeling parents will want to remember, but it is normal, if "normal" is the way a good many other parents have felt too. It would be difficult, perhaps impossible, for any parent to come up with a single "bad" thought, no matter *how* "bad," that who-knows-how-many-other parents haven't also thought.

What *is* bad is getting stuck on any of these feelings, or a combination of them, like a broken record, letting them over-whelm or paralyze you. As one parent puts it very succinctly, "Feelings are not 'bad' or 'good.' It is what you do about those feelings that is 'bad' or 'good.'"

Role of Family: When They Help or Hurt

When parents are so sunk in their own feelings that they can't get going on their own, those around them can make a difference. That's when understanding, supportive family and friends can be so valuable. When Sandee Corcoran learned that her daughter had been born with Down syndrome,

> I sat there crying my eyes out for hours. My mother came to visit me after I had told her, and while I sat there feeling so sorry for Stephanee (and me secondly) she asked me, "Do you see *her* crying? She's healthy, and she isn't crying or complaining about being here." And she was beautiful.
>
> My parents were very supportive; without them, I don't know how I could have handled it. My brothers and sisters love my daughter very much and accept her with utmost love and caring.

Often such support and acceptance is the only push parents need to "get on with it." And many, perhaps most, families rally around, do what families are supposed to do ("they have hurt with us and hoped with us and encouraged us"). But in a situation that can be traumatic for them too, some (off-balance) grandparents manage to become part of the problem: like the grandparents who refused to touch a little boy with cerebral palsy, calling him "poor thing" instead of using his name, or the grandmother of another such child who predicted that she wouldn't be around long, "that God would take her away to a better place."

And perhaps this is the prize family: the grandmother who kept praying that the little boy with Down syndrome "wouldn't make it"; the father-in-law who refused to accept that there was anything wrong with the child and kept saying so; and the mother-in-law and brother-in-law whose only comment was, "It didn't come from our side of the family." That's one of those situations in which you really need a sense of humor, because it hurts too much to cry.

When Family Is Part of the Problem

How do parents cope with unsupportive, nonaccepting families like these? They do cope, of course; they have to. In some cases, it means simply shrugging it off; it's their problem, not ours. We've got enough on our hands with the child and ourselves. Sometimes, it's just a matter of time. Give them a chance, and eventually they'll come around on their own. From Mrs. Steve Cauley:

> I think parents should give their families time to breathe and understand and sort things out when they confront them with a child's disability. The parents sometimes accept things more readily because they have to deal with the situation constantly. Grandparents, other relatives, and friends need more time to sort out feelings and deal with them before being able to talk about them with others. It is sometimes more difficult for them to accept the facts.

But there are other parents who have found it more effective to take the bull by the horns, like Terrie Pearman, the Florida mother of a little girl with a number of disabilities:

My mother was heartbroken because she couldn't help. She was always there, though, to try and boost me and give me support and listen when I had to "curse the world."

But my father stated that there had never been any such problem in our family. I told him: "There is now. And whether or not you want to accept Kelly, you now have two grand-daughters, not one." He is OK now and very involved with the cerebral palsy school in my home town in North Carolina.

As for friends, says this self-assured mother,

> they stayed away at first. They were uncertain what to say. They had healthy babies. Now they accept Kelly because I accept Kelly.

Former "Friends" and Real Friends

One phenomenon seems to be almost universal: the arrival of a disabled baby reshapes a great many social relationships. It re-defines the word *friend,* tends to separate the sheep from the goats. Supposed "friends" come around once to find out what happened and never show up again. Or they do not show up at all or even telephone. They are full of transparent excuses if there is a chance meeting. Mary Borello used to have a very close friend—used to:

> When my friend was pregnant and heard that my daughter Jessica had been born with Down syndrome, she refused to come near her. And even though we had been friends for a long time, she didn't invite us to the christening because— she said—she didn't want Jessica near the newborn baby. I told my friend, "Jessica is *not* contagious. The only thing she can give your daughter is maybe a hug." Didn't help; and now we don't even speak to each other anymore.

On the other hand some of those who ought to leave and not come back unfortunately *do* come back, like the neighbor who told the parents of a baby born with a rare syndrome that they had been a "blessing" to *her,* because they made her realize how lucky *she* was. Then there are friends who show up once a month full of advice and accuse the parents of not loving the baby enough when they do not automatically follow it. "You should let me have your son," one such "friend" told the mother of a little boy with cerebral palsy. "I'd have him sitting up in two weeks." She really didn't know what it was going to take to get the little boy sitting, the mother says. "She just seemed to think I wasn't doing enough. I wouldn't call 'friends' like that helpful."

The compensation, though, is that a whole new set of friendships may develop. Neighbors or acquaintances or mothers who turn out to have the same problems may quickly get to be "close as sisters," and some of them, especially those mothers who've "been there" themselves, are even more supportive than sisters because they've learned how to be.

How to Make Friends and Keep Them

It should be pointed out that if parents of children with special needs get no advance training for their new role and responsibilities, neither do the friends of parents of such children. That includes some who may, because of ignorance, even equate a disability with a disease and ask in all honesty whether Down syndrome or cerebral palsy is "catching." And it includes above all the considerable number who are honestly concerned and caring, about both child and family, but don't know how to handle it, don't know what to say, and therefore choose not to discuss it for fear of hurting rather than helping.

For most parents (though not all) it helps to talk, rather than to keep feelings bottled up inside. It helps to share the burden with people who care about what has happened and will happen, with friends who know the right thing to say and when to say it— perhaps only that the baby is beautiful. Caring friends are sensitive enough to know when not to say anything, when just to *be* there, to hold the mother's hands, hold them, hold the baby, and listen.

Parents should not simply assume, however, that friends will automatically understand what is needed, and how and when to be supportive. Reaching out works both ways. Here are a number of things parents can do to help friends be, and remain, friends:

- Talk about your child as others do about their children, not just about the problems, but sharing the joy over the little bits of progress. But do *not talk* about the child to the exclusion of everything else: friends find it difficult to remain supportive, a Syracuse father feels, because "parents of handicapped children tend to be focused, even obsessed, with the child, and I suspect that that drives some friends away."
- Try not to be too sensitive about thoughtless and hurting remarks ("Wouldn't it be better to put him into a home?") by people who don't really mean to be cruel.
- Be patient, and recognize others' difficulties in dealing with the new situation. When a little boy's problem was finally diagnosed as cerebral palsy, Barbara T. says, *One friend stopped coming over and calling. She couldn't face me, she said. But after three and a half months she finally did come. Once she saw Aaron, she realized that he hadn't changed as a result of the diagnosis; the only thing that had changed was that we knew something about Aaron that we didn't know before. And she has been one of my best friends since then, as far as helping with the day-to-day work.*
- Show friends what their support means to the family ("we let them know we need it, and appreciate it").

When Counseling Is Needed

Sometimes, though, parents are so mired in despair that they need comfort and help beyond anything that even close friends and family can provide. Rabbi George Nudell, the father of a boy born with spina bifida, says that he would first try as a parent to help other parents realize that somehow they *can* succeed in dealing with the baby and their new situations. They at least ought to make an attempt to deal with it. But he also recognizes that that isn't possible for certain parents.

People who can't cope need counseling. There is no single answer; everyone is different. One may need reassurance because he thinks he can't handle the problem, and he needs to be told that help *is* available. Another may have some unresolved trauma in his or her life that needs to be talked about, and once you get the parent to deal with that, he/she will feel better about the baby.

Turning to God

Everyone is different; there is no single answer. Many of those who feel the need for counseling turn to a spiritual guide, their pastor, their church, their faith: "Ask God for help. He has not failed us yet," one says, and another: "Hand it all to the Lord and get on with loving the child as one of God's special children."

And still another. "Without God my life would be much more difficult. So the credit truly goes to my Helper, to Whom I look often." From the very first day she discovered her baby had a disability, one devout mother prayed to the Lord to let her daughter live and vowed to deal, with her faith to sustain her, with whatever problems might come along: "We would be like David and his slingshot against the Giants in her life."

Professional Counseling

There are those parents who need still a different kind of guidance and counsel, who do not have such spiritual beliefs and find baring their souls to close friends and relatives too difficult. They need to talk to someone with professional skills, who can provide understanding and guidance. Increasing numbers of parents with children who have disabilities are now finding their way to psychotherapists without embarrassment, if not immediately after the baby is born then during some later crisis: few parents of such children manage to weather all of the inevitable crises and catastrophes without some such professional help, if only briefly.

For those who are thinking about the possibility of therapy or professional counseling for the first time—and that would include most young parents—but don't know where to look for it, there are any number of places to get helpful suggestions. The family doctor, the baby's pediatrician, the hospital where the baby was delivered and its social service department, local family or disability agencies: all can give names and recommendations, and some even have their own counseling services.

Other Parents as Counselors

And there are other parents. Other parents, even strangers, who have also gone through the experience may often be able to offer a special kind of understanding and solace that neither family nor friends nor professional counseling can. They have "credentials" no one else can offer. Cindy M., whose daughter has cerebral palsy, felt she

> wanted to talk to people who *understood*. My friends and family were great, but were too soothing. I wanted someone to say to me, "Yes, it's the pits! And it hurts like hell!" while showing me not only how they were surviving, but sometimes even thriving.
>
> I now have two close friends from the parents' group. Our conversations are very strange sometimes—it's our way of dealing with stress. We talk to each other in a way we'd never talk to anyone else about our children.

"At this point I was still on my guilt trip. I wanted someone to help me and tell me it wasn't my fault," says another mother, and others attest that parents who have gone through similar experiences or may still be going through them can be much more understanding even than good friends, relatives, or therapists. They discover that, because of the problems they have shared, they are on the same wavelength: it is a virtually instantaneous rapport and kinship.

It is difficult for others to appreciate the healing power of this instant identification. For Mr. and Mrs. Richard Powell, their first meeting with other parents like them was also the first step on the ascent from their personal Valley of Despair.

> When Stephanie was born, we felt totally alone. Our family and friends were there for us, but they truly didn't know how

we were feeling. We experienced very intense feelings of iso-
lation. But the minute we heard the words, "Our baby has
Down syndrome also," those feelings suddenly became less
intense.

"Not Guilty"

Some parents may even have been wallowing in a quagmire of
self-blame and guilt, somehow convinced that they *deserved* the
"punishment" they got. Which human being, devout or not, isn't
able to find something he or she did wrong? But seeing other
parents, meeting so many other people with the same kinds of
problems to cope with (some of them may be "bad," but they
can't possibly all be), makes it clear that having a child with special
problems is not a punishment. No parent does anything to "deserve" it, and no one is especially singled out: accidents happen,
and people have to live with and *learn* to live with the consequences. They must make the best life possible for the child, who
surely didn't deserve to be punished, especially in this way.

Whatever help it takes—other parents, or faith, or professional counseling, or help dredged up entirely from their own
inner resources—for all but a few parents the weeping and the
brooding and the grieving do stop one day. And that is the day
that "getting on with it" begins.

As it did with Barbara V., that mother in Burlington, Iowa,
with two little girls born a year apart, who were both diagnosed
as having autism. To quote her once again:

> That day it was just like God said to me: "OK. Your life so
> far has been fair. Now just take this, and see what you can do
> with it." But I felt like, Don't do this to them. Just do some-
> thing to me instead.

That's where it might have stopped that December day, with
numbness and despair. That was the day in Barbara V.'s life when
she might easily have allowed paralysis to take over completely.
But she didn't, "because then I realized that this did no good. So
I turned myself on, and said Go!"

4
....

"There When I
Need Them"
How Other Parents Help

What helped Barbara V. to "go," to start hunting for the help her two daughters needed, was finding a parents' group, Pilot Parents. Her relatives were well meaning and fairly supportive, but they weren't enough. Friends were sympathetic but didn't really relate; and every now and then there were, and still are, a few thoughtless comments that really hurt.

Worse, she found that sometimes her friends didn't want to hear any more about her kids. And yet she very much needed to talk about their problems, and her own problems, with someone. It was among parents who shared the same experiences that she found sympathetic ears. It isn't true of everyone, of course, but talk to a substantial sampling of parents whose children have disabilities and you get the feeling that the best thing that happens to many parents is other parents.

Just knowing you are not alone can help you keep your sanity. You can compare notes with people who really understand, because they are or were there too.

Some needed help immediately, just to make it through those first terrible days, and often found it among people who were, up to then, total strangers.

The support you receive is very important initially. Just knowing that you're not alone, and that there are people out there who are in the same situation, is a comfort. The guilt is very hard to alleviate; the parents' group helps very much in this regard.

But the kind of comfort parents are able to give each other is not only for those first days. To some parents it is even more valuable over the long haul, as the single best antidote for "parent burnout."

It is important to have an outlet with other parents in similar situations. They can lend support, understanding, and compassion. You can help each other go through the trials, surgeries, and emotional ups and downs. It's nice to know there is someone else there with you.

Some parents do not find their way to a parent group until there seems nowhere else to go. In the case of one Florida mother, it followed an acute attack of "burnout," or something pretty close to it. That day

I wanted just to die, disappear, and have never existed. My son wasn't particularly difficult that day, and nothing bad or out of the ordinary had happened, but I just felt spent and tired and lonely. Nobody seemed to know or care how I really felt about my situation.

Then I called Susan [the director of the parent group], and it seemed like she had been through almost the exact same kinds of experiences. I didn't feel like I was the only one any more, and I didn't have to worry about whether the kinds of feelings I was having were "normal."

We have a nice little group now, and I've found that we all face similar problems. Some are better; some are worse off than ourselves. We all have some negative feelings along the way. It sure helps to have somebody you can talk to.

"Great Therapy"

Parents contact a parent support group and immediately find others there who share their fears and insecurities, who understand and accept what each parent has to do without interfering, who help each other over the rough spots without making a big deal of it. With other parents like them, no mothers (or fathers) have to feel afraid that talking about feelings will be seen as complaining or asking for pity.

Other parents also help to provide much-needed perspective. Sometimes a child makes progress so slowly that parents find it hard to detect improvement. Each stage of growth takes so much longer with some children with disabilities than it does with "normal" kids that it seems to last forever. Nothing can be more depressing than to invest time, energy, and love and to feel that nothing is happening.

That's where other parents come in. Not being involved with the child from minute to minute, another parent may readily see positive movement that the mother who has just been up all night or a great many nights with the youngster is too exhausted to detect.

Meeting all the mothers and fathers is great therapy; just talking and comparing notes is great. Everyone really bonds together and encourages each other's child. Every parent of a disabled child *must* talk to another parent. I feel sorry for those who don't know anyone to talk to.

Learning from Each Other's Experience

There is also a perspective gained from seeing other parents just getting into problems that you had to face with your child months or perhaps even a year or two earlier and from talking with parents of older boys and girls, who can provide a preview of what lies ahead. They've survived; having a child who has a disability— even a severe disability, or a number of them—is not the end of the world. That thought can help you to keep your priorities straight.

All regular ideas of what the future holds are gone. Parents need something to hang onto, some positive ideas of what they face, but from an encouraging standpoint. Usually only another parent can carry that off believably.

Parents of older children can also be extremely valuable in helping new parents to avoid at least some of the pitfalls and mistakes they themselves made. When it comes to day-to-day existence and its problems, parents see themselves as copractitioners, coresearchers, and coworkers on the same project, with a resulting expertise that no one else can achieve.

"Professionals are good," says one mother, who has been involved with a parent group since her son began a preschool program, "but most have not actually had and lived with a handicapped child. It is much easier to talk to someone who understands all the little everyday things that no one else could know." "I'd go to another parent with a question before I'd go to a doctor," says another mother, who has been a member of several parent groups:

> Visiting with the other moms, you have someone to talk to who knows what you face on the *inside* as well as the *outside*. You don't have to do a lot of explaining for them to know where you are, because they already know. You are talking to someone who shares the same fears, concerns and joys, without your having to explain how you feel. They know. They have been there.

When the Helped Becomes a Helper

At some point, after some time, there may be a role reversal: the parent in need of help becomes a parent *giving* help as well. "Sometimes someone else had just been through the same stage we were just entering," says Ann Falstrom, whose daughter has a neurological impairment, "and they could help us." And sometimes she was the one doing the helping and getting real satisfaction from it. "It's always a good feeling when a piece of advice that you give somebody else works for them, and you save them all the trouble that you went through."

There is a certain pride and satisfaction in being able to give as well as to receive. The kind of parent who is able to progress to the point where she or he is no longer just the recipient of help but also is able to help others is likely to go beyond practical advice to lending emotional support when it is needed. And it so often is. Parents who reach that capability may be asked, by their parent group or a social worker, to participate in organized and structured peer counseling, to visit and to help other parents. Some take to the task naturally. Jeanne Struble, the New Jersey mother whose son is blind and has mental retardation, needed no urging to become the guiding spirit of a parents' support group. It was the result of her own philosophy and convictions:

> I am sure you have heard people say that God sends special children to special people, but I don't believe it. I believe that God sends special children to all kinds of people, just to see what they will do about it.
>
> In my case, after I was able to deal with the heartbreak and the asking why?!!!, I tried to turn it all around, and get involved with other parents, to see whether there was any way I could help *them.*

Special children may not be born to special people, but sometimes they can make special people of the ordinary people to whom they're born.

Pilot Parents

Put a lot of people like Jeanne Struble together, and what do you have? An organization, really a movement, like Pilot Parents. The first Pilot Parent Program was formed in Omaha, Nebraska, in the fall of 1970, "based on the philosophy that parents of developmentally disabled children experiencing crises can be helped by parents who have made an exemplary adjustment to their own handicapped child, and who have the capacity and willingness to help others by sharing their experiences." In short, it is the concept of "parents of handicapped children helping parents of handicapped children."

That's the group to which Barbara V. found her way when she was looking for people to talk with about her two daughters. That was in Burlington, Iowa, a state where Pilot Parent groups appear to be particularly strong. Mary McAllister, who has two youngsters with mental deficits, helped to start two of them.

No one could have been more helpless, more in need of help at one point, than she was. After their daughter had been diagnosed, the McAllisters went through extensive testing: the doctor assured them that there was no reason future children should not be normal. And when her son Johnny was born, the doctor examined him and said he was strong and healthy. She felt smug, she says: they had been dealt a blow in life with Christy, but they had survived it; they would be "guaranteed a happy life from now on." But then the troubling symptoms and signs began to appear— again.

> Realizing that Johnny was falling behind other babies was like a slow-motion nightmare. I started to bargain with God. "OK, I'll cope with having two special needs children. Just let Johnny do better than Christy." After a time I pleaded, "Please, let him do the same as Christy." But as time went on, we had to admit he was going to do things more slowly than Christy.
>
> It's funny, but at first I coped quite well. Maybe I was numb from the shock. However, several weeks later true depression set in. I was devastated. I didn't see any reason why either the kids or I should be alive. I seemed to cry continually. My faith in God was the main thing that kept me going.

What made matters worse was that Mary felt that no one around her really understood the way she felt. The McAllisters didn't know any family with even a single child with a disability, let alone two. They were like people in a strange country; no one spoke their language. But eventually the McAllisters did meet other parents and became involved in the Association for Retarded Citizens (ARC). It was through ARC that they first learned about Pilot Parents. Christy was six and Johnny two, when the Mary McAllister who had been there herself, "devastated" and alone, became the Mary who could reach out to other parents. She helped start her first group, in Muscatine, Iowa, as

> a support group for parents with any type of special need. It sounded like a way to reach *all* parents and let them know

they weren't *alone.* Pilot Parents offers friendship, emotional support, and understanding to other parents. I've found many of my good friends through them. Although our children have different types and degrees of disabilities, our feelings are often the same. I must say that part of my strength now comes from helping other parents. And they in turn are there when *I* need *them.*

A Growing Number of Parent Groups

Pilot Parents is by no means the only group offering parent-to-parent counseling and support. Groups exist in nearly every part of the country, under a variety of auspices and names. Their genesis may be as spontaneous as parents meeting in a doctor's office and agreeing to get together. But they are more often the result of a sponsorship—by a disability organization, or a religious or civic group—or they are an outgrowth of preschool and early intervention programs that schedule parent education meetings. (For a list of parent-to-parent groups, see Appendix B.)

Because of the growing number of such groups and the enthusiastic word-of-mouth publicity from their members, some parents are "connected" with a group before they even leave the hospital: if the pediatrician and the obstetrician do not know of a group, the hospital's social service staff or a nurse on the maternity floor often will. And in some communities with a particularly active group, some new parents have even had a member of the group visit and counsel them before they were discharged from the hospital.

Despite the proliferation of parent groups, it may often take a certain amount of hunting around, unless you get lucky, like the mother in a New Jersey community who, "after muddling through the first three months alone," found and contacted a support group she saw mentioned in *The New York Times,* or the couple in a small town who saw a notice of a parent meeting by accident on their local television station.

Quite often parents have found support groups through a letter from one of their members in a local paper, or simply by "asking around." If you talk to enough people long enough, eventually there is bound to be someone who knows someone who knows of a group somewhere.

But if you can't see yourself talking to strangers at a super-market checkout about a parents' group and do not want to leave things to chance, here are some possibilities:

Go Back to Your Family Doctor, Pediatrician, or Obstetrician: Even if he or she wasn't able to supply you with leads before, try again. Your physician may possibly have held back, feeling that the information would not be welcome until you were ready for it. Not every parent is a joiner, and some are more reluctant than others to face up to the disability or to "come out of the closet." Press a doctor who insists that he or she doesn't know of any group to make some inquiries. Someone else in the "doctor's network" may know of one.

Try the Hospital Where the Baby Was Born and Other Local Hospitals: The best bet is the hospital's social service department. A little persistence there may pay off: if they do not know of a group, ask for any possible leads—names or phone numbers. Be prepared to make a dozen or more phone calls for a single contact. If there is a way to reach them, don't overlook the hospital's nursing staff: whatever the reason, parents often report that it was a maternity nurse or a floor nurse who first alerted them to the existence of a support group and gave them a lead.

Work the Phone Book: Look for disability, family service, and child care agencies (perhaps under "Social Service Organiza-tions"). Try the United Fund or the United Way; they may be subsidizing an agency with a parent support group. Make sure not to overlook the "official" health and welfare agencies, state as well as local. And if they do not have a group themselves, never hang up without asking, "Do you know of any agency that might be able to help?" And a useful tip: always try to get the name of a specific person to ask for; this saves a great deal of time you'd otherwise spend negotiating with the switchboard or the recep-tionist who answers the agency phone.

Check the Library; Then Write: Even in smaller communities, the library ought to have a directory of state agencies, and state offices of federal agencies, whom you can contact. And, if need be, librarians are almost always knowledgeable enough to guide you to the right address for your inquiries. One resource the library may have (or ought to) is the Directory of National Information Sources on Disability, published by the Clearinghouse on the Handicapped, Office of Special Education and Rehabilitative Services (OSERS), Room 3132, 330 C Street SW, Washington, DC 20202-2524.

Appendix B: Appendix B lists disability agencies, Easter Seals, March of Dimes, and some parent advocacy groups and coalitions. If you're not certain that you're contacting the right agency, don't hesitate to say so. They will either let you know which *is* the right group, or pass your letter on, or both. For parents of children with rare disabilities or rare syndromes, *The Exceptional Parent,* published at 1170 Commonwealth Avenue, Boston, Massachusetts 02134-4646 in recent years, has probably been the most fruitful clearinghouse.

Your State's Self-Help Clearinghouse: Not every state has one. The idea is still fairly new and is by no means confined to getting the parents of children with disabilities together. Rather, clearinghouses try to help parents and others with special needs to *network:* that is, to put them in touch with existing support groups, or if there is none, with other people with the same problem looking for people like them. If you can't find a listing for a state group, write or call the American Self-Help Clearinghouse, St. Clares-Riverside Medical Center, Denville, NJ 07834; (201) 625-7101; or the National Self-Help Clearinghouse, City University of New York Graduate Center, Room 620, 25 West 43rd St., New York, NY 10036; (212) 642-2944.

Founding a Parent Group

But whether you get the names of local parents from a clearinghouse, find them on your own, or get leads from a local clinic or disability agency, in the end the only way to create parent support may be to found your own group, as did Mary McAllister.

And a great many other parents have, too. There are a great variety of reasons, and just as many benefits: to bond with people who can provide practical support (a mutual exchange of babysitting, for instance, or emotional support), "to be able to talk to people to whom you do not want to explain everything," and "to exchange ideas on ways to stimulate our children's development, deal with common behavior problems, and share our joys and frustrations." Where else would the announcement that a nine-year-old is finally toilet-trained evoke such loud and happy cheers as it did at one group?

Finding other parents poses special problems, of course, in smaller communities or rural areas. One problem, not found nearly so often in the relative anonymity surrounding people in larger cities, may be parents' reluctance "to come out of the closet," in a community where everyone knows everyone else. But even in smaller communities, parent support groups are more and more an idea whose time has come. Someone hears of a successful group in the next county and decides to make some contact; or someone moves from the next county and expects to find a group in this one. Or a half dozen parents get together for a special project, "Help the Handicapped Week" at the local school, and decide to *stay* together.

"The Problems We Share"

It is a sign of the great proliferation of parent groups in recent years that some controversy has already developed as to whether they should encompass all disabilities or a single disability. Parents favoring the latter type of association suggest that only parents who have faced very similar problems down the line can most benefit them. Lori Salvi feels that although parents of newly iden-tified children with disabilities should contact other such parents, any others, immediately ("they can save them untold steps"),

> eventually I would urge them to seek out parents of kids with the same handicap as their child. And even further, if they are single parents, then try to find single parents of a handicapped kid with a similar problem.

> Bonnie Fairchild, whose daughter was born with a hearing impairment, agrees that in such a group "there seems to be an instantaneous rapport with other parents."

> No matter how divergent our backgrounds are, our deaf chil-dren link us together, and we are immediately on the same

wavelength, concerned about the same issues, working toward the same goals. At these meetings, for the first time I began hearing facts about deafness that I could understand.

When a group is just getting started, or where there are only a small number of potential participants, the nature of the disability is almost never an issue. The group is eager to welcome parents of children with any type or degree of disability. Compelled to participate in such an all-disabilities group, the mother of a premature youngster who is legally blind came to feel that it was not a bad idea in any case:

> Blindness, being the low-incidence handicap that it is, makes communication with other parents with visually impaired children an infrequent event. We find, though, that the problems we share with parents of any handicapped children are similar.

If enough parents feel strongly about the issue, the nature of the disability may have some bearing when a new group is being organized: to include or exclude? But whatever kind of group it is, the best thing that can happen for parents who need to "get on with it" and are looking for emotional and practical support is to find other parents, to find a support group, and as quickly as possible.

"The best advice I ever received came from other parents after I joined a parents' group," Bonnie Fairchild says. The contact with others increased her confidence and enhanced her self-image. "Advice and support from other parents revealed my own capabilities as a parent. I began to question and search for excellence in school programs. I began to trust myself."

Bonnie Fairchild's daughter wound up attending Gallaudet College, and Bonnie went on to become president of the American Society for Deaf Children. But, she says, "I never stop learning from other parents."

5

....

"To Be an Effective Parent"
Learning About the Disability

The Learning Process

Looking back from the perspective of the many years since she learned that her daughter was profoundly deaf, and her very considerable experience helping younger parents, Bonnie Fairchild, the mother of the young woman with a hearing impairment, sees the parents' role in helping a child with a disability as beginning with two steps, one obvious, the other almost always overlooked until much later on, when its importance does become clear.

The obvious step: "Learn everything possible about the particular disability" the child has. The less obvious step: "I would advise anyone caring for a disabled child to begin keeping detailed records about the child immediately."

Experiences vary. Some physicians take the time to talk about the disability, what to expect from the child, the kind of programs and services the child can be expected to need, and where to find them. Some explain how important the child's first few years are and the benefits of early intervention programs. One parent still recalls with gratitude the geneticist who gave her a "hotline" number to call to reach other parents of youngsters with Down syndrome and then contacted them for her himself.

But other parents report that all they got was the diagnosis:

When I first brought my child home, I was desperate for information. I didn't even know how to care for someone so disabled.

My wife and I felt like we were still in the dark about a lot of things.

We also felt inadequate, because we wanted to help our son but didn't know how.

Most parents don't know what to do; they have to learn how. They *have* to learn how: what's the alternative? You have to get as much information about the disability and managing it as you can, parents say, so you can know how to deal with it. You have to become an expert, an educated consumer: "The better informed you are, the better care your child will get." You will have an almost endless succession of decisions to make and actions to take: "If you are totally uneducated about the issues, you will not feel comfortable about the decisions you make for your child."

Very often, when parents first get the word that their youngster has a permanent disability, that is really all that may stick with them: the word. That isn't necessarily because it is medical jargon, though it sometimes is. But how many parents know precisely what cerebral palsy or Down syndrome or a "learning disability" is, until they find out that *their* child has it?

Even when the diagnosis is spelled out very clearly, most new parents will not know the right follow-up questions to ask—not only about the nature of the disability, but about what to anticipate and how to manage the child, where to find services: all the things they still have to learn, the special skills needed to parent a child with a disability.

It is not at all unusual for the parents to have trouble getting answers: whom do you ask? You ask the doctor, of course, the man or woman who diagnosed or has been treating the child for all of the medical and physical involvements.

But the problem with many doctors is that they are strictly *medical* doctors. That's good enough, so long as the questions and

the problems are strictly medical. But in terms of the nonmedi-
cal—the problems of managing the disability, coping, dealing with
the child's needs on a daily basis—often parents find that their
physicians are not much more knowledgeable than they are. And
that is hardly knowledgeable at all.

The mother of a daughter with a visual impairment puts it this
way:

> It is a great credit to our society that support services are
> abundant; books on every handicap can be found, but profes-
> sionals are not referring parents to the help they need. I was
> surprised to find the number of sources of information avail-
> able to me. It is sad, though, that I had to find them for myself.

It may take a lifetime of finding and learning. There is always
new information about the disability: methods, programs, treatment, new medications. All have to be constantly reviewed. It
takes patience, determination, persistence, and trying to steal the
time from a day that centers on giving the care that is the purpose
of all the learning. It can feel like being on a carousel: every
question requires an answer, which only leads to more questions,
demanding more answers.

Glennis Lashley, one of whose two sons has a seizure disorder
and the other a learning disability, is one parent who never stops
asking.

> One has to *learn* how to be an effective parent of a disabled
> child. (The purpose of professionals is to make me smarter re
> my children's needs. I pick *everyone's* brains constantly.)
>
> You *must* learn all you can about your child's medical,
> academic, and other needs. *You* are responsible for how your
> child turns out.

Where to Look for Answers

In terms of *managing* the child, learning to deal with the nonmed-
ical aspects of the disability, the single best-equipped person for
the helping role may be a social worker, not only for direct assistance, but for referrals to other sources. Others who may be
able to supply information and guidance include occupational and

physical therapists, nurses, psychologists. Each new contact can lead to several more.

Once a contact has been established, it is a good idea to cultivate it. Some of the most expert "experts" turn out to be most willing to listen (or to read a letter) and respond: you can improve your chances of getting a prompt and responsive answer by making the question as specific as possible.

Local Agencies

Some of the professionals who can provide useful information will be individual practitioners; but many of the most helpful will be on the staffs of local or area agencies, either governmental or voluntary. The telephone book or a local directory will probably list state agencies, although under a variety of headings: tracking down the right one may take time and a dozen phone calls. There should be no problem, however, in finding the local affiliate of the relevant disability agency, if there is one, either directly or through United Way.

These local affiliates will have people to answer questions, and reading matter of one kind or another so parents can pick up enough background to know what questions to ask. Many also have speakers and/or parent education programs, on a regular or occasional basis.

National Agencies

But if there are no local affiliates within the area, many national parent and disability organizations will provide pamphlets, folders, fliers, and booklets, usually considerably more than a new parent can absorb. These supply basic and general information, of course: much of the material may not seem to apply. But a "North Dakota mom" in an isolated area who got much of her information by writing to national agencies makes the point that "you don't *have* to use any of the agencies' material if you don't really want to; but if you do get it, you'll find a lot of help there that you *can* use."

One of the best places for new parents to begin their hunt for information is undoubtedly the National Information Center for Handicapped Children and Youth, Box 1492, Washington, D.C.

20013-1492; (800) 999-5599. And parents often cite the help they got from many of the national disability organizations and agencies listed in Appendix B.

Additional Reading

A great many parents feel the need to go more deeply into the study of their youngster's disability, to get more information and background than agencies' materials normally provide. Among the typical comments: "I have taken upon myself the reading of all the books I could find on my daughter's eye condition and what I can do to help her develop to her utmost potential"; "I read anything about autism I can get my hands on"; "Everything we know about cerebral palsy has been learned from reading any book I can find."

There is one caution, however. Parents need to be careful about *which* books they get their information from. Rapid changes and advances, not only in science and medicine but in how parents can deal with disabilities, make some books obsolete quickly, although more so for some disabilities than with others. Many parents of children with Down syndrome make the point that books only five years old can contain a good deal of inaccurate material, particularly in terms of assessing the future of their children: "Low expectations can be as dangerous as too-high expectations," one parent puts it.

"Books" usually means the local library, though parents with access to the library at a nearby college, university, or school of social work are especially fortunate. Many universities give "friends of the library" cards, usually for an annual fee, to residents of the state. There is now a considerable wealth of books on disabilities, many of them personal histories rather than studies. The hunt for the "right" books may become easier if the library has a copy of *A Reader's Guide for Parents of Children with Mental, Physical or Emotional Disabilities,* published by Woodbine House, Rockville, MD (See Appendix A; in addition to books, this guide lists national agencies and a great many other valuable sources of information.)

The *Reader's Guide to Periodical Literature* lists articles in a variety of periodicals, some very recent. Most of these are addressed to a general audience, and not particularly to parents of children with special needs. For more specialized material, parents will find *Academic Therapy* (Academic Therapy Publications, 20 Commercial Blvd., Novato, CA 94949-6191) especially valuable for educational ideas and resources. And *The Exceptional Parent* is easily the best source of parent experiences and how-tos, as well as information from professionals involved with children who have a disabling condition. One very special service that the periodical has been providing is an opportunity for the parents of children with rare syndromes to make contact with each other.

Parent Groups: Networking

No matter how such contacts are made—through periodicals and newsletters, through physicians, through disability agencies or state clearinghouses, or through parent groups—those whose youngsters have rare syndromes often find the connections invaluable. Through a specialist in genetics the parents of an adopted child with Tridione-Dilantin syndrome found the aunt of two boys with the same disability: "She was able to answer some questions about their growth and development that doctors could not."

A New York mother commented,

> Each family has to deal with the limitations set on Prader-Willi syndrome children and talk to other parents, until they can accept that this is a lifelong problem they have to deal with. Most agencies I went to had no knowledge of our problems; no hospital could give me help; in fact, few doctors knew the syndrome at all. My advice is to find a parent group and ask them where to go for help. I did.

In addition to the letters column of *Exceptional Parent* and the state self-help clearinghouses already mentioned, a valuable source both for information on the child's syndrome and for contacts with parents of other children with the same disorder is NORD—the National Organization for Rare Disorders, P.O. Box 8923, 100 Rt. 37, New Fairfield, CT 06812-1783.

Parents of children with rare ailments are far from being the only ones to benefit from parent groups. When the mother of a boy with a perceptual impairment saw the announcement of a parent meeting, she was dubious that they could help her. She only went around when she "finally got desperate."

After the first meeting I was convinced I should have joined long before this point. The chief benefit from this group and individual parents I have met through the group has been *knowledge.* I would definitely urge all parents to join a group of people with similar problems and pick their brains.

Some parents feel that the greatest benefit they have received from being part of a support group has been a very specialized kind of information: what have been called "tidbits of survival." Take any problem, and some parent is likely to have had to deal with it and to have some tips for other parents, as, for instance, diet: how to get the child to start taking solid food; or personal care: easy ways to bathe the baby who has cerebral palsy; or clothing: the special closures now available for children who can't button; or special equipment: items that can be made instead of bought or where to find hearing aids at the lowest cost.

Other tidbits of survival can help parents in just coping: how to get a baby who cries all the time to stop; how to deal with strangers' stupid comments in public places; how specific behavior modification techniques can eliminate tantrums.

Experiences of other parents can indicate where to find programs: the infant stimulation or early intervention program that somehow none of the physicians knew about. Or—and this alone makes the "parent grapevine" unique among sources of information—it can tell parents which doctors, which therapists, which programs, and which agencies are most skillful, most helpful, most worthwhile, and which are worthless. "I hoped to bypass some of the unqualified practitioners and unnecessary red tape," one mother indicates. "Parents told me whom to see, described the benefits and pitfalls of certain schools; they also recommended our present doctors."

These are the advantages of finding, and asking, those who have walked the same path before you.

Keeping a Record: Writing it Down

While not its primary purpose, keeping good records of your child's history is essentially linked to, and part of, the learning process. Details of the child's history may be invaluable not only for any medical and other professionals whom the parents will be consulting, but to the parents as well, because the record is specific for this one child, rather than general for all children with similar (but never identical) disabilities.

But even on the purely practical level, somewhere along the way nearly everyone who has experienced parenting a child with special needs learns how valuable, and sometimes crucial, it is to keep as many records as possible on the child. Ideally, the record keeping should begin with the birth records, everything dealing with mother and child, and go on from there.

One of the most useful parts of the record, part of every parent's "survival kit," is the contact list that develops over time. Even names and phone numbers that are absolutely unforgettable turn out to be frustratingly forgettable just when they're most needed, like the name of the doctor who gave Baby her shots.

One mother keeps the names, telephone numbers, and addresses of every doctor, therapist, and practitioner she has ever seen about her son. She even lists the names of individuals she's spoken to only on the telephone, if they've been helpful in providing information. Her contact list also has the same information on all hospitals, schools, and organizations she has dealt with in any way, including—most important—the names of the individuals she worked or spoke with (along with a thumbnail characterization, if she thinks she'll forget who the person was or what the contact was about).

That mother keeps her contact list in a three-ring looseleaf binder, as she has done from the beginning, and recommends it for its flexibility. Except when she's using it for something else, she usually keeps it handy (next to the phone) for quick reference.

No two parents keep exactly the same kind of information in the file or notebook, and some do a lot of changing around: after a while, the number of clippings from magazines and newspapers tends to get so great that usually they have to go into a separate file. Eventually, most restrict the child's file to purely personal and pertinent information.

Here are some other kinds of information parents often include:

- ✦ **Emergency telephone numbers:** These include first aid or ambulance service and police and fire departments. Important suppliers and providers, for example, oxygen supply house, prosthesis repair companies, paid and volunteer transportation services, are also listed.

- **The child's (and sometimes the parents') ID numbers:** Any time you deal with a government agency, such as Social Security Administration or Medicaid, you may need Social Security numbers, case or file numbers, Medicaid numbers, and perhaps more, private medical plan ID numbers, for example. They should all be there, readily available: having them is no guarantee of speeding up the process, but not having them when they're asked for is an almost certain guarantee of slowing it down.

- **The child's medical history,** *a whole section in itself:* If the baby was born with the disability, this includes prenatal information about both mother and child (such as problems during pregnancy and previous miscarriages) and perhaps about the rest of the family (genetic background, any other children with disabilities in the immediate or extended family). Also included are details about the birth and shortly after: Was the labor difficult? What was the baby's birth weight? How soon did the baby cry? Was the baby in an incubator? Why? Similar data, where the disability is the result of an accident or illness, are important. In either case, include copies of hospital and medical records where obtainable, either directly or through physicians.

- **The child's medication record:** It is amazing how easy it is to forget the names of drugs and medications, why they were prescribed, what they were supposed to accomplish, what they did accomplish, and any negative side effects.

- **Informal notes on conferences and consultations:** After consultations with physicians and therapists, note the questions you asked, and the answers you got, the professional's recommendations, and the follow-up. With organization and agency conferences, note the purpose of each conference, the participants (including notes on whose ideas really carried the most weight), the conclusions, and suggestions. If the conference is very important in the life of the child, it's a good idea to get an OK to bring a cassette recorder, if possible. No doubt then about who said what and why. (But if there is a hassle about it, parents say not to push it: it's not usually worth rocking the boat.)

- **The parents' observations on the child's behavior:** Physicians, therapists, teachers, and other professionals, at least those who recognize the contribution parents can make to the child's therapy, education, or other program, often welcome parents' observations. If they don't, they are worth keeping anyway for your own sake, as a record of changes, growth, progress. When you're most discouraged because "nothing is happening," there's the proof in black and white that it *is*.

✦ **Notes on conversations, face-to-face or over the phone:** It is especially valuable to keep notes on conversations with agency and school officials: they may not hold up in a court of law, but the parent's notes on a promise or agreement— made but not kept—can have a most persuasive effect. Sometimes, that is; there is no point in going overboard on this.

✦ **Correspondence:** This category is the letters to and from government and voluntary agencies, suppliers, school officials: whoever has been contacted about the child's needs and problems, including public officials and political figures, if you have called on them for help.

✦ **The child's educational history:** As with the child's medical history, this should be a section unto itself. It should include preschool programs and schools attended; infant stimulation and early intervention programs (with starting and finishing dates); names of teachers, therapists, and resource personnel who work with the youngster; copies of report cards and test results; and comments from school people. (And it offers a chance to dote: some parents also include samples of the kind of writing and artwork done at each level.)

✦ **Copies of all assessment and evaluation reports connected with the child's education:** Parents are entitled by law not only to a copy of all assessments, but to copies of test results, a written explanation of what the tests were and why they were given, what they were supposed to show, and which kinds of help they were supposed to suggest. There is no reason the parent cannot add some relevant—or even irrelevant and irreverent— comments.

✦ **Copies of every IEP:** The IEP is the child's *Individualized Education Program,* the "heart" of his or her education. Each has a very specific and immediate set of goals and objectives and is designed—among other purposes—to help parents monitor progress. (See Chapters 15 and 16 for a full discussion of the IEP.)

Of course, individual circumstances vary so much that the file or record may include any number of other types of materials. A rule of thumb for parents: when in doubt, write it down. It is impossible to predict which document, which event, will turn out to be important. And keeping a record can be useful not just to parents and child: with some children there are often multiple disabilities, and many doctors to see. It is wonderfully helpful to the doctor to see the record spread out: to see what has been tried, what worked, and what didn't.

But most of all, studying the record and learning as much as possible about every aspect of the disability can help parents with their most important responsibility: making the best choices, the best decisions they can.

6

....

"A Hard Decision to Make"

Genetic Counseling, Pregnancy, and Abortion

Chad's cerebral palsy was diagnosed at birth. Because he was their first child, his parents were doubly fearful: for him and for the other children they had hoped to have. "As a couple," his mother recalls, "my husband and I had always wanted a big family. But with the possibility that any more children we might have would be handicapped, too, we felt deprived of a dream for our future."

As it turned out, the family's "dream" was restored when Chad was tested and evaluated at a cerebral palsy clinic: they were assured then that there were no hereditary factors involved. They have since been "blessed" with two more youngsters.

In fact, hereditary or genetic factors are responsible for only a very limited percentage of the 250,000 American babies born each year with physical or mental defects. Cerebral palsy, for example, which affects one of every two hundred newborns, is not hereditary, but rather a motor function impairment resulting from brain damage before, during, or just after the baby's birth.

Besides such "accidents," a variety of other nongenetic factors can cause infant disabilities. For a number of reasons that are not heredity-linked, two out of five babies born to young teenagers are likely to be disabled, for instance. One of the most common is a very low birth weight, less than four pounds, six ounces. And although a very small number of Down syndrome cases, which occur no more than once in every seven hundred births, results from genetic factors, the risk is higher for mothers over thirty-five than for others.

Genetic disorders *are* responsible for three or four of every hundred infants being born with a disability. The real dimensions of the problem emerge from another statistic. It is currently estimated that some 22 million men, women, and children in this country have, or will develop, some sort of genetic disorder or a disorder with a strong genetic component.

In addition, gene-related disorders have a disproportionate impact on infants and children: nearly one-third of all admissions to children's hospitals involve youngsters with some sort of genetic disease. Many of the ailments are extremely grave: congenital diseases now account for between 25 and 35 percent of all infant deaths, aside from the many fetal deaths that are the result of chromosomal abnormalities.

Yet few couples seek genetic counseling before marriage, or before the first pregnancy. Those who do are generally likely to be couples whose family histories, on one or both sides, leave no doubt that such guidance is necessary. Others, like Chad's parents, are driven to seek such guidance only by the arrival of a baby with a birth defect.

A great many other couples who might also benefit never go for such help. For example, it might or might not bring some measure of comfort to parents feeling guilty for having had a baby with a disability to know that there might be a rational explanation for the disability, but it can undoubtedly help them to make decisions on family planning, if that is their choice. Although not all risk factors are genetic, it is likely that there would be fewer youngsters born with a disability—not only first children but later children as well—if more couples were made aware of the more than twenty-four hundred gene-related diseases and disorders that are known to exist. Among the most widespread (and therefore best known) are the following:

- ◆ **Cystic fibrosis,** which affects the functioning of the mucous and sweat glands and is the most common lethal genetic disease among people of northern European descent
- ◆ **Muscular dystrophy,** a progressive deterioration of function

- Glaucoma, a major cause of blindness
- Hemophilia, defective blood coagulation that can lead to hemorrhaging
- Sickle cell anemia, a blood disorder most common among black children, but also affecting some Mediterranean and Asiatic groups
- Tay-Sachs disease, which causes fatal brain deterioration and primarily affects children of eastern European Jewish ancestry (plus some others, including inbred populations of French Canadians)
- Thalassemia, a group of hereditary anemias mainly affecting those of Mediterranean or Asian descent
- Hypercholesterolemia, a defect of cholesterol metabolism, which heightens the risk of heart attacks in mid-life
- Huntington's Disease (also called *Huntington's Chorea*, also known as "Woody Guthrie's disease") a progressive degeneration of the nervous system

Others of the hundreds of gene-related disorders have so low a rate of occurrence that couples may not even suspect a possible problem. Janice Garrett's son was born deaf.

Additionally, when he was eleven years old, an opthalmologist diagnosed retinitis pigmentosa [a serious visual impairment]. Deafness and retinitis pigmentosa together are called *Usher's syndrome,* a recessive genetic syndrome affecting about 4 percent of the congenitally deaf population. Thus our son is now classified as deaf-blind.

Prime Candidates for Counseling? Who Is "at Risk"?

That kind of information makes family histories almost the only clue to the relatively large number of men and women who are carriers of potentially harmful genetic traits. With some of the more common hereditary disorders, it is possible to predict with some accuracy the degree of risk. A healthy mother, for example, may carry the gene that puts any male child born to her at 50 percent risk for hemophilia. Or when two healthy parents both carry the same abnormal gene, as is sometimes the case with cystic fibrosis, each of their offspring is at 25 percent risk of being born with the disease.

Advance investigation would appear to be particularly advisable for couples with certain geographic or ethnic backgrounds, given the known genetic linkages. But there are others at higher-than-average risk of having a child with a genetic defect:

- Couples from families with a known history of an inherited disorder
- Couples who have already had children with chromosomal or genetic defects, such as Tay-Sachs disease or Down syndrome
- Families with a child who has mental retardation from no known cause
- Couples with close relatives who have children with such unexplained disabilities or with genetic defects
- Those who have experienced difficulties with fertility or with infertility
- Women with a history of three or more spontaneous abortions or who have had a baby who died in early infancy.

A California father who became interested in the causes of birth defects after his daughter was born with cerebral palsy offers some confirmation of this last. He reports that not only did his wife have a miscarriage several years ago, but that she "has noted that other mothers of babies with cerebral palsy also have miscarried in the past."

Genetic Counselors

Even when a birth defect shows itself with one child, another child born to the same parents will not necessarily have the same impairment. A genetic counselor, on the basis of the considerable information available to her or him, can advise parents whether the defect is gene-related, and whether the risk of similar defects in another child is high, moderate, or low.

The doctor may be able to indicate some options for preventing a second occurrence or even to dispel the parents' fears entirely with the information that the defect is not gene-related at all. For example, if the mother has had rubella (German measles) during her pregnancy, only that one fetus was affected, and the mother's ability to bear normal children in the future is not in any way impaired.

A greater number of hereditary problems are being detected earlier today than in previous years because nearly all states require that certain tests be performed on all newborn children. There is good reason for this; some birth defects, including hypothyroidism and phenylketonuria (PKU), can be treated successfully if caught early enough. In the case of PKU and many metabolic or endocrine disorders of genetic origin, prompt dietary and other treatment can prevent mental retardation and early death.

Tests are also routine when Down syndrome is suspected, since that defect—hereditary in only about 3 percent of the cases—is the result of an extra chromosome easily detected during testing. Many parents of children with Down syndrome have said that they received not only confirmation of the disability, but also their first genetic counseling, after such testing, and found the guidance helpful in making their family decisions for the future.

Testing is actually just one aspect of genetic counseling, the first step in establishing the inheritance pattern. That may also involve additional testing for the child, for the parents, and even for various members of both families. Entire families are now tested to find the genetic "fingerprint" for the most common types of muscular dystrophy. Tests that can detect carriers of certain disorders chiefly affecting specific geographic or ethnic groups have now been developed; these make it practicable to screen selected people for the suspected genes. For example, approximately 10 percent of all black persons in the United States are carriers of sickle cell anemia. A simple blood test can detect the gene.

Counseling may also include the construction of a complete family medical history, perhaps even going back several generations. That kind of probing helps the geneticist to establish the precise nature of the birth defect. It isn't always that easy: recent studies have indicated that certain disorders caused by environmental factors may mimic or disguise themselves as genetic abnormalities. And it is possible for some genetic defects to be confused with others.

"Just in Case" Counseling for all Prospective Parents

Where couples are aware that there is some risk that their children may be born with hereditary defects because of their backgrounds or family histories, genetic counseling might well be indicated even before the first pregnancy. But what of those prospective parents who are not aware that there may be any problem?

George and Liba Nudell, whose son was born with spina bifida, which affects one of every five hundred newborns in the United States, feel that some sort of genetic counseling—prepregnancy counseling or prenatal counseling—is important for *all* prospective parents. They speak from experience: They were the couple who needed to and were able to make a quick decision to have surgery performed on their newborn son, whether or not the CAT scan showed that he "had no brain"—the doctor's warning.

> What had helped us to prepare was that the natural childbirth instructor had mentioned birth defects, and even before Elazar was born we had spent some time thinking and talking about it. The instructor suggested spending five minutes talking about it, no more, so that if you had to make a snap decision, you would already have broken the ice. And that's what we did.
>
> And we recommend that procedure to anyone we know who is pregnant. And I went back to the natural childbirth class and told the instructor and the class that if they hadn't yet sat down and asked themselves, "What should we do if the baby isn't perfect?" they should do so. Just in case.

Certainly any prospective parents who have reason to suspect that they may transmit genetic defects to their children should ask their physician for a genetic workup, as well as some discussion of the possible outcomes. If the doctor indicates that he or she is not very familiar with the steps involved in genetic testing and counseling, the couple should not hesitate to ask for a referral.

Couples may also refer themselves. For the address of the nearest genetic counseling center, couples should contact their local March of Dimes chapter. Or they can contact the following organizations:

Alliance of Genetic Support Groups
1001 22nd St., Suite 800
Washington, DC 20037
(800) 336-GENE or (202) 331-0942

National Center for Education in Maternal and Child Health
38 and R Sts. NW
Washington, DC 20057
(202) 625-8400

The National Center has published *A Guide to Selected National Genetic Voluntary Organizations,* listing more than 150 service and support groups concerned with genetic disorders and birth defects.

If the disability may be genetically linked, many of the national disability agencies also offer materials relating to testing and counseling. Couples contacting the local March of Dimes chapter should also request a helpful and easy-to-read pamphlet, entitled *Birth Defects—Tragedy and Hope,* and a booklet entitled *Genetic Counseling.* Both may also be obtained by writing to

March of Dimes/Birth Defects Foundation
1275 Mamaroneck Ave.
White Plains, NY 10605
(914) 428-7100

What to Expect from Genetic Counseling

In many cases, it is now possible for a genetic counselor to predict with some degree of accuracy the likelihood of both congenital defects and later-onset inherited disorders. Largely because of basic research over the past few years in the field of human genetics, medical science has made considerable progress toward understanding and detecting numerous inherited disorders and other birth defects.

And by dealing with all the factors that can cause genetic birth defects, as well as environmental ones (infections contracted during pregnancy or the effects of drug abuse, sexually transmitted diseases, smoking, or drinking, for example), the genetic counselor attempts to provide the information couples need in order to decide whether to risk producing a defective child, and whether and how they may be able to avoid that risk.

To some couples, the possibility of having a child with a birth defect is by no means a fearsome prospect: note the increasing number of childless parents now adopting children with special problems. (And many adoptive couples have taken more than one such youngster.) Nor does confirmation of the possible risk always resolve parents against having additional children. After Elazar Nudell was born with spina bifida, his parents learned that

> there is an increased chance that the next child will also have it. It makes us afraid, but it is not going to stop us from having more children. We'll take another one just like Elazar.

For many others, even for couples who love and want children, it is not an easy decision to reach. When Nicky Payne was born with a rare eye abnormality called *anophthalmia*—he was born without eyes—the parents learned that the condition is "sporadic; that is, there was no definite pattern to prove that it was genetically linked." Since the linkage was only a possibility, they decided to chance having another child, there was no birth defect, and they are happy: "I think since Nicky's little sister came along, his development has progressed much faster." But Paula Payne makes the point that

> when parents are thinking of having another child after having a handicapped one, it is a hard decision to make. Aside from the other things, they must also keep in mind the genetic factor. Some defects have been proved hereditary; some defects they are not sure about.

Informed Decision Making

Considering that there are many couples who, after genetic counseling, conclude that they cannot cope with even one child with a severe disability, it is not surprising that some parents of a child born with a genetically linked birth defect do refuse to consider having another. Those who want larger families choose instead to adopt.

The decision not to risk having other children with inherited defects or even a single one, may well involve some difficult secondary issues for which the couple might find counseling helpful: sterilization of one of the partners, for example, or pioneering techniques—artificial insemination, *in vitro* fertilization, or ovum transplantation—that can require an exploration not only of their medical aspects, but of the legal, moral, ethical, and psychological issues and implications.

Prospective parents should also be aware that counseling has its limitations. The mother of two daughters with autism found that counseling services were not very helpful to her, because the causes of autism are little known: there is no certainty that it has a genetic linkage.

Nor is genetics an exact science. Even after being reassured by counseling, a Virginia Beach mother had herself tested during her second pregnancy, because her previous child had been born with a form of spina bifida.

When spina bifida was detected during this pregnancy, it was of course quite a shock. The genetic counseling we had previously received informed us that spina bifida was not something that would occur again. Now we know better, both because of experience and competent genetic counseling.

Another mother who received genetic counseling after her daughter was born with Down syndrome also received assurances regarding future children—"the most positive statement at that time in our lives"—but still chose to have amniocentesis during her next pregnancy "to be sure."

Testing the Fetus

Amniocentesis is the procedure most widely used to determine, among other things, whether there is any defect in the fetus. It is simple and painless though it presents some problems, which the physician will undoubtedly discuss with the prospective mother/parents. After about the fifteenth week of pregnancy, a long needle is inserted through the mother's abdominal wall into the uterus and a small amount of amniotic fluid is extracted. The needle does not touch the fetus, but the amniotic fluid contains fetal cells.

These cells provide information on the genetic makeup of the fetus, including the presence of suspected genetic defects. The test also shows the sex of the fetus, which can be important when there is the possibility of a sex-linked disorder such as hemophilia.

In recent years, several other diagnostic procedures have been developed. In 1983, the U.S. Food and Drug Administration approved a new blood test, called the *maternal serum alpha-fetoprotein (AFP) test,* which checks for neural tube defects that involve the spine and the brain. In spina bifida, for example, tissues fail to close properly, and the spinal cord may protrude from the infant's back. This test is performed during the sixteenth to eighteenth weeks of the pregnancy, with additional tests following if a positive reading is obtained.

Another procedure is becoming more and more widely used. Known as *chorionic villus sampling* (CVS), it is performed no later than the tenth or twelfth week of pregnancy, earlier than other tests, and generally yields results within twenty-four hours. In this procedure, a flexible plastic tube is passed through the vagina and cervix into the uterus, and a small amount of tissue from the membrane surrounding the fetus is removed for testing. It is estimated that there is a one-in-three hundred risk of spontaneous miscarriage from the procedure.

CVS appears to be able to detect the same defects as does amniocentesis but somewhat earlier. Some physicians believe that barring negative information, CVS may eventually replace amniocentesis to a great extent, at least for women who present themselves early enough in their pregnancies for such testing. It lessens the risk for the woman because there is no penetration of the abdominal wall, uterine wall, or amniotic cavity.

An alternative—and safer—technology for isolating and testing fetal cells, which avoids the risk of miscarriage entirely, was licensed in 1990. This procedure requires only a test of the pregnant woman's blood; but because the analytical techniques still need to be refined, the method may not be widely available until the mid-nineties.

Sound waves are also being used to detect abnormalities in fetal development. Another new technique, called *sonography,* bounces sound waves harmlessly off the fetus, and an outline of the fetus appears on a computer screen. Although the procedure often shows the sex of the fetus, it is used primarily to detect anatomical abnormalities and certain functional problems, such as disturbances in the fetus's heart rhythm.

A special type of sonography is in part responsible for another dramatic development: *surgery on fetuses*. Using continuous sonography and very delicate instruments, surgeons have, for example, succeeded in relieving fluid buildup in the fetal brain, thus preventing brain damage and increasing the odds for a normal baby. Other possibilities of the technique are still being explored.

Of all the testing procedures, however, amniocentesis is still the one performed most often. And although the odds are about two hundred to one that even at age thirty-nine a woman will bear a normal child, the procedure has become almost routine for the increasing number of older women who become pregnant.

In 1978, there were only about three thousand such tests. The most recent estimate is that there are hundreds of thousands each year. While a New Jersey hospital quotes a figure of $560 (plus physician's fee) for the procedure, other published figures range from $170 to more than $1200, though it is not clear whether this includes both laboratory and physician's fees. For the vast majority of expectant mothers, the tests have brought good news: in only some 2 to 5 percent of the cases has there been any evidence of a defect in the fetus.

When the results do show that the fetus is defective, that news can be shattering. And when the choice is having a baby with a birth defect or aborting the fetus, there is not likely ever to be a decision more agonizing.

Ever since the Supreme Court legalized abortions (in *Roe v. Wade*) in 1973, polls have shown that between 80 and 85 percent of the public agree that an abortion should be legal if there is a strong chance that the baby will be born with a serious defect, an indication of the general sympathy for prospective parents faced with such a harrowing choice.

Courts have also been sympathetic. In 1979 the New Jersey Supreme Court ruled that a physician who failed to advise an expectant mother that there was a substantial risk that she would bear a baby with birth defects could be sued for "wrongful birth" when the woman subsequently gave birth to a child with Down syndrome. In *Berman v. Allan* the court held that by failing to inform the woman of the potential problem so that she could choose to have the fetus tested, the physician had deprived her of her right to have an abortion.

Similar decisions in other states have awarded parents estimated expenses for the medical care and education of children born with defects that prenatal testing might have discovered, had the mother chosen to exercise the abortion option.

Yet in the end, with or without public opinion—and assuming that abortion remains a legal option—it is a decision that each couple, or sometimes only the mother, must face alone. Even among parents of children with disabilities there are differences, strong feelings on *both* sides of the issue. Here is one such reaction, from Frances S., whose son was born with Down syndrome:

> If I had a close friend or relative who was over thirty and pregnant, I would strongly advise amniocentesis and abortion, if the procedure revealed Down's. You learn to live with the pain, but it is always there. Sometimes I feel that the word *special*, as in *special child*, is the most painful and ironic word in the language.
>
> I would tell my older, pregnant friend this, so she would know what lay in store for her if she didn't terminate the pregnancy—a lovable child with considerably more potential than might be apparent, and a lot of pain and heartache and deep suffering that is beyond tears and time.

But Fay Moore is one of those parents who found through amniocentesis that her baby would be born with Down syndrome—as her first child had been—and still chose to have the baby.

> I had an amniocentesis before Aaron was born, so I knew about him beforehand. I am not real fond of surprises. I am absolutely glad I had my amnio. I find that I can better deal with any situation if I have all the facts in hand.
>
> Obviously we decided against abortion for Aaron—though we carefully weighed both alternatives. I learned from this experience that you must assess each situation as it presents itself, in order to make a decision. Abortion is a personal decision, not an academic one. We are glad we decided as we did. Aaron is a delightful boy. His smile makes up for all his handicaps and problems.

Physicians also feel strongly about the choice, pro *and* con. When the Virginia Beach mother learned that she was carrying a second child with spina bifida,

> the obstetrician that diagnosed spina bifida was adamant that I have an abortion. He didn't even want me to go home and think about it. He wanted me to go through with an abortion right then and there. He said he was basing his advice on another child he knew with spina bifida, and all of the operations and problems that child was having.
>
> I left his office, called the local medical school, and met a more supportive doctor. During the rest of my pregnancy and delivery, all of the medical staff were supportive.

There can hardly be any decision more personal, but others who care are bound to have opinions too, as that same mother discovered.

> My family was angry—they felt that I should have aborted. Most of my friends were indifferent. We chose not to abort because we simply believe that life begins at conception.

It is a very personal decision and almost always a very difficult one. All that couples or single mothers can do in considering their options is to try to be sure that they receive comprehensive information to help them with their decision. Competent genetic counseling can provide not only the facts, but the broadest possible understanding of the situation and issues involved, as a basis for intelligent decision making.

All sorts of factors—family, health, economic, psychological, religious, ethical—contribute to the decision, and all can have weight in making the choice, as can talking with other parents, seeing similar children. Logically, it would seem to be a given that no one would deliberately choose to have a child with a birth defect rather than one without one. But even with the new fetal testing procedures that make it possible for more people to choose to wait, and hope for another chance, the fact is that many families have chosen to have such a baby rather than not to have it.

Holly W. was twenty-nine when her second child was born, a little boy with Down syndrome. She decided immediately that if she became pregnant again she would have an amniocentesis, but only to be prepared for eventualities: she did not believe in abortion. She was insistent on having a third child, no matter what.

Perhaps the best advice on family planning came from my O.B. [obstetrician], who said, "I can tell you the facts, but you and your husband have to live with your decision; I do not. So I will not tell you what to do."

7

······

"The Doctor Studied Medicine; I Studied My Child"

Choosing Physicians and Therapists

Could any human activity possibly be more individual, more personal, than carrying a child in the womb? Yet the climactic moment of giving birth becomes a team effort, especially in a hospital: someone else takes over, gives instructions, takes charge, especially when the baby is expected to have a birth defect.

When the baby is born with a severe ailment or a serious problem, even though it may not be life-threatening, there is an augmented team, a heartening array of specialists and technicians to take charge. What can parents contribute except their fears and prayers?

In the blur of those first traumatic days or weeks, when they find themselves with so much else to think about, it is natural for parents to assume, more often than not, that *someone,* like all those very competent someones in the hospital, will always be "in charge."

Someone always is, but who that "someone" is may come as a shock. Although some parents do get referrals to competent professional help even before they take the baby home, in all too many instances they discover that once outside the hospital door, they themselves are the ones in charge.

Of a boy with cerebral palsy: "We were told the diagnosis and were then left to our own devices to find help or information." Of a baby born with developmental delay: "No advice from the hospital or doctors from the time she came home from the hospital until she saw the neurologist." Of a little girl born with Down syndrome: "I remember being amazed and angered by the absolute lack of information from hospital personnel in terms of literature and sources of help. I thought to myself: How could I even begin to know what to ask?" And of a child with impaired vision: "Although the emotional support of the pediatrician was terrific, we got very little advice from the hospital itself. No one knew where we could turn for help, and that was perhaps the loneliest period of dealing with blindness."

Without any special advice from the little girl's pediatrician and ophthalmologist, a Colorado mother gave her baby who was born with limited vision no more care than she had given her other two daughters. But later, when she learned all the things she could have been doing for her, "it really frightened me that I had been doing absolutely nothing."

Decision Making: A Learned Skill

Most parents cannot do nothing: Disabilities often create and dictate their own urgencies, to find help *now,* or find help *again,* or find help *elsewhere.* And it is not only a matter of finding (Where?), but of deciding (Who? Which?). From those first days and on and on, in some cases for a lifetime, the name of the game is decision making for parents of a child with special needs, far, far more than for parents of other children; like it or not, ready or not.

There are those who never come to like it. There is no choice, though, *but* to be ready. To a very great extent, the life and well-being of the child are defined and determined by the decisions the parents make, every day, like it or not, able or not.

That means it is necessary to become—sometimes almost from day one—as able as possible as quickly as possible. You must learn where to find, and how to choose, a physician, pediatrician, pediatric specialist, pediatric neurologist, other specialists: a neonatologist, ophthalmologist, audiologist, orthopedist, psychologist, and therapists: physical, occupational, speech, and hearing;

and psychotherapists. Often many are highly specialized, highly skilled. How does a parent know which one is the right one?

The hospital, or the physician, or another professional, ought to be able to provide a referral, or at least a recommendation. If no other resource is available, and help is urgently needed, there is the phone book or the local medical society. But that should be a last resort: names and numbers tell you nothing about competence, knowledgeability, suitability, personality, quality.

Where it exists, anywhere in the area, a much more reliable resource would be the local chapter of a disability organization. They may have their own tested and trusted list of practitioners. They may have their own clinical team or be able to refer parents to such a group at a nearby hospital or to a private group.

As good, if not better, for referrals, though perhaps more difficult to locate, are other parents. One parent even refers parents' evaluations to those of professionals, who may or may not be prepared to make a recommendation. And another:

> Other parents help the most. The question of choosing doctors comes up so frequently in conversation with other parents. It seems to preoccupy them. They have had a bad experience with one doctor and have gone to another and another. They are the real experts. Get together with other parents who have—whose children have—the same problems.

Doctors to Avoid

If there are no parents around to consult and you're forced to fly blind, there may be no way you can altogether avoid some bad experiences. One limited study of parents of children with disabilities reported that one-third felt that the health-care professionals they were currently in contact with were not doing a good job.

Parents tell too many horror stories about their experiences to leave much doubt that there are some health care professionals out there, fortunately a relatively small number, who ought not to be involved in any way with children with special needs. Though there is considerable overlap and intermixture, they tend to fall into three basic categories: the ignorant, the incompetent, and the insensitive. Unfortunately, these characteristics do not advertise themselves in advance. Once they manifest themselves in practice, though, parents are advised to *run, not walk, to the nearest exit:* it is the only way to limit the damage.

The hallmark of the *ignorant* practitioner is usually the advice that you *do nothing.* Watch out for the physician who tells you you're overanxious when you detail your child's symptoms and assures you that "he'll grow out of it," long after your child should *already* have grown out of it, whatever *it* is. And who, when you protest that nothing is happening, tells you that you're "resisting" or "hostile" or subtly implies that you are probably feeling guilty about "causing" the disability. What comes across is that you are not helping with the problem: you *are* the problem.

For example: three—count 'em, three—pediatricians recommended that a little boy with autism be sent to a preschool program that would make him "normal" and prescribed psychotherapy for the parents.

Two parents discovered they were being "treated," instead of being interviewed, by the psychotherapist they'd hunted up for their son: the therapist "didn't believe" in learning disabilities.

A physician in Michigan did "the old clap test" in front of a little girl's face

> and when she jumped, declared that there was nothing wrong with the kid's hearing, and not to worry. But there *was* something wrong, and that stupid advice delayed our having audiological testing done, and taking the steps that were necessary to educate our daughter appropriately. I've talked to a number of other parents of hearing-impaired children who have told me that they had the same experience.

The Incompetent

As opposed to the "do-nothings," the incompetent doctor will generally recommend doing *something.* It is the something, the treatment they recommend, that usually identifies them: like

> ◆ The South Carolina doctor who wanted to operate on a boy's foot—but not the foot with cerebral palsy, his good foot—and then later operate on the bad leg to make it meet the good leg. That didn't make sense to me, and I

refused it. He said I'd be sorry I didn't listen to him. But I wasn't.

* The psychologist who recommended tying a little girl with Gilles de la Tourette syndrome to her bed, or that the mother drop her off at the nearest medical center with the message "I can't take care of her any more."
* The physician who decided to use an experimental technique on a youngster with cerebral palsy: he injected alcohol into the boy's legs to reduce the spasticity. The procedure only resulted in much prolonged pain for the child.
* The pediatrician who insisted on treating a small boy for bronchitis long after it became clear he wasn't responding to medication. When the parents finally got a second opinion, they found out immediately that the child was asthmatic.

The Insensitive

The insensitive are doctors who, for one reason or another, see the child as a "handicap" rather than as a human being, or clinic specialists who do not see the whole child, but a body part: He's here for an eye problem; I treat the eye. For the finger, go to a finger man.

Perhaps parents read too much insensitivity into that kind of attitude. After all, some specialists treat everyone that way. But there is no mistaking other examples of a special brand of callousness toward youngsters with a disability:

* The Louisiana physician who was actually afraid to touch a little boy named Isaac, who has cerebral palsy.
* The occupational therapist who would lay a little girl with cerebral palsy on the table and then tell her to do this, do that, roll over, in the same tone in which you might give commands to a dog.
* Surgeons who suddenly question the need for an operation, when they discover the patient has a disability.

Stephanie Nankervis, not only a mother, but the executive of an Association for Retarded Citizens chapter, provides special insight into the thinking of one such physician:

When Christopher was seven months old, he still had the intestinal obstruction and was throwing up much of his food. I called the surgeon and asked his advice about having the operation. He said that as long as Christopher was otherwise healthy, there was no hurry. Then I asked him whether, if this were a *normal* child, he would have the same advice.

He told me that he wouldn't hesitate or wait if this child were normal. I scheduled the operation right then. That was a lesson in the value of professional advice—it can be very prejudiced and detrimental to the welfare of a person who is handicapped. It depends on the value a person places on one who is disabled.

Finding the Right Practitioner

Here are some tips and guidelines from mothers and fathers who have been through the mill, to help you find a "good" doctor for your child. Your experience with one of the not-so-goods need not last longer than a single visit.

Find and hold onto the health care professional who values the child with a disability as a child; who hasn't forgotten how to care for, and about, the child; who touches the child, sometimes when it isn't even necessary; who hasn't forgotten that the healer's oldest skill was the "laying on of hands;"

- ◆ who is willing to take time with child and parent, even if it means longer than the usual perfunctory office visit;
- ◆ who answers questions in English, not medicalese or therapeutics or professional jargon;
- ◆ who is willing to listen, not only during an office visit, but after you leave the office, on the telephone when there's a problem that needs answering *now*. A California physician encouraged one mother to phone her regularly, even at home, for years. And an Iowa doctor arranged with a mother to call him once a week: *He could sense an underlying concern and just plain would talk until it came rolling out, even when I didn't realize what was bothering me. He earned every cent I paid him, and then some.*
- ◆ who trusts you, who respects your judgment enough to give

you every bit of information possible and then to present
you with the options;

✦ who welcomes your opinions and suggestions, asks for your
   observations, and recognizes that such information and insights may be a most valuable diagnostic tool;

✦ who treats you as part of the team, talks to you expert to
   expert, and *listens* to your questions or comments.

Avoid the practitioner who not only knows all the answers and
what is best for the child (though it is possible that he or she may
know a great deal) but considers you a time-waster and troublemaker if you question or disagree with *anything*. Avoid the practitioner who ignores you or seems to treat you like a dimwit.

I'm sure there are many good doctors, therapists, and counselors [says the mother of a boy with mild cerebral palsy], but
there are also many rude, inconsiderate know-it-alls who think
parents are stupid and don't know anything. These "experts"
expect us to follow their suggestions just because we are parents, and they think we don't know any better.

When I found out about my son's problem, I read every
book, article, and magazine about cerebral palsy. So when I
go to doctors, I ask questions. If they cannot spare five minutes
to help me understand, I don't go back.

When a professional respects the parent, sees him/her as a
team member, and invites parent input, the *child* benefits. One
mother didn't like the side effects of the medication prescribed
for her son's hyperactivity. She did some reading and searching
on her own, heard about an alternative medication from another
parent, and told her doctor. He agreed to try the substitute, and
it worked out. He respected the mother and had the confidence
that her respect for his competence would not be destroyed by
his acknowledgment that he could learn from her. It doesn't always
hold, but it is much more likely to be the *in*competent who balks
at letting parents "get into the act."

The physician knows medicine, the therapist his or her field,
far better than you do. But you know your child better than either.
And as against their weekly hour or two with the child, you may
be spending 7 days, 24 hours a day, 168 hours a week parenting:
most of those hours awake and seeing the child in all kinds of

situations, not the special conditions of the practitioner's office. "The doctor studied medicine; I studied my child," one parent says flatly.

Trust the practitioner whose ego is healthy enough to be able to say "I don't know the answer, but I'll find out." Trust the doctor who *does* know the answer but, unsure what to do about it, isn't too defensive to refer you to a specialist, a diagnostic team, or an evaluation center. A good doctor will suggest a second opinion and help you to find the supplemental or supportive therapies and services prescribed.

Getting a Second Opinion

Not all medical care professionals, even good ones, hold with parents getting second opinions: they speak of it as "doctor-hopping" and "shopping around" for a better prognosis, an opinion they like, or even a "magic pill" to "cure" the disability.

But the mother of a boy with a hearing impairment makes no bones about it: "We are always in the market for fifth and sixth and even seventh opinions when it comes to Michael's deafness," because "this area called deafness has few knowledgeable professionals—literally no medical types to speak of."

What if there *are* answers, but the answers all differ and make no sense? Joan Simon knew there was a problem with her daughter very early on, and refused to stop hunting for help.

> We went from doctor to doctor. Several said our daughter was absolutely normal. Other diagnoses varied from hopelessly retarded and schizophrenic to emotionally disturbed, and many diagnoses in between, including being a victim of poor parenting.

The little girl was not properly diagnosed as having autism until she was six. Only then could the parents know what kind of help to look for. They

> finally found a knowledgeable, supportive child psychiatrist, who prescribed drugs for our daughter's hyperactivity and got us on a behavior modification program to deal with her behavior problems. That set our lives back on an even keel.

For another couple who ran into a similar situation—"no two doctors worked with each other, we got conflicting reports, we could not put our faith in any of them"—the clinic and the diagnostic team approach worked out very well. They checked out every cerebral palsy clinic in two states by phone, found one that gave them "good vibrations," took the child there, and "in three days learned more than in the entire three years before."

Sometimes that "second opinion" can pay off immediately: a diagnostic team or a new physician with new insights and approach, and presto!: the "magic pill" turns out to be nothing more than a fairly standard medication that controls the seizures.

For one reason or another, not all parents find their way to a good diagnostic team. The Texas mother of a little boy with cerebral palsy poses the problem such parents often face: "If we see three doctors for one problem, each has a different diagnosis, different advice, and different medication. Of course this creates a big problem: whose medical expertise do I listen to?"

It is a matter of ignoring some of the advice, picking and choosing among the rest, making your own decision. Alanon, the Alcoholics Anonymous affiliate, has a saying: "Take what you like, and leave the rest."

How? Some parents rely on "gut instinct." "People must learn to trust their guts and do what they think best." "Sometimes a parent has to go with gut feelings about a program, or about people, or about the future of a child." "Do what feels right for your child. My gut instinct proved to be the best way to go, time and time again."

The More You Know . . .

In the end, any choice parents are forced to make among conflicting alternatives *will* have to be based partly on instinct. But they can help to eliminate some of the guesswork by doing what most do anyway, but doing it more intensively: *learning everything possible about the disability*. Read everything, study everything available about the disability or the special problem. Go to meetings, ask questions, and talk to other parents: who chose which way to go, and how did it work out?

Even in the midst of every other urgent demand on parents' time, emergency or routine, self-education has to get a top priority: It takes informed judgment to know when to take advice, when to disregard it. It can be taken as a given: the more you know, the better it will be for the child.

And the more you know, the better you will be able to stand up to those health care professionals who, in their determination not to allow parents to have any "false hopes," come across as prophets of gloom and doom and who are—though proving it may take years—not infrequently wrong.

"No One Can Tell You the End"

It is not simply that parents are told a child is "hopelessly mentally retarded" or will never walk; or, after an accident, will never be able to do anything more than lie in bed and "vegetate." Valuable time may be lost in the child's development if parents unquestioningly accept a neurologist's advice to "take her home and just feed her: he didn't hold out much hope for our daughter's development." Or when therapists tell the mother of a little boy with cerebral palsy that the therapy is a waste of time and money: "We get tired of hearing 'he won't' or 'he can't.' They don't *know* what he can or what he will do."

An Iowa couple was similarly advised not to search for therapy or other help for their daughter who was born with brain damage: no matter what they did, she would only progress at her own limited speed. They ignored the advice, set up an exercise program, and "discovered she was very bright and vocal."

Despite professionals' "realism," other parents have persisted and helped their "vegetables" to walk and talk and go to school. "Doctors are not infallible," one parent says in explanation, "and they cannot possibly tell you the end from the beginning."

Parents still get prognoses all too often about what their children can or cannot do that are "down toward the low end of the scale" and do not cover the full range of possibilities, says Florene Poyadue. She is Executive Director/CEO of Parents Helping Parents in San Jose, California, and is a parent educator and advocate.

I've heard professionals say that it's because they don't want to give parents false hopes. What I tell doctors and pediatricians at our briefings is that people cannot live *without* hope. "You do not have to give them false hopes, but I also do not want you to dash every hope to the ground. If you want people to work with you, and work with their children, remember that people have a very difficult time putting time and energy into something they have no hope for.

"If you will simply be honest," I tell them, "about both the high end and the low end of the scale for children, whatever the disability, we can go ahead and do our own hoping. There is a difference between giving hope and allowing people to have hope. You don't have to give us hope if you can't honestly do so, but don't take it away either."

If any parent chooses to believe in "miracles," it is not necessary to find a physician or a therapist who does too, so long as he or she will not prevent the *parent* from continuing to believe in them and will help with any and all of the practical steps and therapies that may just make those miracles happen.

A Way to Monitor Progress

In terms of therapy, parents must think in terms of one step at a time rather than one day at a time: "Where are we heading?" instead of "Let's wait and see." It is precisely that approach that educators now take toward children in the Individualized Education Program (IEP), which is the core concept of Public Law 94-142, and in the Individualized Habilitation Program (IHP), that state and other institutions need to develop for their residents. There are no guarantees of results, but there must be a clear indication of the results being sought. Goals and objectives, including the parents' goals for the child, should be spelled out along with a timetable for achieving them.

Usually, the therapist's goals are or should already be there, whichever the type of therapist (physical, occupational, speech, even psychological and certainly behavioral). But articulating the goals by spelling them out in some detail and adding a timetable (even though experience may later necessitate changes) give the parent a useful yardstick with which to measure progress. Too often the therapist's "it takes time" masks the fact that nothing is really happening. A detailed plan or program, preferably on paper and including the timetable, allows the parent to discover that fact sooner rather than later and take action.

It is admittedly a fairly new approach, based not only on parents' experiences but on the concept of parents and children as consumers, and not every therapist may be prepared at this point to agree with and to it. That does not mean that parents—if they still have confidence in the therapist—should automatically reject him or her and find another. Even without an individualized therapy program, parents can continue to monitor the progress of therapy and child as they have always done.

Some parents may not want the added burden of this program. What a written program does, in fact, is to increase not only the therapist's responsibility, but the parent's as well. Instead of making a single decision and waiting for results, parents must make repeated assessments and decisions as they monitor progress against a specific plan and schedule: stick with or change objectives; stick with or change therapies; stick with or change therapists. Changing requires a decision, but so does staying put.

Parents as Decision Makers

More decisions are required in lives that many parents find already too full of decisions needing to be made. But over the years, who else can be responsible? As the child grows, as the needs and problems change, who else can find, monitor, and change physicians and therapists and other health care professionals, programs, schools, services, and suppliers? Who else amid all these changes are the constants in a child's life, the only ones always there?

For specific time periods, one or another of the health care professionals may serve as the child's case manager. But trained or not, most of the time the parents have to take over. And all of the time, it is they who have to make final decisions. Trained or not, in one respect parents *are* best equipped for the job: "Knowing my son better than anyone," a Minnesota mother says, "I *wanted* the responsibility."

For the parent fearful of making a mistake, it helps to realize that doctors and therapists are not necessarily infallible, either. Wanda T.'s daughter has cerebral palsy:

> I have learned that professionals are also human beings, subject to mistakes and bad judgment. Therefore I consider all advice, but weigh it against my eight years of nonprofessional

expertise—as a mother—and decide what is good and what is not so good advice.

There's an essential clue there, should you wind up making the wrong choice, on how not to lose time sticking with that mistake. Two questions to the physician or therapist in advance may help: 1) What results can my child and I expect from your course of treatment/therapy/medication? 2) When can we expect to see those results—or at least some signs of them?

The answer to the first question may not be that good things will happen but that the treatment will keep bad things from happening. If you need to ask more questions, ask them: every answer adds to your knowledge. And if you're like the Texas mother faced with three different diagnoses, three kinds of advice, it may be frustrating, but don't lose the chance to learn three times as much—it will only help you in choosing.

Two additional pieces of advice come from parents with many years of experience: the first from Janice Garrett, whose son, now twenty-two, is profoundly deaf:

> The best advice I ever got was from a psychologist who told us, "Make the decision based upon the best knowledge and advice you have at that point. And don't, at some later time down the road, look back and wish you had done something differently. In other words, don't cry over spilt milk."

The other bit of counsel comes from Elaine Clearfield, whose daughter, born with mental retardation, is now twenty-four, who urges young parents to "become experts on their children's disabilities":

> Mothers should feel they are the experts. And if they are not experts, they can become experts if they want to. In the end, what it comes down to is that parents have to believe in their own ability to do what is best for their disabled child.

8

"Part of Your Life, Not All of It"

How Not to Become a Handicapped Family

There is no question that the arrival of a child with a disabling condition can create great stresses in a family or intensify those stresses already present. And it can drive couples apart. But on the evidence of parents' experiences:

- A family with a child who has a disability does not have to be a handicapped family.
- A family with a child who has special needs and requires special care does not have to disintegrate under stress.
- It is not the child's disability that handicaps and disintegrates families; it is the way they react to it—and to each other.
- Finding a way to deal with the added stresses, minimize them, overcome them—by sharing them—can glue a marriage (and a family) together more firmly than ever.

Despite the general impression among professionals as well as parents that marital breakups are substantially higher among families that have children with special needs, the research is inconclusive. Some studies report no statistical differences, but other findings, based on limited studies, range from one citing "severe disharmony" among nearly a third of families with such a child to another claiming that "two out of three marriages ended in divorce before the handicapped child attained the age of six," to still another indicating a 75 percent separation and divorce rate among families of institutionalized "abnormal" children in one midwestern state.

Perhaps more among medical professionals than among parents, it is often believed that a child with a disability can destroy a marriage simply by being. Parents of a newborn son with Down syndrome were even warned by their doctor that taking their infant son home from the hospital instead of placing him in an institution immediately might break up their marriage.

Some husbands and wives tend not to blame the child's disability so much as the other partner's reaction to it. For instance, the father of an eight-year-old with cerebral palsy who is also a health care professional says with some pain:

> My wife and I separated over a year ago, and our divorce will be final this month. I attribute a great part of the problems in our marriage to the stress brought about by our son's condition, specifically the surgeries, recovery from surgery, continual trips to various clinics, and so on.
>
> In addition, my wife became obsessed with his handicap: whenever we went out socially, it was her sole topic of conversation. And it was the same at home.

The opposite side of the same coin: "My husband wouldn't accept that there was anything wrong with the boy, never would, never did," says the devoted mother of a youngster with Down syndrome. "When my son was fifteen, he divorced me." Mothers— even those with outside employment—rarely see such nonacceptance as an option for themselves, however.

Affixing the blame naturally depends on who is telling the story. But there seems little doubt that in the past—when fewer mothers worked outside the home—some fathers were far more likely not to accept the fact of the disability, perhaps because they were away from the baby so much of the day that they were then not as closely bonded to the child as the primary caregivers were. Sometimes a father's apparent lack of involvement is really a lack of confidence or understanding, a distorted notion of "mother knows best."

Or perhaps the child who has a disability poses a problem for a father's self-image: "It was impossible for my husband to think he had anything to do with having a handicapped child. He never had anything to do with his son."

"You might have to choose between your marriage and your child," says the mother of a little girl with multiple disabilities. "It's really unfortunate when that happens, but if you're really strong, go with what you believe in. I made my decision; my children are everything to me."

Living With a Child Who Has a Disability = Tension

The truth is, when the child who has a disability becomes part of the family, the tensions begin to mount, and it is too easy for couples to find fault with each other, dump guilt on each other. The anxieties often begin to grow from the moment parents get the news. One mother stayed up all of the night before her baby, who has Down syndrome, was due to come home from the hospital, frightened by visions of what might lie ahead.

The reality can have a nightmarish quality, too. Only someone who has been there can truly appreciate the pain and the effort it takes to care for the child who has somehow stopped in mental development as a two-year-old, yet has the body of a man or woman.

Living with a child who has special needs can be like living inside a pressure cooker. The less the child is able to function, the greater the stress on every other family member. The expenditure of both physical and psychic energy is so great that everyone tends to be on a short fuse. "With a child who requires a lot of attention and patience," says Karen Ruschill, whose five-year-old son has one of those "invisible" mental disabilities that still have not been clearly classified, "the stress load can be unbearable."

You ask yourself why you had to be punished for having a special child: "Why can't I have a *'normal'* child?" Things become affected by your attitude. You take it out on your husband, your children, your friends, anyone who comes near you.

Parent and professional groups are increasingly concerned about an even more total form of rejection, child abuse. Where it is happening, it is likely to be a dark family secret. But a study of child abuse cases that have surfaced shows that a disproportionate number of these children are disabled. (See Chapter 11.)

Yet for every parent who lashes out indiscriminately, there is another who turns inward, turtles up, crawls into a shell. "I remember how very alone I was for months on end," says a mother who still doesn't have a "label" for her nine-year-old, "not able to discuss my hurt and agony with my husband, who was also in such pain." It is as if a door stood closed between the two, with neither able to turn the knob, and as one parent puts it, they wound up "crying in separate rooms." For such couples, it helps to find a way to "cry it out" together.

Some parents can't or won't cry at all. When only one partner breaks down, he or she may interpret the spouse's failure to make a display of feeling as a *lack* of feeling. That behavior, though, may be a different way of dealing with feelings and may be a great source of strength to the other partner, provided that partner is given to understand the nature of the ostensible calm.

The Safety Net

Other couples speak of their experience in coping with a child with a disability as bonding them closer together, making their marriage stronger and firmer, building on the commitment to each other that was there in the first place, like the parents of a little girl born with spina bifida:

> After our daughter came home, and everything started to sink in, our periodic depression and "bad days" were hard, and the strain became tough. What got us through that, and continues to be our safety net even now, is that we talk a lot about everything, and both of us are very committed to keeping our marriage healthy, by talking things out often.

It is the rare family that does *not* have to devise some sort of "safety net," or coping mechanism, to deal with the repeated emotional traumas of caring for a child who requires special care and attention. Couples do not have to cry together, but the health

of the marriage and the welfare of the child and others in family
demand that they do find a way to *talk* together. It can begin, if
possible, with those first moments of grieving. Linda Clement's
daughter Caty was born with Down syndrome:

> While we were in the hospital we had many, many thoughts,
> but none of them included not taking her home. We did admit
> to each other, however, that it would be so easy if we would
> wake up one morning while I was still in the hospital to find
> that Caty had died during the night. This would have removed
> the situation from our hands.
>
> I've always been so grateful that my husband and I were
> able to talk so openly to each other and be able to discover
> that one of us could not think anything that the other one had
> not already thought. That helped to remove all guilt.

Not every couple has the special kind of relationship that
allows them to communicate so freely and rewardingly from the
outset. Parenting a child effectively—any child—requires even
couples who have difficulty in communicating to do so as best
they can. Where there is a child requiring constant care and constant decisions, couples *have* to find a way to talk about their
feelings, expectations, and hopes, and the child's problems. And
they need to find the way to talk out any disagreement about the
management of the child.

Involving Both Parents

Of course, there are simply too many decisions to be made for
parents *never* to have disagreements. Disagreements are not necessarily unhealthy: unhealthy is not being able to resolve them.
"If the two of you can communicate, then you can conquer, and
the one who wins is the child," one mother comments.

And, another points out, there's a second and equally good
reason for talking things out. "Resolve differences quickly, as
coping and helping are a lot better together than apart."

In the all-too-common case of the father's withdrawing from
involvement with his child or appearing to want to withdraw, one
solution is for the father to become involved (or to get the father

involved) in learning as much as possible about the child's problems, too.

Particularly in the early days and months, when neither parent is likely to be very knowledgeable about the disability, it is a mistake to let one parent do all the listening and studying and learning. The divorced mother of a girl with mental retardation blames part of the couple's marital problems on the "father's inability to accept her problems [and] his lack of involvement (i.e., consultations with doctors, teachers, and other professionals) in the diagnosing of Libby's disabilities."

Within the limits of the parents' working hours, every attempt should be made to schedule visits to doctors, therapists, and other health care and education professionals so that husband and wife can go together. Parent and disability group educational meetings are often arranged for evenings, so that fathers and working mothers can attend. And whenever one parent can't make it, the parent who goes should pass along the important information as fully as possible.

Ways of Communicating

Each family needs to find its own best communication pattern. In some families, spur-of-the-moment discussions work out well; in others, it may be more productive to set aside specific times for regular conferences. Except in special circumstances, these should not be parents-only conferences, but family meetings with the children. Some parents hesitate to have the youngster who has the disability present, but one mother makes the point that "this is where many families go wrong, in not including the child in making decisions about himself."

Couples should make it a point not to disagree on important issues in front of their children. Family meetings can offer a healthy deviation from that pattern: obviously the only way to arrive at an agreed-on approach to caring for the child is to examine and evaluate all of the possibilities. The time not to disagree, the time to be consistent and concerted, is in following through on what has been decided. One mother wryly notes the consequences of inconsistency: "We have real trouble with that, and our son knows it, so he uses it all the time to manipulate us."

This same mother notes that she and her husband "always

have some differing opinions in dealing with our son's daily problems." The solution is for each parent to give a little ground: "What we do after we understand each other's feelings is to compromise."

Compromise is recommended, but sometimes easier said than done. When each parent feels strongly about a point of view unacceptable to the other, here are some guidelines parents suggest:

- Never decide today what you may be able to decide more peaceably tomorrow: "We've delayed big decisions when we couldn't agree, using the time to gather more information, go for a second opinion, talk it over some more."
- Try one parent's approach for a limited period: "My husband felt the therapy our son received at school was adequate, and the expense for private therapy was too great. We came to an agreement to give my idea a trial period. After a few months my husband was in full agreement to continue with the private therapy."
- When the disagreements span a wide range of issues, and a longer period of time, agree to allow one parent—perhaps only temporarily—to be the child's "case manager": "Let the parent having more responsibility for raising the child make the basic decisions and support him or her in every effort to obtain the best environment and education for the child with open discussions as to how best to achieve the ends chosen by the spouse having primary responsibility for the child."
- Agree on an "emergency procedure": When a situation must be handled on the spot, "allow the party who seems most determined in a specific episode to take control. Afterward, definitely talk rationally about the episode—not in front of the child—and keep an open mind. Usually a mutual understanding for the future can be decided on."

But allowing one parent to become the decision maker, whether in an emergency or as "case manager" over a longer period of time, does not mean making that parent the sole caregiver.

Too often the responsibility for nurturing the child with a disability falls automatically, and entirely, on the nonemployed mother: "I work hard and come home dead tired," the father says, and who is to deny it? But there is no work fathers do that is more tiring and tension-producing than having to care for a child with special needs for a large part of the day. In a "who's tireder?" contest, don't bet against the mother.

Whether or not it is a two-paycheck family, the father who cares about the child has to be willing to share in the care *of* the child. That doesn't necessarily mean splitting every chore fifty-fifty, but it does mean looking for ways to lighten the mother's load to whatever extent possible.

Siblings

There is no reason that brothers and sisters can't shoulder some of the responsibility, as well, in any family. But in a single-parent family, there is almost no way the mother of a child with special needs can manage without help from the older children: as baby-sitters, taking the child for a walk in the park, learning to change diapers—you name it. In any family, though, the trick is to begin involving the other youngsters early enough that it's nothing more than "doing what comes naturally." Linda Clement's younger daughter Caty was three-and-a-half

> and her sister Annie was about six, when she asked what Down syndrome was. I explained to her that basically it meant that Caty would learn more slowly than most children, but that in nearly every other way she was like other kids. Annie's reaction was: "So what? I'll help her learn."

There are any number of reasons why the child's brothers and sisters need to know as much as possible about the nature of the disability, according to each one's age and ability to understand and deal with the information. But there's no more important reason than their understanding and acceptance of the sibling's need for a disproportionate amount of the parents' time and attention.

That sounds fine, in principle. But in real life, although siblings may understand, they will still be jealous and somehow feel short-changed: "I'm nothing but a second-class citizen in this house," an older brother told his parents. The real feelings of a younger brother suddenly surfaced and jolted his parents: "Boy, I wish I were blind. Those blind guys get all the breaks." Did he really feel that way? "Not all the time, but sometimes it sure seems that way."

Theoretically, every child in the family should get equal treatment, attention, affection, time with every other child. But it is impossible not to make the child with special needs "more equal" than the others: he or she needs more of everything. The others have to get less, and parents like Carol J., who has a gifted child and younger twin boys, as well as the youngster with cerebral palsy, feel totally frustrated:

> The hardest part of being a family with a handicapped child is giving everyone the attention and time needed. We are in our late thirties, and our time is all for our children. But time for everything and everyone is impossible at this time in our lives.

"Quality Time" for Siblings

Accepting the realities, what parents suggest is that siblings get not equal time, an obvious impossibility, but "quality time." No matter how much time supervising and caring for the child with the disability takes, parents cannot forget the other children in the family. Somehow it is necessary to arrange for times when the others can have one or both parents' attention entirely to themselves, to know that they too are loved and wanted.

When the child who has a disability is still young, that may take some serious arranging: asking friends or relatives to take over for short periods, or hiring a babysitter, or finding a respite care program (discussed in the next chapter). But later on, the child ought to learn to respect the needs of brothers and sisters.

Yet, even with such "quality time," there are likely to be occasions when siblings can feel overwhelmed by the unfairness of it all. One source of help is the growing number of community sibling support groups. Some have been organized by agencies dealing with specific disabilities; others accept all siblings who feel the need to counsel with their peers. One such group is Siblings for Significant Change, 105 East 22 St., Room 710, New York, NY 10010; (212) 420-0776.

Some of the groups are part of the Sibling Information Network, Connecticut University Affiliated Program, 991 Main St., Suite 3A, East Hartford, CT 06018; (203) 282-7050.

There are also an increasing number of local and national seminars under social work and disability group auspices. And North Carolina, for one, has set up "Let's Grow Together" workshops for siblings.

Brothers and sisters of children with disabilities can get a free booklet entitled "Am I the Only One?" from the United Cerebral Palsy Association of Western New York, Children's Center, 4635 Union Rd., Buffalo, NY 14225; (716) 635-4440.

Other Ways of Coping for Siblings and Parents

Another source of help for siblings is professional counseling, both for individuals and for groups. The group may be a peer group, or it may be for the entire family: siblings are not the only family members who sometimes resent that so much family activity must revolve around, and take second place to, the needs of the family member who has special needs.

Not everyone feels that psychological counseling is always recommended in such situations. Such therapy is more likely to be helpful when the depression or anger is not reality-based or when it seems disproportionate. Mollie W., who has three daughters, the youngest with autism, is one of those parents who does feel a counselor might be helpful to many families.

Having Deanna has added a lot of stress to our family. She takes a lot of my time and energy, which in turn affects the other girls and my husband. There is a lot of anger, because of the "why us?" that we all feel. I'm not sure that we have totally gotten through the grieving process; maybe we never will.

I am not sure that a family can survive this kind of crisis without very supportive friends/relatives or counseling. Too many feelings come into the situation to go on ignoring them. I personally would like to get my entire family to a counselor to deal with all the anger and denial, etc. We have to learn to accept what has happened to our family unit.

Where the depression doesn't seem acute enough to demand counseling, it may be helpful to do something new and different; there is nothing more energizing than learning something new. As long as it excites the learner, it doesn't matter what it is— ceramics, Hindustani, break dancing, knit-one-purl-two—the effect will be therapeutic.

Some families find the strength to cope with what has happened to the family unit through their faith.

I am told that 60 to 80 percent of families with disabled or handicapped children end in some sort of marital problem or divorce. For my wife and me, who know the Lord (we are Christians), we have been able to give Him our burden and have rested in His care.

More succinctly, "I am a Christian," another parent says. "God gives me strength."

Parent Support Groups

Other parents have found the help they were looking for in parent support groups, not one kind of help, but a number of different kinds, underscoring the point that to keep from becoming a handicapped family, each family needs its own kind of help. It may be the "insights from couples in a similar situation" on handling profound depression. It may be "good advice from a parent group" when husband and wife can't agree on the way to handle problems.

Families can get the names of individual counselors or counseling services and agencies from any number of sources, but a parents' group "can not only give you referrals, but tell you about the counselor's style" and help parents decide which door is likely to be the best for them to knock on for help.

Husband-wife groups are particularly valuable in providing role models for fathers who are having trouble accepting either the reality of the child's disability or their responsibility in helping to cope with it. Carrie N., whose daughter has cerebral palsy, originally sought out a support group because she felt "all alone out there." But when the couple attended a conference together, there was a welcome bonus.

It was a wonderful experience, especially for my husband, who had been letting me "take care of our daughter." He needed to know other parents—men—who also had special children. My husband's favorite part of the seminar was entitled "For Men Only." He never told me much about it, but it really changed his attitude.

Support groups can help families (especially mothers) come to grips with another, self-destructive attitude. Nothing handicaps a family more than being totally absorbed in the child who has special needs and requires special attention. Yet many mothers, and to a lesser extent fathers, feel guilty about having any concerns, any interests, any life that does not center on the child. Almost inevitably, love turns to resentment; it can even become hatred.

The experience and encouragement of others like them, who have been there, often help parents to get that particular guilt monkey off their backs: "The group gave us much emotional support on how to help ourselves first, so we would be able to help our daughter."

Any family with a child who has a severe disability has special stresses and more than usual problems. But the family that defines and limits its life by the child's needs, that allows that child to disorganize it, to break down completely the way normal families operate, is bound to become a handicapped family, less capable after a while of meeting the child's needs.

It takes experience to recognize that. The luckier ones are those who can learn from the experiences of others that parents must be kind to *themselves* and their other children, even if only now and again, if they want to continue being able to give their best to the child who has the disability. Take some priority time away from the child, whether it is a daily "time out," or an occasional treat—a movie with the other kids, an hour in the bathtub—and above all, a night out just for husband and wife. "It is not always easy," says one mother who found a way to do it, "but even if it comes down to just doing one hour a week of something for you yourself, it will help."

So, from others who have gone through it before you:

- Don't devote your total life to the child. You have to consider all your needs, and not just the child's disability.
- You *must* take time for yourself, your mate, and your other family. If you don't take the time, you can lose all sense of reality and be of no help to the child *or* yourself.
- Be careful, as the days go by, that the child with the disability becomes a part of your family's life, not all of it.

9

"How Your Child Will Benefit Most"
Institutionalization: Not the Only Alternative

Obviously, no one but the physician can determine the extent of the newborn's disability, the need to attach the infant to life-support systems, and whatever other active medical care and treatment are immediately required. But in those first few traumatic days a considerable number go further: suggesting, advising, recommending, urging, even pressuring parents to "put the baby away," for the baby's sake, the parents' sake, the family's sake.

Not a few parents recall that experience and their own rejection of the advice, born of the recognition that the physician's advice to institutionalize immediately, however well-intentioned, is in fact an intrusion. The basis for institutionalizing a child with birth defects is only rarely medical (outside of hospital care, of course). However parents phrase it, their decision, even if it is only an "if" decision, a fearful "for now" rather than a confident "forever," is always based on quality of life: the family's, as well as the child's.

The sureness and speed with which the greatest number of parents reject the recommendation to institutionalize is grounded in faith, or better said, in each family's own kind of faith: religious ("God sent her to us. My husband and son and I will always love her and take care of her") or moral/humanistic ("I would never put a pet dog in a kennel for the rest of its life, so I surely would never put a human being, no matter how ill, in an institution"), or belief that parents have the right to make miracles if they can. ("When the time came for us to leave the hospital, my husband said we would try home and see if that worked, before we would ever try anything else," one mother says, and another says, "We had to at least try; and we needed her to be with us to do that.")

Yet at some later point in their lives, and their child's, even the surest may be forced into "thinking the unthinkable": considering placing the child, temporarily or permanently, outside the home, on the basis of what is best for family and child both.

The reasons can be compelling: a youngster with whom the parents cannot communicate, "unable to go, or to tell me when he has to go, to the toilet. And unable to walk: I could not make him wear his braces because he's so heartbroken when he's uncomfortable." The survival of the family may be at stake: coping with the child at home is, or turns out to be, beyond the family's strength or ability. It may be their inability to find—or worse, to pay for—supportive services. It may be changing relationships and conditions and circumstances. It may be the one inevitable circumstance: aging.

Aging Parent, Aging Child

If there is a single concern that bonds and distinguishes parents of children with more severe, or multiple, disabilities, it is the question: What happens to my child when I grow too old to care for him or her, or when I die? There are in fact some who find themselves obsessed with the problem from the baby's infancy. And many more treat "permanent placement" in the same way as making a will, as a way of looking after loved ones, to be considered before the need becomes urgent.

> I intend to institutionalize my child at age twenty-one, an age when most children leave home. When we are gone, this will be his life. I would like to help with the adjustment and be satisfied that it is the right choice.

For a single parent, worried that no one else will "be around" to take over the responsibility, the decision may come earlier rather than later, as it did for one mother in the Southwest.

I have been divorced for ten years. I am now fifty-four years old. The fear of sudden death on my part, and what would happen to my daughter should I die during the night, forced me to consider placement.

When you are young, you can beat all obstacles. When age begins to move in, you find you can't. Facing the reality that my child can never be left alone in an apartment or home, can never earn a living, can never cook a meal or do the laundry, is the most agonizing experience of my life.

For sixteen years I have directed my energies to keeping her out of an institution, and tomorrow I am going to place her there. I don't regret in any way the years she has been with me. I only wish I were younger.

When an older child, perhaps a teenager, is able to move into a group home, in many respects parents can feel consolation in the similarity of the move to other young adults' leaving home: the age is right, and the atmosphere of the new home is noninstitutional.* That still doesn't make it the easiest of decisions. But it is infinitely less painful than when parents are forced to weigh the placement of a much younger child.

The Severely Disabled

What makes the decision particularly difficult for many parents of a young child is that at the outset they are "so sure" that they *can* manage. And if affection and determination were all it took, they could. But here, as in other contexts, love is not always enough. There are other circumstances that may force families to consider early out-of-home placement. Although a variety of factors will inform a family's decision, there is no question that the nature and severity of the child's disability is the number one consideration. Often the most difficult children are those with

*For a perspective on noninstitutional community living for people with even very severe disabilities, see Chapter 20.

"invisible" disabilities: hard to diagnose, almost impossible to live with.

Jared Doze was a Kansas youngster who had been diagnosed as having epilepsy, with acquired aphasia and a behavior problem. He was functionally deaf; he did not speak. Yet at ten his photograph shows a boy with an all-American smile, charming, a fine physical specimen, completely normal-looking.

By the time he was a year old, Jared had become "a behavior problem." By the time he was five, his other problems had surfaced. The family was then living in Oklahoma. There were four other children, two of them babies.

> In 1978 Jared was involved in a communications program, where he saw different doctors who studied him and then all came together to tell us their findings. They had decided that Jared was animalistic; was dangerous to us, our other children, and himself; and that he should be institutionalized. They told us there was no help for Jared and that he should not be in our home. My husband was ready to kill. I could see it in his eyes. When we left the conference, we were both crying, and Kent said Jared would be institutionalized over his dead body.

Yet in three years this loving family was forced to accept the fact that they could not give Jared the help he needed at home. To get him that help, they decided to place him in a private residential school. What had finally tipped the scales was the realization that being at home was not really helping Jared: he needed not only love, but a kind of care the family was not equipped to give him.

The moment of parting was understandably "very traumatic." But Vicki Doze

> did not feel guilty. I knew it was the best thing for him, and that we owed him that chance. It would have been selfish to keep him home just to spare our feelings.

But Jared's out-of-placement turned out to be therapeutic, not just for him, but for the rest of the family as well.

> Our social life was zero. No one invited us to their homes. Mealtime was such a hassle that we quit inviting our friends over to eat when Jared was three. We never went anywhere.

Our friends became few, and we did not see our relatives much because it was too awful to travel.

I remember shortly after taking him to school, my husband and I went to a funny movie. We could not laugh; we had forgotten how to laugh. We had to learn how to let go and relax. We had been living and surviving on pure stress.

Jared stayed at the residential school for four years, but all that time his father continued to feel that the family was not complete "without everyone at home." But when he was brought home in 1987 he was still so violent—threatening his family, kicking holes in the walls, breaking furniture—that he had to be placed in foster care. He was in and out of foster care until May 1992, when he came home—hopefully for good.

Jared is now eighteen, six-feet one-inch tall, has won many ribbons at the Thomas County (KS) Fair for his pencil drawings, and is a fine basketball player who dreams of playing for the Denver Nuggets "because they need help." He began talking about four years ago when he apparently outgrew his seizures. A special teacher first began to teach him to read three years ago, and he reads now at the second grade level. Jared needs a full-time interpreter in school because of his hearing impairment, but he will be a senior in the local high school this year. In the past two years he's learned to keep his temper within acceptable limits most of the time. "He wants so much to be a normal teenager," Vicki Doze says, "though he knows he's different. We have to keep reassuring him that he's not dumb, that he is just starting later than other kids."

There are services in northwest Kansas now that the Doze family helped to get going because Jared needed them, Vicki says proudly. But Jared is their greatest pride:

Eighteen years ago we were told that he was so severely mentally retarded and had so many other problems that he would never be anything more than a vegetable. There were times when I just wanted to give up, but in the end because of Jared we have become stronger and tougher than other families.

I'm so glad now that we didn't give up. Because today Jared shows—with his drawing, with his personality—that he's gone from an almost-vegetable to an almost-normal teenager. I'm glad I didn't give up, because Jared really has something to give to the world.

Respite Care as an Alternative

Where the stress and strain is less constant and unremitting than it was for the Dozes, the family may be able to take the pressure off from time to time through a respite program or services. Finding a way to get themselves some time off, even as little as a few hours a week, may help delay or avoid entirely the need for permanent change. This may be especially helpful when there has been a sudden change in the family's circumstances: separation, divorce, remarriage, a new baby, or the illness of the parent who is the primary caregiver.

The sometimes desperate yearning for a chance to "take a break" is a bond shared by most parents of youngsters with special needs. "I have never considered institutionalizing my son. However, I have often felt the need for respite." And another parent: "Our child is part of our family. His physical needs are difficult, but we have found in-home respite care allows us the intermmittent break we need to continue."

Respite is a term so flexible that it can mean anything from an hour off for shopping to a week's vacation with the rest of the family. In its most time-honored form, respite is simply a sister (or brother) or a mother-in-law who comes in for an afternoon to let Mom go to the hairdresser's. Or the babysitter who makes it possible for husband and wife to get out to the neighborhood movie or for an evening with friends. Respite care can come from a friend or an agency or service that provides paid respite aides, or from exchanging respite services with other families who also welcome it. It may be inside or out of the home: not just a cooperating family's house, but as part of a center program. It may even be stretched (with somewhat older children) to include a week or two for the youngster at summer camp.

One family is quite deliberately using out-of-home respite care to prepare themselves for their son's (and brother's) permanent placement in a residential facility, already arranged, but still several years off because of a long waiting list. They feel that because he has mental retardation, cerebral palsy, and epilepsy (only partially controlled), he needs more help than they can give him.

Another family testing their feelings about out-of-home placement for the child who has Down syndrome is following a different approach. They might eventually put up the little girl for adoption, if they do decide that it would be better for her. To help them make up their minds, an agency has placed their daughter with a foster family specially trained for such temporary placements, with experience in parenting children with special problems.

That family welcomes the chance to take the pressure off without committing themselves permanently. Some of their problems have nothing to do with the child, and if things ease up, they hope eventually to bring her home again.

Adoption

In many cases foster care is seen from the beginning as a step to adoption—a step more and more preferred by parents of children with disabilities in recent years as an alternative to institutionalization, and particularly as more and more couples are indicating a willingness to adopt children with permanent or severe disabilities. Some families have adopted as many as nine such boys or girls.

Frequently the foster care or children's agency has to all intents and purposes already taken the child over from the natural family and is providing training and support for the foster parents and the child until permanent adoptive parents can be found. It is not unknown for the foster relationship to "take." A 1985 Michigan court case, for example, found a black couple, not related to the child, battling white foster parents for the right to adopt a seventeen-month-old racially mixed Down syndrome baby. Similarly, Henry and Gale Hedgecock had been foster parents to several babies before Craig came into their lives.

> The case worker said he was probably blind; he is a miracle child, as so many premature babies are. Our family motto was "survival of the fittest," and Craig *is* a survivor. When he was three years old, our own children (three of them) wanted to adopt Craig. And we did.

Sometimes, in the case of certain types of mental conditions, an in-home placement is made in which neither agency nor parents is aware of the problem. It may not make a difference: the executive of Spaulding for Children, a New Jersey agency specializing in the placement of difficult-to-place children, describes a family that discovered that their teenage foster daughter was psychotic: "They went ahead with the adoption anyway," he says, "because they viewed her as *their* daughter who needed help. *Their* daughter."

In the past decade or so there have come to be more and more couples, and single people, with or without children of their own, who are willing to adopt a child known to have a permanent disability. For some time, in fact, prospective parents have had to put themselves on a waiting list to adopt a baby with Down syndrome, and children with various other mental and physical disabilities are also finding adoptive parents far more frequently. The prospect does not appear to be forbidding or off-putting to childless older couples, or to couples who have been waiting and searching for a child to adopt for a longer time.

Margie G., who is the mother of two children with, and one without, a disability, doesn't feel that it takes special or extraordinary people to adopt, considering the rewards.

> Knowing you cannot have children somehow makes you want them more, and the disability is minor, especially when whatever else they may or may not do, they love you, and you are a family.

For parents who have come to feel that they have no choice but out-of-home placement, local social service agencies are usually the best at-hand source of information on adoption possibilities and procedures. A priest, minister, or rabbi may also be able to provide some guidance. If no local source is available, among the best sources are:

Adoptive Families of America
3333 Highway 100N
Minneapolis, MN 55422
(612) 535-4829

Aid to Adoption of Special Kids/AASK
3530 Grand Ave.
Oakland, CA 94610
(415) 451-1748

Children's Adoption Resource Exchange (CARE)
1039 Evarts St. NE
Washington, DC 20017
(202) 526-5200

Children's Defense Fund
122 C St. NW, Suite 400
Washington, DC 20001
(202) 628-8787

National Adoption Center
1218 Chestnut St.
Philadelphia, PA 19107
(800) TO-ADOPT

North American Council on Adoptable Children
250 East Blair
Riverside, CA 92507

When Institutionalization is the Only Choice

If the decision to place comes when the children are older, teenagers or nearly so, the only possible placement may be in institutions, no matter how reluctant parents may be. At a time when every state is pushing for the deinstitutionalization of persons with even severe disabilities, it is ironic that community programs that might help such people to remain in their homes have been cut or eliminated entirely, those that existed, that is. The financial burden that this places on some families may leave parents no alternative but to institutionalize their child.

Patricia McGill Smith, a Nebraska parent who is now Executive Director of the National Parent Network on Disabilities (NPND), noted some time ago that in Nebraska

> there are a number of parents currently on waiting lists. This has caused a number of things to happen. One leadership parent placed her son in a state institution recently. Another parent, who was recently widowed, placed her son in a church-related private institution. Another tired and despondent young mother did the same. Many other parents are baffled as to how to get systems to respond to them.

> The only advice that can be given in such cases, if there is a possible choice among placements, is for parents to try to check

them out in advance of making the decision. Not all institutions today are the human warehouses to which society's "rejects" were once relegated, but some may be. Not all institutions are establishments operated for the benefit of their staffs, though clearly some are (otherwise why would the residents' last meal of the day be at 4:30 or 5:00 P.M., with bedtime at 7:00 or 8:00, even though it may not get dark in summer until ten?).

But the situation is changing: many states are now experimenting with and establishing smaller facilities, such as group homes in the community, and are financing voluntary programs by disability groups to operate supervised apartments and other innovative projects. Local chapters of disability organizations—if they do not run such programs themselves—may know of possibilities not too far away. Social agencies, local hospitals, physicians, other parents may all have clues to such newer nontraditional placements.

But there is no substitute for parents' checking them out themselves, not only before placement, but as frequently as possible afterward. Aside from any effect parents' visits may have on institutional standards (it would be optimistic to suggest that it is very great), every study of institutional care has shown that the residents who receive the best care and the most attention are those who receive the most visitors.

When Stress Becomes Unbearable

Except in a medical emergency, the decision to place a child outside the home is rarely a sudden one. The situation in the home deteriorates gradually, over a long period. Parents "wear out" under the daily burden of care, or, as the child grows older (and bigger), temper tantrums and other behavior become more difficult to cope with.

The survival of the family may be at stake, literally as well as figuratively: "It got to the point where I had to come between my son and my husband to keep him from killing the child," one mother says; and another: "I must tell you that there were times when I wanted to kill the kid, and myself, for that matter."

Even under such circumstances, with each parent knowing what the other knows and both under great stress, they may have different feelings about what should be done. When a Florida couple learned that their baby daughter was deaf, had microcephaly, cerebral palsy, and a seizure disorder, the mother recalls:

> My husband told me that he did not love her, and he wanted to give her up for adoption. He said he was just not strong enough to handle what was in store for him for the rest of his life.
>
> I told him I understood, but could he really give her away, knowing that for the rest of his life he would have a daughter but could never know how she was, or whether she lived or died?

At this juncture, it may be helpful for parents to discuss their feelings separately or together with a professional counselor, a psychologist, a social worker, or a minister. Even if they do so separately, it is important that not only the parents but any other children in the family be given an opportunity to get help in dealing with the situation and the situation to come.

Advice from other parents is usually valuable in a different way. It can be extremely helpful to hear others who share the same problems and the same values, and who may have faced the same situation, discuss not just both sides, but every side and every aspect of the decision.

"A Very Personal Decision"

Advice can be helpful, but only when and if parents want it. Unsolicited advice—whether from other parents, the best intentioned of professionals, or loving relatives and friends—can equate with pressure. It is especially difficult to take if the decision has to be for institutionalization. It is best to deal with such advice bluntly, parents say.

> Tell them how you feel straight out, and tell them that it is your decision, and to please let you handle it the way you feel your child will benefit most.
>
> This is a very personal decision. My only advice to other parents on how to decide is to follow their own hearts. No matter what they decide, they don't have to answer to anyone but themselves.

What it comes down to is that no matter how well-meaning the advice of others, no matter how experienced and competent the comments and suggestions of professional counselors, only the parents, the family, and the child have to live with the decision. And their decision must be based on factors only they can really know; it is a decision never taken without pain, and it is the best decision they are able to make, for themselves, their family, *and* the child.

Do what *you* feel is right. Not everyone should keep the child. There are circumstances where it may prove too much to handle. Just don't feel guilty about your decision.

10

"I've Gotten No Help from the System"

The "Miracle" of Life, the Cost of Living

They only let me hold my baby for a couple of minutes. Then the nurses took him away, and ten minutes later the doctor came into my room. My baby would never walk, he said; he'd have no bladder or bowel control, could have mental retardation, and needed emergency surgery right away. What BJ had was spina bifida. And then they whisked him away by helicopter for the operation.

Since that first six-hour surgery to close his back and insert a shunt—a tube to drain excess fluid from his head—Bryce James Gillies has had frequent additional surgery: for a life-threatening bowel obstruction, for his club feet, on his hips. The first time BJ came out of a body cast, he broke a femur just by rolling over; the next time it was both femurs and an ankle. Today a standing frame helps to prevent further breaks.

From early on, BJ has had too many appointments with health care providers to count—the orthopedist, pediatrician, urologist, the spina bifida clinic. At home, his parents learned to catheterize him every three hours and to change the casts for his club feet once a week.

In addition to medical attention, BJ has also had an occupational therapist, physical therapist, social worker, personal care attendant, child care provider, teachers, and a speech therapist. It took six different assessments—and six months—to determine that BJ had mental as well as physical deficits. The assessment process was necessary to get him into an early intervention program (at age two). That's also when he got his first wheelchair.

Now that he's three and in preschool, "You can't keep up with him," says BJ's mother, Lynn Gillies, "and he's a happy, social kid."

Some other happy youngsters also needed a lot of extra attention. Michael Caruso, also three, has had a total of seventeen operations. He was born with hydrocephalus; his physicians also thought he might be blind and couldn't be sure what other problems there were.

What Sarah Caruso remembers most about the early days is feeling "devastated." For four or five months—"but it seemed forever"—mother and father dealt with one critical medical issue after another. It never even occurred to them that there might be "something else." But when Michael was seven months old his parents sought out a developmental specialist and "that was our first contact with reality," Sarah says.

The doctor made it clear that Michael would not be "just a year behind," as they'd been hoping. When he also suggested the possibility of institutionalization, "We felt as though there had been a death in the family. But it was therapeutic for us; we got moving."

And some of the worst possibilities never happened. Michael isn't blind—he has very good close-up vision. He is now sitting up and has complete use of the left side of his body; someday he may even walk. Sarah thinks he's a "miracle child," because "his cognitive abilities are very strong, and he has a complete range of emotions.

"But what is really so great about him," she says, "is his spirit, his zest for living, his pure *joy* of living."

"I'm Very Proud"

Even more moving is the story of a baby named Emily Abel, who is now eighteen months old and will be going into an early intervention program in two more months. She was born with myotonic dystrophy, a genetic disorder; in 1992 geneticists discovered that this disorder is unique in that it grows more severe with each generation. Ellen, the baby's mother, has had to cope with a milder form of the disorder all her life.

At birth, Emily went right into a respirator. When she was diagnosed, Ellen Abel recalls, "They told me she wasn't going to live a year. She was too weak, she wasn't eating." Even now the baby has to be fed through a G-tube (a gastrostomy tube), which is inserted through an incision in the stomach wall. Ellen Abel recalls those early days with pain:

> She couldn't cry, she couldn't do anything. She was very le-thargic, very floppy. They also told me she was cortically blind and had cortical atrophy. It was no kind of life for anybody.
>
> So when she was a month and a half old we decided to pull all life supports from her. The doctors at the hospital said, "We're going to give her the benefit of the doubt—that she'll tire after two hours and die." And they gave her morphine because they didn't want her to gag. We had everybody there—priest, my husband, all my close friends, everyone you can imagine.
>
> But she didn't die. She just lived. She breathed on her own. And she made it all through that night with no problems. The only thing they did was they gave her a little bit of oxygen through a nasal tube—which was fine with me.
>
> It's hard to tell people what I go through now on a day-to-day basis. I don't ever get a free moment, except Mondays, when I get respite. I have to mix and puree her food so I can get it through the G-tube; when she gets sick—even a cold or an earache—it's always life-threatening. But she's not blind, she just learned how to sit up, and when she starts in the program—three hours a day three times a week—I won't have to stay there, so it will be a real break for me.
>
> I'm very proud of what I've done so far. Emily has turned my life around, but there's no question of institutionalizing her. I don't think she's bad enough to be institutionalized.

The medical "miracles" begin at birth—but they are often needed for a long time afterward. Nicole Anderson was born two months prematurely and spent the first two weeks of her life in an incubator with an apnea monitor, to guard against interruption of her breathing. That was the beginning. Since a developmental pediatrician made a diagnosis of cerebral palsy, she has had three orthopedic surgeries and services from more than seventy-five professionals, her mother estimates.

Of all the newborns whose lives are touch-and-go at birth, a very high percentage are those born prematurely, often with an extremely low birth weight. Some 250,000 babies a year are born in this country more than two months early and weighing less than 5.5 pounds; some 45,000 weigh less than 3.3 pounds.

The medical rarities of a generation ago have become matter-of-course. Medicine has pushed the "natural limit of viability" lower and lower: By 1960 babies weighing only 3.3 pounds were being routinely saved; in the nineties, newborns weighing as little as 2.2 pounds survive. It is a tribute to those who provide what is termed "high-tech aggressive neonatal care," using an array of sophisticated electronic equipment, resuscitating babies born "blue" and "dead"—and keeping them alive.

A far greater number of "preemies" and other "at-risk" babies survive to leave the hospital than used to, but, as one physician has said, "We can save them, but we can't repair the damage."

The Cost of Caring

If there has been any ray of sunshine in Ellen Abel's life, it is that she hasn't had to worry about the financial cost of Emily's care. All of the medical bills, including those for the nurse who comes in to look after the baby, have been paid by the county, through the area's regional center, which in California provides case-management.

The other source of financial assistance for medical bills for families with a member who has a disability is private insurance—up to a point. When Eric Lescarret stopped speaking at age two, Judy Lescarret had to seek out her own therapists. The diagnosis was autism. The family's medical insurance covered all of the therapists Eric needed—except one: the speech therapist who worked with him for three or four months. For that they were billed $3,000; the insurance company wouldn't pay it, so they paid it off little by little.

In San Jose, Sue Sitler's husband's insurance pays for special glasses for their son, Travis, who was born with a congenital visual impairment. But the insurance company balked when she wanted to take Travis to a specialist in San Francisco. They gave in when she told them, "You find a pediatric ophthalmologist down here who has dealt with Travis's problem, and I'll use him."

Ideally, private insurance should work the way Nancy Crowe's California HMO has: "We have not seen one medical bill since Jonathan was born," she says. Jonathan requires constant medical attention because of his many problems; he has had two shunts, numerous MRIs, CAT scans, and other tests, as well as second opinions from Stanford to San Francisco. Nancy is rightly grateful: "They've never raised any objections or mentioned a maximum," she adds.

One of the major problems that many families with a child who has a disability encounter is that health care coverage comes with the job—and often stays there. An example was reported in *Epilepsy Today:* When Eric Johnson's father changed jobs in Oklahoma, his new employer had the same health insurance carrier as his old one, so the Johnsons assumed that there would be continued coverage for their four-year-old son, Eric, who has epilepsy, cerebral palsy, and other disabling conditions as the result of a birth injury. But under their new policy—repeat: *same insurer*—they discovered they would *not* be covered. The disability had now become a "pre-existing condition" not entitled to coverage.

What made the situation considerably worse is that it was not just Eric who wound up going without health coverage. In order to pay for the antiepileptic drugs Eric had to have every day, the entire family had to go without health insurance. They could not afford both Eric's medications and the $200 monthly premium for family coverage.

A Minnesota father was luckier. When he changed jobs, he discovered that the new carrier that covered the family would not do so immediately for their baby, who had "pre-existing conditions." Their good fortune was that coverage would begin after a year.

In other families lucky enough to find that they have locked-in coverage before their baby is born with special needs, the family member whose employment provides the insurance may find himself locked into the job just to ensure coverage.

"Insurance Is a Real Concern"

Katie Ganley is seventeen months old. She has a seizure disorder with developmental delay. Before she was diagnosed, her mother was planning to finish college and go back to work. That's not the only plan that has had to change.

> Before this happened, my husband was thinking of changing jobs. But given the need for insurance, and the fact that she may not be accepted by another plan because of the pre-existing condition, he hasn't pursued that. That is a real concern, because we can't just pick up and change jobs. The insurance benefits are just too important to us.

But when there is a child in the family with a mental disorder or emotional problems requiring long-term treatment, "locked in" may not be locked in at all, or may mean only a ceiling on payments. Dixie Jordan, who is Coordinator for Emotional Disorders for the Parent Advocacy Coalition for Educational Rights (PACER) in Minneapolis, knows several such families:

- The father of a child with schizophrenia lost his job. He was fortunate enough to have the money to buy health insurance on his own—except that he couldn't find a private company that would sell it to him for his son.
- Another private insurance company had a maximum clause in its coverage. There was a little boy in the family with an emotional disorder. Two weeks after he was hospitalized for treatment, his coverage ran out. The family had no funds for either further hospitalization or for home-based treatment and medication. The boy wound up sitting in a corner of his room every day.

Deb Jones was another mother who ran into a similar coverage ceiling. Her adopted son, Roger, had a psychotic break his first day in school. Deb found that her private health insurance had a maximum of $50,000 for problems like Roger's—still not definitely diagnosed, but possibly manic-depression, possibly schizophrenia—and there too the coverage quickly ran out. Though Roger needed continued hospital care, his mother couldn't pay for it. And when she turned to the county's social services, they would agree only to his placement in a residential treatment center, which was not what he needed.

A father writing in *Exceptional Parent* described how—while his daughter was still in the hospital—his private insurance company raised his premiums by 125 percent and warned him to look into Medicaid coverage because his policy might be cancelled altogether—the "greed factor of the private insurance empire," he calls it.

Even families with continuing health coverage from private carriers are not safe from the widening spiral of exclusion—if they make the mistake of having a child with a disability. Reports in March 1992 described how after three-year-old Marisa Renshaw was found to have only one kidney, the family's group insurance company began to double the family's premium each year, the maximum increase permitted in California. Eventually the premium soared from $1,552 to $16,000 annually, a payment the family couldn't possibly make. In practical terms their insurance became *un*surance.

Major problems with Marisa's kidney, but no other part of her body, are now covered through a catastrophic health insurance plan of California Children's Services, and the Renshaws' other daughter has an individual Blue Cross policy with a $1,500 deductible. Mr. and Mrs. Renshaw have no coverage, however, and like so many other families in the same situation, they are terrified that if either has a serious illness, the medical bills will bankrupt them and result in the loss of their home.

One of the pressures currently building for some sort of national health insurance plan is that among the 35,000,000–40,000,000 Americans without such coverage, there are about 10,000,000 children. Fortunately, most youngsters manage to avoid conditions or diseases requiring long-term care and treatment, but for the more than 300,000 children with severe disabilities or illnesses, there is little question that health insurance is a must.

A report by the Pepper Commission on Long-Term Health Care, a congressional group named after the late Congressman Claude Pepper, affirmed that most families with a member who has a disabling condition are caught between a rock and a hard place. "Public financing for home- and community-based long-term care is quite limited," the report says, adding that "private long-term care is not an option; insurers do not sell policies to persons who are already impaired;" they "have not marketed long-term [health] insurance policies to young adults and children" with disabling conditions. It is families of the person with a disability who "provide the bulk of long-term care," the report concluded.

"Kids Live Now"

And if they can't? The single mother of a little girl in the Midwest who has multiple disabilities, without health insurance and faced with mounting bills, told Virginia Richardson, PACER Manager of Parent Training:

> I feel like my baby got caught in a machine, and my decisions were made without me. Now I'm bearing the consequences of that, and I would like to ring peoples' doorbells and say, "This is what you've left me to deal with, and I've gotten no help from the system."

Virginia, herself the mother of a daughter with mental retardation and epilepsy, makes the point that

> We deal with much more complicated kids nowadays than we used to, because kids live now who used not to live. We have the technology and the know-how to save lives. Now we need to assume responsibility as a nation for the cost of care afterward. Right now it's destroying families. If society says that everyone has a right to live, then it also has to provide medical and other care afterward as a *right.*

The Association for Persons with Severe Handicaps (TASH) is among the national groups advocating for such a program. In a policy statement, TASH has noted "the responsibilities of society and government to share with parents and other family members the support necessary for infants with disabilities [and] . . . the obligation of society to provide for life-long medical, financial, and educational support to persons with disabilities . . ."

"There are countless children . . . whose lives have been saved or enhanced by these medical advances," the Association for the Care of Children's Health adds, "and many whose complex and chronic medical conditions require ongoing care and support from the health care system." Yet "increasing numbers of children are living in poverty with little if any access to health care." For such children, "burgeoning medical technology and the emerging crisis in health care financing are dramatically affecting the delivery of health care."

As evidence of what the crisis means—and perhaps the most compelling reason for national health insurance—is a 1991 study by Dr. Paula A. Braveman and a team at the University of California at San Francisco that found that newborns with severe low birth weight, infections, or birth defects whose families lacked health insurance coverage for them got substantially less medical care in the hospital than did insured infants. Not only was less care given to uninsured babies, but they were discharged from hospitals sooner than those with private insurance or Medicaid coverage. Translation: those who needed care the most got the least.

The gloomy forecast is that an even greater number of families may be the victims of this kind of discrimination in the near future. A December 1991 report by the Center for National Health Program Studies at Harvard Medical School showed the number of persons without any insurance coverage at all had increased by 1,300,000 in the previous year alone. The two reasons given confirmed what parent advocates already knew: private coverage is less affordable, and insurance companies are increasingly declining to write policies for people with pre-existing conditions.

But it might have been far worse, one of the coauthors of the report, Dr. David U. Himmelstein, indicated, if the Medicaid program had not been expanded last year to cover many pregnant women and children in low-income families. "Without the expansion of Medicaid," he noted, "the ranks of Americans without health insurance would have swelled by 4,400,000 last year," instead of the actual 1,300,000 increase.

The Medicaid "Safety Net"

With so many families unable to get private health care insurance, many more families than previously are turning to Medicaid, only to run into the barrier of income eligibility. Medicaid is the federal-state program that provides health care coverage for families, provided they qualify financially.

"The health insurance industry forced me to turn to Medicaid," David Penzenik of Indiana told a congressional committee, for whom he was testifying on behalf of the United Cerebral Palsy Associations, in 1990. His son has multiple disabilities, and in the process of trying to get the boy the help he needed, said the father, "I have learned a great deal more than I ever wanted to know about the health insurance industry."

In order for his son to become Medicaid-eligible, the family had to "spend down" all of its assets, not just using up savings, but cashing in IRAs and even life insurance policies. But even after they were accepted, they found Medicaid had drawn the line as to what was "medically necessary." They still had to go to private charities, family members, and friends for funds to pay for such items as a wheelchair lift to get their son into the family van, one of the items that Medicaid ruled was not a medical necessity.

Why the need to "spend down," to spend away the assets that might be needed in another family crisis? Because of another policy, usually referred to as *deeming*. Under Social Security Administration regulations, all family resources, with certain specified exceptions, are "deemed available" for the care of a child with special needs.

Forced by overriding need to tackle the "deeming" concept, some parents have fought for and won the help necessary for their children. Among them were the parents of a nineteen-month-old Indiana baby named Matthew, who had vision and hearing impairments and a cognitive disability. They would have had to impoverish themselves in order to pay for the many health services and equipment Matthew needed to survive, including a ventilator, an apnea monitor, a G-tube for feeding, and a nurse twelve hours a day.

Medicaid turned them down. But as a result of a direct appeal to Health and Human Services Secretary Louis Sullivan—with the support of Indiana's political leaders and some intense parent-group lobbying—they were granted a waiver setting aside the family's resources as a source of care for Matthew and making the baby's own (nonexistent) income the basis for establishing his eligibility.

That "set aside" waiver dates to 1989. There is nothing automatic about its application in other states, since each administers its own state Medicaid program. There are therefore fifty different sets of regulations. But it did set a precedent that has been followed, though to only a limited extent, elsewhere. Deb Jones had to find that out for herself:

> When Roger first got Medical Assistance [the Minnesota term for the state's Medicaid program], I was told by the county social worker that I had to liquidate all my assets to under $2,000. I refused; and when I went and checked the law for myself, I found that there were actually two ways to determine Roger's eligibility—either on the basis of the parent's income or on the child's income and assets, because he is mentally incompetent. I don't know why they didn't tell me that; I know they knew it.

There is a good deal of such anecdotal evidence which suggests that in a period of tightening budgets at every level of government, states are doing their best to keep eligibility and expenditures for children with disabilities down as much as possible. Whether it is based on policy or personality, foot-dragging can have some saddening consequences for families. Dixie Jordan describes one family that had a son with severe emotional problems at home:

> They were in desperate need of help for him, so desperate they were even willing to accept institutionalization. She called Medical Assistance, and they sent her application forms, but to her they were so complicated that she was unable to fill them out. She had no transportation to go down to the office either; and they wouldn't send anyone out to her house to help her with the forms.
> The result was that the family—and the son—never did get any Medical Assistance. And then one day the boy took his sister's eye out with a pair of scissors. And as if that wasn't more than they could handle, the parents were then charged with neglect.

What Parents Have Done

But at a time when parents in need of help are largely faced with such barriers, systemic or otherwise, it's worth noting that parent action has succeeded over the years in actually broadening the eligibility criteria. Despite Medicaid's built-in bias toward institutional care, not only for children with disabilities but for the elderly as well, a number of waivers now exist to provide home- and community-based care rather than institutionalization for children with certain specific types of disability. Most require proof that it costs less to care for a child at home than care in an institution would demand.

The first such waiver dates back to 1982 and is generally called the "Katie Beckett" waiver, after the little girl whose mother, Julie, decided to take action against Medicaid's bias in favor of institutions, which would have kept Katie institutionalized rather than let her go back home for less costly medical treatment.

After Julie Beckett, an Iowa parent leader, sued and won, a number of states amended their plans to include the provisions, and a substantial number of others began to provide individual "Katie Beckett" waivers to help children stay home.

Nicole Anderson got one in Minnesota to keep her from going into an institution. The funds were needed for a part-time personal care attendant in her home, because Maria Anderson is a working mother. They were lucky, Maria says; each state and county has only a limited number of such waiver slots, and, understandably, there are always waiting lists for them.

One other expansion in Medicaid eligibility has been important to families. In 1988 Medicaid regulations were amended to provide federal matching funds to states for the cost of "related services" called for in a child's IEP (Individualized Education Plan) or the Individualized Family Service Plan for the family of an infant or toddler. Parents need to check whether this provision applies in their own state, however. While the states were already mandated to provide nine core medical services to eligible children, twenty other programs are optional, meaning that the state may choose to include or exclude them.

One of the core services is a provision for examinations for all Medicaid recipients as part of the Early Periodic Screening, Diagnosis, and Treatment (EPSDT) Programs. And in April 1990 the Health Care Financing Administration issued new regulations that required that any disabilities uncovered during these examinations would also have to be covered under the state's Medicaid program.

But at a time when "budget crunch" has become a household word, parents may find that funds for related services are increasingly hard to come by. One judicial ruling in particular is worth noting, not only because parents sued when they were denied Medicaid coverage and won, but because it has far-reaching implications for other parents as well.

In February 1990 a court ordered Medicaid to pay for a private-duty nurse—as a "related service"—for eleven-year-old Melissa Detzel so that she could continue to go to school. Melissa breathes with the help of a ventilator and gets her food and medication through a G-tube. To the judge who made the ruling it was clear that without the nurse's help, Melissa would be deprived of her right to a public education, and he so ruled.

It may seem all the more ironic, therefore, that some families have had to sue their school systems to *prevent* the use of their Medicaid and/or their private insurance coverage to pay for related services specified in the child's IEP. Students are entitled under the law to receive such help at no cost to them or their families.

But under the pressure of shrinking budgets, some school administrators have attempted to persuade, or pressure, parents to use the child's medical insurance to pay, even telling parents that "It's the law." Others have sought to finesse the problem by simply asking for Medicaid ID or health insurance policy numbers and then proceeding to bill the carrier without notifying the parents.

Parents are under no legal obligation to furnish such information. On the contrary, they should be aware of the possible danger of permitting schools to use the child's coverage to pay for related or other services. Some policies place a ceiling on yearly or lifetime coverage for certain conditions, which the school's action may be depleting. The use of the family's private insurance may result in increased premiums, or even cancellation or refusal to renew the policy. Farther down the road, it may affect the child's insurability. And there is no benefit accruing to the family from allowing the practice.

Supplemental Security Income (SSI)

Medicaid was created as a federal-state program to pay for medical care for low-income, low-asset families. It is administered by the states; parents, and even welfare staff people, are not always aware that in addition to Medicaid, children with disabilities may also be eligible for monthly cash payments under the Social Security system's Supplemental Security Income (SSI) program.

Her son, Roger, had been receiving Medicaid assistance for a number of years, Deb Jones recalls, but had never gotten SSI payments until he was thirteen, when she learned about his possible eligibility "almost by accident":

> Even though I had moved from a rural area into the city by then, I was not very knowledgeable about regulations and such. One of the social workers in the treatment home where Roger was told me about SSI, almost by accident. But when I asked the county social worker about it, since they were paying for Roger's care, she demanded that I go and apply right away. Somehow she'd never thought to tell me about it before.

The reason it is important to know the state's rules is that in many states, though not all, SSI and Medicaid are linked. More than 290,000 children under the age of eighteen receive SSI benefits annually, and about 100,000 more claims are filed each year. The amounts change from year to year, but in 1991 eligible children could receive payments of up to $407 a month (though most checks were, in fact, lower). Twenty-three states also made supplemental payments of their own. Filing is done through the local Social Security Administration offices; a twenty-four-hour hotline will provide the location of the nearest SSA office.

In the past, Social Security was able to reject applications not only because of its "deeming" regulation but also it insisted that the child's disability had to "match" or equal a condition that would disable an adult. In February 1990, however, the United States Supreme Court ruled, in the case of a Pennsylvania boy named Brian Zebley who was cut off from benefits in 1983 despite having congenital brain damage, mental retardation, poor vision, and partial paralysis, that the SSA's "child-disability regulations are inconsistent with the statutory standard."

As a result of that decision, as many as a million children denied benefits between January 1980 and February 1990 became eligible, not only for possible benefits but for retroactive payments, as members of what has been dubbed the "Zebley class." Parents were to receive a notice from the SSA that they might be eligible and that their child's case was being reviewed. If parents did not receive such a notice, or wanted quicker information on possible eligibility, a toll-free hotline was set up—1-800-523-0000. In addition, if the original application was for Medicaid as well as SSI, the retroactive payments might cover that as well.

In January 1991 the National Parent Network on Disabilities, which has participating groups throughout the United States, held a series of training sessions for parent volunteers. The sessions were held in various parts of the country, and were aimed at helping parents navigate their way through an often difficult system.

In addition, in 1992, a group of children's advocacy organizations launched the Children's SSI Campaign to provide information to families about applying for the benefits. The SSI Campaign is a joint project of the Mental Health Law Project, Community Legal Services, the National Center for Youth Law/Youth Law Center, and Rural Legal Services of Tennessee. Also participating are the American Academy of Pediatrics, the Spina Bifida Association, and the National Association of Social Workers. The campaign may be reached at: 1101 Fifteenth St., NW, Suite 1212, Washington, D.C. 20005; (202) 842-3100.

Tax-Deductible Expenses

No matter what help they may receive, families will still have to pay for a great many items and services out of their own pockets. Among the few financial breaks they get is the fact that many such "special" expenses are tax-deductible.

Medical expenses, including health insurance premiums, payment to therapists or care providers, transportation to the doctor's office or an early intervention program, and even counseling for the parents (provided it is prescribed by a physician) are arguably tax-deductible.

If you're a new parent and are making such deductions for the first time, tax experts recommend attaching letters from your child's physician and yourself, explaining the nature of your child's disability and indicating what aspects of the required care you are not receiving reimbursement for. Include whatever additional information you feel may be relevant. The more complete the documentation, the less the likelihood that you will be questioned, perhaps even at a later time, by the Internal Revenue Service, which has up to seven years to audit any return you file. That is a good reason for keeping cancelled checks, receipts, correspondence, and other items relating to the deductions you've taken for the same length of time.

Local IRS offices can supply publications that explain these deductions in some detail, but pamphlets issued by local and national organizations concerned with disability may prove to be even more helpful. Some of the tax aspects of caring for a child with special needs are so complex, however, that local parent groups often invite helpful accountants and/or tax attorneys to speak and answer questions.

Other Sources of Help

In addition to tax information, national organizations can provide a great deal of helpful information on the treatment and management of the child's disability. They are not geared, however, to provide financial assistance directly to families, though frequently their local chapters and affiliates can and do.

United Cerebral Palsy Associations, The ARC (formerly the Association for Retarded Citizens), Muscular Dystrophy Association, Spina Bifida Association, and National Easter Seal Society are among the national groups that have large networks of local affiliates, therapy centers, and/or education and rehabilitation programs. They can be helpful with advice and guidance, regardless of the nature of the child's disability, and some are even able to offer assistance in obtaining necessary aids or equipment for the child.

It is also worth exploring possible help from local fraternal, service, veterans', or civic groups, such as the Kiwanis and the Lions, particularly in rural areas or isolated communities. In Sanger, Texas, for example, the Lions not only helped a little boy get his first hearing aid but also sent him to a camp for children with hearing impairments. In a New Jersey town, the Elks provided oxygen tanks for home use and a portable unit for the car, so a couple could bring their daughter home after a seven-month hospital stay. Some parents have gratefully reported that their children were treated and cared for in one of the Shriner Hospitals; local groups of that organization have also helped with financial aid.

One other organization may also be helpful. Providing a variety of assistance, including financial assistance, to children with disabilities is:

Telephone Pioneers of America
22 Cortland St., Room C-2575
New York, NY 10007
(212) 393-3252

If You Can't Be Rich . . .

Even if parents are lucky enough to get help from such volunteer groups, and from government sources, caring for the special needs of a child with a physical, mental, or emotional disability continues to impoverish many families. The cost of a night out is a major expense; vacations become impossible "luxuries."

Even parents who are able to keep their heads above water will echo the New Jersey insurance executive whose daughter has a severe hearing loss. "I think that parents of a deaf child should be rich," he said. "In fact, even if your child is only hard of hearing, it's not a bad idea to be rich."

One thing is for sure: having a child with a disability doesn't help anyone to *get* rich. Even when private health insurance companies and Medicaid cover most of the child's medical expenses, there are special services and situations that are seldom if ever covered—speech therapy is one example—and parents report that even prostheses and adaptive equipment, which would appear to be necessities, are sometimes challenged.

It's always a shock to find that something that seems like an absolute essential for the child's care and treatment is not covered. Every once in a while, parents' ingenuity helps.

What is now generally called Attention Deficit Hyperactivity Disorder (ADHD) is a behavioral disorder of childhood characterized by a short attention span, excessive impulsivity, distractibility, hyperactivity, and inappropriate behavior. But before it was called ADHD, and to some extent even now, therapists called it minimum brain injury or brain damage, minimal brain dysfunction, neurological or perceptual impairment, food-additive-triggered hyperactivity, specific learning disabilities, and attention deficit disorder—some of the terms medical descriptions, others behavioral.

A boy in the Midwest, who has to remain nameless, was diagnosed some time ago as having ADHD. His treatment was covered without objection by Blue Cross, but then the family switched to an HMO (health maintenance organization). Still no problem, but when they decided to switch back, Blue Cross refused to cover the son's ADHD on the grounds that their policy did not include mental health coverage. The boy's mother picks up the story:

> We've gotten really clever about it, because after that no one would sell us mental health coverage, no one. But finally we remembered that in the past the problem has been called minimal brain damage, minimal brain dysfunction, and a lot of other things. So during the diagnosis we asked our doctor not to call it ADHD any more but to call it hyperkinetic syndrome of childhood, because the insurance *will* cover that—even though it's the same disorder.

11

"They Fare Better in Life"
Avoiding Disaster: Early Intervention

Mac Shapland is now seventeen. The pediatrician at the hospital where Mac was born thought he might have an unusual condition resulting from an illness his mother had had six months earlier. The doctor told Ceci Shapland, "I'm going to write an article about you," as they looked at the new baby.

It didn't occur to the doctor, however, to offer Ceci any guidance for dealing with Mac's birth defects at home. Nor did a second, kindlier pediatrician, who didn't refer her elsewhere or suggest any further assessment either. On the contrary, he told Ceci to "take him home and watch him." At first she did so, but at nine months she'd had enough of watching. She took Mac to a children's clinic and finally learned he had cerebral palsy and mental retardation. That was in the seventies.

By the eighties many parents and health care professionals were fully aware of the consequences of such delays. To quote one mother:

> Instead of my daughter's receiving the best of help, to develop her mind to the fullest, time is flying by and . . . this child's future is uncertain. So much has been learned about how much

more educable children are before the age of five. Parents should realize that the word *wait* is a disaster.

Some, but not all, physicians, pediatricians, and therapists were already warning parents a decade or more ago about the likely results of *not* beginning therapy as quickly as possible. The North Dakota mom of a boy born with spastic quadriplegia, a form of cerebral palsy, recalls:

> The neonatologist at the intensive care nursery showed me how to exercise my son's limbs at three weeks old. I did the exercises ten times daily, every day, and I credit them with keeping him from developing permanent contractions or dislocations. My son started informal therapy at three months and formal therapy at eight months.
>
> My advice to other parents would be to get the child into physical, occupational, and speech therapy as soon as you possibly can. It was extremely helpful to start therapy early, and I'd tell others the earlier the better. I have noticed a *vast* difference between my baby and other children who started therapy much later.

The difference is evident whether the infant has physical or mental problems or both. One controlled study of children born with mental retardation, for example, found that seven out of ten in a special nursery school showed an increase in IQ test scores of ten to thirty points, whereas the scores of similar children who received no special help during that period actually went down.

Researchers long ago determined that *deaf and dumb*—once a commonly used phrase—were not linked aspects of the same disability. They found that children born with hearing impairments, if helped early enough, could readily learn to speak and/or sign: they weren't "dumb" either physically or mentally. They were simply among the many children with disabilities who were being additionally handicapped in those days by help denied or delayed.

By the beginning of the nineties, the evidence was quite clear, and generally being applied. Jessica Borello was born with Down syndrome. Soon after her daughter's birth, Mary Borello's genetics counselor

> told me straight out that the children who get early intervention fare better in later life than those who don't. She gave

me a list of phone numbers of programs in our area to call. She told me to talk to the people, but not to go by what they said, to go there and see the programs for myself. And that's what I did.

One that I explored told me they'd never had a baby this young; Jessica was only a month old then. And I thought to myself: if you never had anyone this young, how would you know how to deal with them? But when I went to the one I finally chose, there were infants there who had started when they were two weeks old, and I saw that they seemed to know how to handle them. That center was run by ARC.

One week later Jessica was in the program, getting a lot of stimulation, and physical therapy to get her muscles in tone, and tastes in her mouth, and different textures to feel—that kind of thing. She went for two years—two hours once a week—until she was ready for the next step.

In many hospitals that kind of referral is routine. As soon as a Miami youngster was diagnosed with Down syndrome, "the hospital responded with help from their social workers. I was told about the special programs available for infant stim (stimulation)," the mother remembers. "Immediately I began the paperwork for enrollment."

The most common source of referrals seems to be social workers, either in hospitals or in social agencies. A fairly large percentage of parents report, however, that they first heard of early intervention programs by accident—from the friend of a friend or relative, from a chance encounter in a supermarket, from a news item or feature story in a local newspaper. They then did what Judith Davis did: she went through the local telephone directory and located the nearest cerebral palsy center. "Without any doctor's referral," she says, "I arranged an interview and an examination, and my son started in the baby group before he was a year old."

It can be a frustrating experience. It was especially so for Lynn Gillies, who is a nurse:

All the social worker in the hospital where BJ got his surgery did was give me a packet of information about spina bifida. When I asked about occupational and physical therapy for stimulation, I was told there was no such thing, just do "normal baby things" with him. Even the occupational therapist at the hospital never told me about early intervention; obviously she didn't know about it.

But I knew it was out there somewhere. I found a program on my own, by opening the phone book and calling every government agency I thought might have any program, or any lead to a program, or anything that could help. What I found was a social worker who was a gem; with her help we got BJ into the birth-to-three program of our school district.

Families that live in an area with a number of programs, and have the luxury of choosing, should be aware, as one parent points out, that "not all early intervention programs are equal." Two of the three programs that Vicki Hart's school system suggested she check out said they couldn't handle her daughter, Angela, who has Down syndrome, because the little girl was "too hyperactive." Vicki found the third "not stimulating enough" for her daughter and eventually enrolled her in an out-of-district ARC center.

After parents find an appropriate program for their infant (with some children who have severe or multiple disabilities that isn't always easy), and they see the positive results, many complain that there just isn't enough time allotted for their baby. The OT (occupational therapist) was coming to June Ganley's home only five hours a month to provide infant stim (stimulation) and teach her the basics. But June felt that her daughter, Katie, wasn't getting enough stimulation and that she needed something "more intense." Their HMO "won't pay for that kind of therapy for chronic conditions," so they're paying for additional OT for an hour a week.

Meeting Other Parents

When mothers bring their infants and toddlers to center-based programs, they are nearly always rewarded with an unanticipated bonus—interaction with other parents.

Sarah Fliegel, whose son is now thirteen, still recalls that first contact with another parent whose child had cerebral palsy:

Suddenly I was not feeling alone any more. All those feelings of "Why me?" and being struck by lightning—being the victim,

if you will—all of a sudden you get more perspective on the
fact that you're not the only one. Like you're all in it together,
and you can begin to feel that you can help each other through
the tough times.

Judith Ingle has only had contact with one other mother, a
friend of a friend, whose baby was born with Down syndrome.
Judith's daughter was an infant, the other's was five, and they
never met, but they spoke often on the telephone, sometimes for
hours. What she remembers most about those conversations after
two years is not so much the valuable tips on how to manage her
daughter—"one day at a time"—but how much better she felt
about life after she hung up the phone. She found even more
emotional support from the parent group at the center:

> I think it is great therapy for parents, too. Just talking, com-
> paring notes is great; everyone really bonds together and en-
> courages each other's child. Every parent of a disabled child
> *must* talk to other parents. I feel sorry for those who don't
> know any others to talk to.
>   It was good to meet other parents who were struggling—
> some more, some less. Being active in our group has given
> me the feeling of being able to do positive things for my
> daughter, rather than just sit around and fret. I think parents
> benefit even more from the infant stim programs than the
> children.

Most center-based early intervention programs require the
parent (almost always the mother, of course) or caregiver to stay
with the baby during the three hours or so a week that the baby
is there for therapy or infant stim. Parents are usually not treated
simply as observers. They're shown how to provide the same
hands-on exercises at home and urged to speed the baby's progress
by spending time during the week repeating them.

In programs where parents are made to feel like partners rather
than students, and their input about the program is welcomed,
parents get a particularly strong psychological lift. Kate Cuthbertson began receiving intensive services when she was eight
months old at an early intervention program of this type. Says her
mother Diana, "Joining a program which had at its heart the belief
that parents are the experts regarding their children was tremen-
dously empowering and got us off to a good start."

Fathers Too "Do That"

Many centers also ask parents to attend evening parent meetings or groups. With the exception of one-parent families, some effort is usually made to get fathers to attend, too. When one father complained that that was asking too much of him, "because I put in a hard day's work," his wife reports she quickly got him to "change his tune" by asking him very quietly: "And what is it you think I do all day long with your child?"

Perhaps the most successful method programs have found for initially involving fathers is to set up informal father-and-child get-togethers on Saturday mornings. Frequently they attract only a handful of fathers at first; but when the word gets around, more and more may show up.

In fact, some fathers need support as much as mothers do, or more, even though they're not as involved in the minute-by-minute care of their child. Some even break down and admit that they feel bruised and isolated, just as their wives or partners do. Whether they do or not, discovering a support group often turns out to be a real emotional charge. As it happened, Bobby Allen's father went to a support group meeting at Parents Helping Parents, in San Jose, California, before his wife could attend one. The way Diane Allen tells it,

> He went to meet other families with Down syndrome children, and he came home with a smile from ear to ear. He told me, "It's great. They vary like everybody else. Some of them have more disabilities, some less, some are functional, some not— they're just like other kids, they're all individuals."
>
> He was encouraged because he had made contact with other families of children that have Down syndrome and had seen that they're all different. And he's still just as involved as I am. He wants to know everything that's going on and is always telling people about his son.

Sometimes "care without father" may be the fault of the agency sponsoring the program. According to some parent reports, programs sometimes make only a pro forma attempt to include fathers in the activities. One father remembers that when he tried to participate, agency administrators acted surprised—"as though children with disabilities are born fatherless." Other fathers got the feeling that the reason they were ignored when they showed up wanting to help was because the people in charge felt that "men don't do that" or that "men don't know how."

That feeling extends beyond infant stim programs to other areas. One father quoted in an Association for the Care of Children's Health (ACCH) publication says: "Professionals are a difficult lot to deal with. They have some specialized training, so they think they must have all the answers. At least they seem to think that because we, as fathers, have not had that specialized training, we could not possibly have anything meaningful to say about our child's condition."

Others feel that such negative attitudes may extend to mothers as well, with no sexism involved. "Professionals seem to have too much regard for their own training," another father says, "and many times the parents have been better judges of what their child will do." In fact, because such professional attitudes are not uncommon, giving parents an enhanced decision-making role in the care of their children is a core concept of the 1986 legislation that expanded infant stimulation, early intervention, and preschool programs.

"The Infants and Toddlers Act"

The amendments that year to the original Education for Handicapped Children Act gave parents a special role in a new discretionary program under which states were encouraged to deal with the special needs of infants and toddlers and their families through home-based, family-centered assistance. By empowering parents in very specific language, the regulations for the law made it clear that it was *parents* who were to be the key figures in their child's programming.

One of the objectives of what has come to be known as the "Infants and Toddlers Act" was to lower to three the age of eligibility for all children with disabilities for special education and related services from the public school system. In focusing on the needs of younger children from birth to three, the law also requires that when programs on their behalf are eventually implemented, the family of each child served has to have a written Individualized Family Service Plan (IFSP).

Embodied in that mandate are two catalytic concepts: first, that the service program deals with the needs of the entire family, and not just the child with the special needs; and second, that it is the parents who are in charge of that program, aided by professionals as "consultants." While the regulations for implementing the IFSP call for a professional case or service manager, they note that "parents retain the ultimate decision in determining whether they, their child, or other family members will accept or decline services."

In summarizing the elements of family-centered care, ACCH notes that "the family is the constant in the child's life, while the service systems and personnel within those systems fluctuate." One mother puts it even more simply: "Teachers and therapists come and go; parents are for life."

In preparing to implement the program, professionals are going to have to rethink their methodology, Professor Ruth Cook suggests. She is the director of Early Intervention Services at Santa Clara University in California and teaches future professionals.

We've come to realize now—significantly so—that the special-needs child is part of a larger family system, and that's one of the greatest advances I've seen. Parents are now going to be involved as major decision makers; that means that professionals are really going to have to change considerably, to look at parents' priorities and their new rights, to really collaborate with parents in a much more respectful way, and to accept this as a team process.

That requires not only a tactical and philosophical conversion of professionals who've been in the field a long time but also a conversion of the agencies for which they work. It is easier to get a change in philosophy, in attitudes and values, if we can get a systems change at the same time.

I see a great many professionals out there who really do believe in true, open, and respectful collaboration with families, but they're hamstrung by the agencies for which they work. It's one thing to have a convinced teacher, but if you don't get the principal to come along in terms of attitudes and philosophy, it's hard for that teacher to do all he or she would like to do. I think it is going to take us at least another five years to really get IFSPs going. I think it will take a lot of groundwork.

In most states IFSP programs may not be completely in place until well into the nineties. States were given five years to implement their programs, with federal grants providing special incentives and a special U.S. Department of Education program, the National Early Childhood Technical Assistance System, to aid them in the development of their services—outreach, evaluation, and treatment—for children with special needs from birth to three. Maryland, probably one of the most advanced states, if not the most advanced, started its fourth year in 1990. That year all twenty-four of the state's jurisdictions were required to set up model demonstration projects, and as of December 1 some 2,000 children had been served.

But the "tactical and philosophical conversion" Professor Cook described is underway, as a 1991 report of the Task Force on Developmental Disabilities of the National Conference of State Legislatures indicates. "Increasingly states are moving," the report declares, "to a system that empowers families to participate in the process and to choose services that best meet their needs . . .

"Support services should be available to families from the onset of the disability and should be designed to reach out to families. . . . Families should be allowed to control resources, making the system less 'provider-driven' and more 'consumer-driven'. . . . Strengthening the family structure may be less costly to the state than funding expensive alternative residential options for children."

The Center on Human Policy of Syracuse University has confirmed that not only do family supports keep families together, they are also a cost-effective use of tax dollars. The center studied children who had lived first in institutions and later on at home, and found that the cost of home care to the government was only a quarter to a fifth of the cost of institutional care. One likely explanation is that parents as the mainstay of home-based programs draw zero dollars in wages and salaries—that's about as cost-effective as it gets.

"A Lifelong Commitment"

Nancy Crowe is also helping in the "tactical and philosophical conversion of professionals" Professor Cook spoke of, as a parent advocate and trainer of other parents in advocacy for their children. She came into that role at Parents Helping Parents at a point in her life when she was "really angry," she says. Her son, Jonathan, is ten and a half, has multiple physical disabilities, and is "cognitively in the range of a three- or four-year-old."

She came to advocacy because

> The problem was that I was becoming more aware that Jonathan was a lifelong commitment, that there wasn't going to be a normal kindergarten for him and all the other normal things. It was the point in my life when reality was really real.
>
> I was feeling intimidated by the professionals who worked with Jonathan. Maybe I didn't know what I was asking. I was disagreeing with them and sometimes expressing it, but sometimes feeling so overwhelmed that I let them persuade me in my ultimate decisions. And feeling very frustrated as a result.
>
> I decided that if it was going to be a lifelong commitment, then I needed to learn everything about the system I could possibly learn, so that when I went into those meetings I could feel comfortable about making decisions about Jonathan, making decisions I felt confident were right for him.

Now she is training other parents to be able to make decisions about what is best for *their* children. "I also give them confidence, by confirming and reassuring them that they're doing the right thing with their child, and at the same time trying to provide them with some guidance so they will *know* they're doing the right thing."

Clearly, preparing for the implementation of the IFSP approach will be a two-way exercise: while professionals will be educating parents about systems and services, parents will be educating professionals about themselves and their families—their strengths, weaknesses, foibles, needs, values, and desires—everything that makes a family a family. It is probably not a bad thing that Congress gave the states five years to begin the IFSP aspect of the program, hopefully to be implemented in 1992, but with the likelihood that it would go into effect later in some states.

Other elements of the "Infants and Toddlers Act" have progressed somewhat faster and further. Federal funding is an attractive carrot: the *Federal Register* noted that this is the only grant program at the national level "that focuses exclusively on the provision of services to children with handicaps from birth through age three," and by December 1990 states reported serving nearly 250,000 infants and toddlers in infant stimulation, early intervention, and preschool programs.

The difficult part of getting such services for their youngsters, some parents report, is breaking into the system in the first place. Sue Sitler had that problem. Her son, Travis, now five, was born with a severe congenital visual impairment—he can barely distinguish colors or sense high-contrast objects. He didn't even look at lights until he was eight months old. When he was four months old, Sue checked with the regional center (she lives in California) to see if she could get funding for an early intervention program for Travis.

They said no, he's only blind. It wasn't among their criteria for help. They didn't even bother to do an assessment; they just said no. And no matter how I put it, they still refused; so I said I was going to file for a fair hearing. Then their attorney called. I really wasn't up to it, because I was so angry, and it took so much for me even to talk on the phone because I'd get so emotional.

But they came out and did an assessment, and in the end they did grant the funding. After a while I started finding other parents in our area who had gotten funding the same way, and other parents who had been denied, and who never did anything about it.

So Travis got into a home-based rehabilitation program until he was eighteen months old. They sent out a social worker and an occupational therapist every week for him. And they also did more than anyone else for me emotionally, because they always asked how my husband and I and the other children were, helping me emotionally while they were teaching Travis to crawl.

At eighteen months we were contacted by the school district and got into an early intervention program three days a week, with help in making the transition from the people who'd been with Travis all along. It was a center-based program for visually handicapped children only—there were other programs for kids with other disabilities. His group averaged around six kids, with a teacher and two aides. He was there three days a week for three hours each day, from the time he was eighteen months until he was three.

At that point he was in a preschool program, but it was with the same teacher, in the same place, and the same hours. At four and a half, when he was ready, the schedule expanded to five days a week, the regular preschool schedule. We will probably hold him back from kindergarten an extra year, and enter him in a resource-room kindergarten when he's six.

Transition to Preschool

Since Congress mandated special education services for children from three through five and made schools responsible for outreach, the transition from early intervention programs is usually just as easy as Travis's. The ages of the "promotion" may vary; by the time Jessica Borello was two, she was so advanced that they started her on her transition at that point. She is in her old early intervention program one day a week, and the other four days she is in what is really a preschool setting for all kids from two to five.

The "Infants and Toddlers Act" mandated that states accepting federal funds under the program would have to offer special education and related services to eligible children with disabilities between the ages of three and six no later than the 1991–92 school year. By the summer of 1991, forty-eight states, all but Oregon and Alabama, had undertaken to provide such programs. But that is a misleading statistic: only two states, Idaho and Kentucky, were reaching more than 6 percent of the preschoolers with special needs in their states. And services might range from full-day sessions five days a week to as little as half an hour one day a week.

The problem is familiar to long-time program watchers, though exacerbated because states are retrenching their own financial aid to all social and education programs. As it has consistently done with other special education programs ever since it passed PL 94-142, the Education for All Handicapped Children Act in 1975, Congress underfunded the early intervention and preschool programs by some $60,000,000 in 1991 alone.

The underfunding tends to hit hardest in rural areas and major urban centers, in some cases areas where state and local governments have done their own budget cutting as well, with a disproportionate effect on poor and minority families with children with special needs. In the end that becomes a costly misjudgment. A 1985 study of the Head Start program, which serves mainly children from poor families but also a sizable number of children with disabilities, demonstrated that every dollar invested in that program had saved five dollars that would have been required later on to help those same youngsters.

A Bonus: Respite

One bonus preschool and some early intervention programs provide for mothers and caregivers from their always-on-duty, often-harassed days, is a brief respite. Many mothers, in what younger parents may think of as "olden times," though it was only fifteen or twenty years ago, never spent more than an occasional hour or two away from their children. Today preschool and center-based early intervention programs that do not require parents to be present at all times offer mothers a respite-on-schedule those earlier mothers were never fortunate enough to have.

A new baby always means some stress for the family, but seldom beyond the limits that most parents can handle. In some families with babies who have severe or multiple disabilities, the added stress may at times be overwhelming. Laurena Miller, Health Resource Coordinator for Parents Helping Parents, describes one such instance:

> One parent who telephoned was majorly stressed out. As she was talking to me, the baby was crying, her voice was rising, her train of thought was all over the place. She kept saying, "I'm holding the baby and she won't stop crying," things like that.
>
> It took a while, but I was able to talk her down, get her to calm the baby so that she could calm down herself. I made it clear that the more out of control *she* was, the more the baby picked up on that and went off too. I was relieved when I got her calmed down, because when I first started talking to her, my professional assessment was that she was a candidate for throwing the baby out of the window.

Juana Gomez (not her real name) has a two-year-old with Prader-Willi syndrome. She hasn't yet discovered how to cope with the incessant demands for food that are the characteristic of that disorder. She insists that while the doctors have told her what the underlying problem is, none has ever advised her how to manage or control her son. Often at her wits' end, she sometimes spanks her son to get him to stop demanding food—only to have him come back in an hour or two, begging again. Her only hope, she says, is to connect with other Prader-Willi parents who have learned how to cope.

Counseling in time, whether from other parents or trained professionals, can lower the stress level of mothers and caregivers to manageable proportions, but the potential for child abuse is there. The 1974 Child Abuse and Prevention and Treatment Act required all states to establish definitions for child abuse and reporting guidelines. In 1986, for example, Utah identified some 5,100 victims of child abuse and neglect, more than 600 of whom were identified as having "special characteristics." More specifically for children with disabilities, the 1988 Child Abuse Prevention, Adoption, and Family Services Act includes recognition that children with disabilities, more helpless and vulnerable than others, need special protection.

Prevention makes more sense. That's the conclusion that most parent groups dealing with the potential have come to. Like Florene Poyadue, head of PHP, who once returned a call from a mother who told her she was so "stressed out" she was afraid she'd hurt her son and herself. Florene was able to get her calmed down; years later at a meeting, the woman introduced herself and said the return call came just in time. When Florene reached her, she had had a gun in her hand and was ready to kill her son, who has autism, and herself.

"There was more to it than just a mother saying she was afraid she'd abuse the child," the parent leader says. "What she was really saying was: 'I do not want to hurt my child but someone has to give me relief from this constant stress. I need respite.' "

No question, parents say, that respite is a major unmet need. To some extent early intervention and preschool will help, as they are already doing. But by and large, respite care programs for families with a disabled member are still a thing of the future.

Doing Something about It

Also largely in the future is another program that will do much to relieve family stress—the Individualized Family Service Plan (IFSP). As one indication of the new status given to parents by the law, it includes a provision that parents who choose to may be trained as case managers or service coordinators for their own family IFSPs, and be paid for doing so.

Minnesota was one of the first states to begin implementing the program, and Lynn Gillies, who is a nurse by profession, had been serving on a committee to work out the details. She felt not only that her son, BJ, could benefit from it, but that she had a pretty good notion of how it should work.

When BJ was two, and the school system said it was time to develop an IEP for him, I said I wanted to try an IFSP instead. It's true that anyone receiving services through the school district has to have an IEP; but since I knew what an IFSP was supposed to be, and we already had all kinds of home services for BJ, I just went ahead and did it. I became the facilitator, the one who contacts the different people involved in the child's care, and arranges the place and time for the team to get together.

So we did it at a potluck in our home. We had the child care provider, the physical therapist, the personal care provider, the special ed teacher, neighbors who saw BJ a lot, relatives, siblings—of course, BJ was the center of attraction. Everyone concerned with his care was there, and we discussed BJ's strengths and problems. The question was: what does BJ need and what can we do?

We had a big easel in the middle of the room. First we wrote down all the areas of concern; then we narrowed them down to priorities, so we could decide what to work on first. Call it brainstorming, but we explored different ways of combining all the caregivers to implement each priority.

When we were done, I put most of the IFSP on paper. Yet even though I'd been on that subcommittee, there were still a couple of things that I couldn't transfer to the set forms they had at that time.

The IFSP was still not an accepted document then; the school system was not required to pay any attention to it. So once they got the IFSP we had done, they took their part out and made an IEP out of it.

Lynn is obviously proud of what she and her "team" accomplished, but in retrospect she's not sure she'd recommend that other parents try it. There are some key problems to work out, she believes:

I think it is very difficult for a parent to be the facilitator. It was really difficult for me to organize the whole thing, and to keep in touch with everybody. I think it should be an outside person, someone a little more objective than parents can be.

In some ways it creates problems you don't need. For one thing, having to view the family as professionals is real threatening to trained professionals at this point. It may be too soon.

Also, from my experience I don't think the different systems work well together: education has its focus, social services has its own. It's kind of like no one wants to let go of their little piece of the pie. Maybe that's why in most places they still haven't been able to decide who the facilitators are going to be when the IFSP has to be implemented—teachers, social workers, therapists, who?

12
....

"Let's Go for It"
Mainstreaming — Integration — Inclusion

Angela Hart has just started regular kindergarten, with an aide in the classroom beside her, and so far she seems to be keeping up with the class. When the regular kindergarten day ends at 11:15, she gets her speech therapy, physical therapy, and occupational therapy, and after a lunch break she goes into the transitional kindergarten class, where she was supposed to be going full-time. She is part of an all-day special education program for youngsters who are not ready for regular kindergarten. Some will stay on for another year of "getting ready," others will go into first grade along with Angela. The difference is that Angela is *already* associating with and interacting with the "regulars." Vicki Hart says

> It's really a question of being knowledgeable and knowing what to ask for. They didn't offer it, and to tell the truth they didn't even know about inclusive education. They still keep calling it "mainstreaming," even though by now they know it's not mainstreaming, it's something different.

Vicki says she found out about inclusive education from SPAN, the New Jersey Statewide Parents' Advocacy Network, and in fact helped to form the state's Coalition for Inclusive Education.

The confusion of terms is readily understandable. Many school systems are still struggling with the concept of "mainstreaming," the term applied to educating children with special needs in the "least restrictive environment" (LRE) as required by Public Law 94-142, the Education of All Handicapped Children Act of 1975. Accomplishing that was intended to bring such children into the mainstream of public education.

The result was an immediate sprouting of "special" classes. "Special education" quickly became a growth industry separated from "regular education." The "special" students were technically in the mainstream because they were in the public school system, but they were rarely fully immersed in it.

There were immediate results and manifest benefits—a real schooling from specially trained teachers, and frequently a sense of real accomplishment. But there was that "special," rather than least restrictive, environment, which meant that children with disabilities were separated from others their own age, their neighbors, playmates, and siblings. Sometimes that meant not just being in "special" classes but being bussed or vanned to schools far outside their neighborhoods. "Special" classes, despite their benefits, certified that such separated children were not like the others. Separation didn't guarantee that they would always remain "different," but it didn't help to make them less so.

In the eighties, spurred on by the testimony of older parents who had seen the results of such "education with a difference," parent advocacy groups initiated a campaign for "integration" into real LREs. Spelled out that meant bringing children with special needs back into neighborhood schools and into regular classrooms, if necessary with "pullouts" to "resource rooms" staffed by "resource teachers."

The transition was never completed; "mainstreaming" and "integration" coexisted, but neither seemed altogether satisfactory: children were still being "separated." As Marge Goldberg, co-director of PACER, the Minneapolis parent advocacy group, puts it:

> There has been a great deal of research on what students gained from resource rooms and special classes against what the same types of students who have been educated in regular classrooms, with the support services they need, have gained.

And that research can't all be wrong; it indicates that children with mild-to-moderate disabilities at least weren't gaining from the resource room what we thought they were gaining.

It's because separation is exclusion; it's because it is a stigma. Other students immediately say about their peers with disabilities, "Oh, those are *those* kids, those are the retards, those are kids who don't belong." By keeping those exclusion programs in the schools, you almost guarantee that there will always be kids who are different, who are not accepted by the other kids. Once you pull students out of a class, their space is gone.

"You Have to Fight for Integration"

In addition to such testimony from parent advocates, adults in the disability movement have testified that such separation and stigmatization during their growing years has made it more difficult to become fully participating members of the community. Ed Roberts, president of the World Institute on Disability and a leader in the fight for passage of the Americans with Disabilities Act in 1990, notes that

One of the things that's really going to help us to change social attitudes is the integration of young people in the school system. And that's why it is so important that we not allow children with disabilities to be shunted aside into some education unit. Parents have to learn to fight to get their kids into local schools and integrated there.

It's been the law since 1975 that kids be put into the least restrictive environment, but that law has never been more than partially enforced. I think advocating for special settings is a mistake: there they focus not on full people but on their disability. Segregation in any sense is bad. Kids need to be *included* in order to become social people, to become independent.

Roberts is paralyzed from the neck down, but he says, "I'm damned independent when it comes to my head." He contracted polio at age fourteen but went on to become an A student in high school—only to be told by the principal that he couldn't graduate because he hadn't taken driver training and physical education. He and his mother took their fight to the school board, "which agreed the decision was ridiculous and ordered the diploma issued." Roberts believes

> Parents have to realize that sometimes "No" is absolutely unacceptable. You have to go on. You have to fight for your rights, for integration. It's tough to be singled out as a troublemaker, especially if you're fighting to get your kid into a neighborhood school. But you're fighting not just for his schooling, but for his future: when kids with disabilities go to school with kids without disabilities, those other kids will recognize the disabled kids as part of life, and people will not be labels first, but people first.

Doing "What I Had to Do"

One such "troublemaker" is Vicky Jones, of Burlingame, California. She has two sons with autism or autisticlike behaviors. When she asked that her eight-and-a-half-year-old, Christopher, be placed in a regular classroom after five years in special education, the administration there "acted as though we were the only parents who had ever complained." Not only that, but they insisted they felt "accountable" to the "regular" parents, who would surely have "a negative reaction" because Chris would be getting more than his share of services.

But Vicky "did what I had to do:" she countered by threatening to keep both boys out of school until and unless Chris was "regularized."

She won; and "in spite of fears that other parents would object, no one has. Actually people have been very friendly and supportive. And I feel that any child, regardless of the nature or severity of their disability, should have a chance to experience their home school from kindergarten on. As the saying goes, 'Special education is a process, not a place.' "

There is a postscript: "After years of our district having no knowledge of or interest in the ideas of integration and full inclusion, we have a new superintendent who wants to try it (gradually) on a districtwide basis. We have therefore formed a task force to explore the idea, which includes regular and special education parents, regular and special education teachers, district principals, psychologists, and so on."

One mother who is currently struggling with her school district to get her daughter into a regular classroom is Trudy Grable, of San Jose, California. When her daughter was seventeen months old, a team at a major hospital did a full assessment of Lauren, she says, "and telephoned me at work to tell me she had mental retardation. Perfect timing; I had to go on my shift right afterward."

Lauren has been in special settings all along, and at age six she is still in a special class. As often as her mother has requested it, the school has never offered Lauren the possibility of getting into a regular class at her neighborhood school; the response is always "there's just no money to do that." In addition, the special education director felt that it would be an uphill battle with parents and teachers at Lauren's home school, despite Trudy's offer to do parent and teacher education herself.

Trudy was determined; she then started an integrated play group in her home, with children Lauren's own age, and invited the special education director to observe Lauren "in a setting with her nondisabled peers." She converted him into an ally. Yet at this point Lauren is still "excluded." And at this point Trudy has also joined an inclusion task force:

> Until I learned about inclusion, I never thought there was that kind of option for Lauren. Whether it will work for her will only be known after it's been tried. It may or may not, but it's worth the effort, because unless kids like Lauren have the opportunity to be with nondisabled models, they can never be socially aware of what's expected of them.
>
> There are a lot of barriers, including Lauren's sometimes inappropriate behavior and her seizures, but I'm willing to try, just to give her the opportunity. I think if she can have appropriate role models, she will achieve better success in life when we're gone. Our goal is to have her become as independent as she can be.

All the evidence indicates that children with disabilities are readily accepted by others if the inclusion begins in kindergarten or first grade.

Diane Cuthbertson, executive director of New Jersey's SPAN, recalls an incident involving her daughter Kate. The mother of one of the little girl's schoolmates mentioned that she'd seen "that little blind girl" in the Halloween parade. "You mean you saw Kate!" the boy said. "She can really sing!" Because to him the essence of Kate was singing, not blindness.

Increasingly, therefore, parent advocacy groups have begun to call for the full inclusion of children with disabilities—even those with severe or multiple disabilities—in regular classrooms in neighborhood schools.

"Kids Growing Up Together"

In the LaGrange (Illinois) Area school district, a consistent pioneer in the development of special education programs, instead of children with special needs being taken out of the regular classroom to a resource room, the resource room is taken to them. The resource teacher is in the regular classroom along with the class teacher. The philosophy of LaGrange's Department of Special Education, which serves twenty suburban communities, is that "the integration of children with disabilities into regular education enriches the lives of all the students."

A "first-grade educator" in The Association for Persons with Severe Handicaps (TASH) *Newsletter* attests that while "the single most significant factor in the integrated setting is the impact of the nondisabled students on their peers with disabilities, . . . as one engages in the integration process in the classroom, the benefits to the nondisabled peers begin to surface and become self-evident."

What is also evident is the coexistence of all three approaches to meeting the LRE requirement: in the 1988–89 school year, 31 percent of children with disabilities were in regular classes, 37 percent were using resource rooms, and nearly 30 percent were still in separate classes or schools.

If disabled and nondisabled young people grow up together—especially if the integration starts early—there are no labels and no stigma attached to those with disabilities. Florene Poyadue, of PHP, tries to encourage other parents by telling them about her son, Dean, who was born with Down syndrome:

> They're worried their child will be laughed at. We have a great trust here at PHP in parents making their own decisions about

their kids, so we give them information and try to help them see the possible benefits of integrated classes. If you're saying that you don't want your child laughed at out in the world, maybe one of the ways to keep that from happening is for little kids to start growing up together. The regular kids who've grown up with my son, Dean, are ready to pop anyone in the mouth who says anything bad about him, because they see him as just one of the guys.

For Some "It's a Risk"

As convincing as these reasons for inclusion are, not all parents are convinced. Ever since "least restrictive environment" came into the educational vocabulary, there have been parents who preferred the benefits of special and separate education to those of socialization with nondisabled peers.

Lucinda Gabri, whose son, Christopher, now fifteen and a half, was born with Down syndrome, is one such parent. "I never wanted him to be mainstreamed," she says with conviction, "because I never wanted him to have the responsibility for being successful, and as a parent that's how I envisioned mainstreaming."

That feeling started with Christopher's infant stim programs and continues now that he's in high school. He has never attended a neighborhood school, and at this point the local high school's child study team doesn't feel that he could be successfully mainstreamed there—in part because he hasn't been exposed to and doesn't know any of those who might be his classmates now. Lucinda explains her rationale:

> I think inclusive education is a risk. It has to be a very strong collaborative effort by parent, child, child study team, teacher, and principal—in fact, all of the building personnel. If any of these pieces is not in concert, I don't feel that it works.
>
> But the key piece to successful integration is the parent. I have a good friend whose disabled son is in regular kindergarten, and all that's happened in the first three months was that she's there almost all the time. She's had to be constantly involved. I don't have the luxury of doing that. If I were to put Chris in an integrated setting, I feel that I would have to be the monitor, and I can't because I'm a working parent.

The main argument other parents offer against inclusion is that the quality of the child's specialized education almost invariably falls off. That feeling is particularly noticeable among parents of children with hearing or vision impairments. Some also tend to be skeptical about the presumed benefits of full-time association with nondisabled peers. Says Sue Sitler, whose five-year-old son, Travis, was born with a congenital defect of the retina that left him with almost no useful vision, "I know that what you gain in education you lose in socialization skills, but I think it's different for kids with visual impairments."

She wants Travis "integrated with sighted children as needed," but she feels he can only get the necessary basic education in braille and in orientation and mobility techniques by being in a resource room under the tutelage of teachers accredited in the blindness field, and not with what are termed *itinerant teachers* who must share their time with children in seven or eight different schools.

I would want a lot of his classes to be mainstreamed with sighted friends, as needed. But what I don't want is for recess to come, and he's the only visually impaired kid in the school, and the other kids go out to play and he just sits there. I've talked with twenty or thirty parents in the last two years who said that that's what happened to their kids, and it's the pits. And I've talked to older kids who are blind, and they say that the most traumatic time for them is recess or phys ed, because those are the times when they're completely alone.

Sue has heard about school systems, at this point usually the more affluent, that foster the inclusion of children with special needs by providing them with a full-time aide in the regular classroom, but she is not persuaded:

A hearing-impaired kid told me that for them their buddy is their interpreter. And one blind kid I know, the aide did everything for him, and it wound up the aide and the child always together, and it did not encourage any kind of interaction with the other kids in the class. And besides, Travis is not going to have an aide with him for the rest of his life.

Yet Susan Baker, the mother of a little girl named Jennifer, who was born not only blind but with mental retardation and a number of physical disabilities, says she and her husband disregarded "the conventional wisdom in our country" that a child like that "is incapable of doing much of anything." Writing in *Future Reflections,* the National Federation of the Blind magazine for parents of blind children, she describes how Jennifer entered first grade at age ten: "She had not been in the graded program because they did not think she was capable of doing it."

Next month Jennifer will be going from sixth grade into seventh grade. "She is the only blind child in her school," her mother says. But "she has been mainstreamed in science and social studies for the past three and a half years. She has maintained a straight A average," and "as she reads [in braille] and her world experience broadens, her IQ goes up. When we first had her tested we were told she was moderately retarded. On the next test she was mildly retarded. On the last test, given about two years ago, she tested out at the borderline retarded level."

The American Council for the Blind *Braille Forum* cites one other approach to solving the dilemma of special education versus integration which it indicates has actually been going on for decades: visually impaired students who "simultaneously" attend both a residential school and a public high school in the same town.

"Parents Should Have Options"

Florene Poyadue, who fought to have her son, Dean, attend regular classes, in large part so that he could grow up with the other boys from the neighborhood (Dean is now completely accepted by them) recalls that

> When Dean was in a regular class, even if he couldn't grasp everything, he was being exposed to much broader information and knowledge than he would have been if he'd never been there at all. And there's the benefit of the social growth he's gained. I'm not urging that parents need to be fighting the system all the time. But the more we can get our children into regular situations during their school years, the better life is going to be for them later on.
>
> When parents say their kid won't learn as well in an integrated setting, I can understand that because it's partly true. If a kid is in a regular class with teachers who are uncom-

fortable with him and who have no expectations of the kid, who don't know how to interact with him and don't know how to use resource specialists, it's true the kid could potentially lose out. But aren't there also low expectations of the kids in many special education classes?

So when people at the school say to you, "Either you want your kid over here in special education and educated, or you want him to be over there in regular education and not get an education," don't accept that at all. That's *their* mentality— an either/or situation. *We* have to say: "Why *won't* he learn in regular education? What do we—you and I—need to do to make it work?"

I think the most important thing is that parents should have options. Too often they're not given a chance to make those decisions for their children. We *need* options for our children, we need to have choices.

Agreeing that "there should be options available," Paula Goldberg, PACER co-director, feels that "some kids with very severe disabilities may need resource rooms, but certainly not as many as are placed there now.

"There is need for movement to have children with disabilities integrated into regular classrooms, even those children with severe or multiple disabilities. Such movement is an essential element of integrating them into the neighborhoods and communities in which they live. Parents need to think about the fact that their kids will one day be adults who will surely want to be part of the community."

"Not Enough Is Being Done"

Whether they might choose to have their children integrated or even fully included in regular classes in neighborhood schools or not, many parents find their school systems locked into approaches and structures that make such choices hard to come by. In Massachusetts, for example, since the seventies—that is, before the passage of PL 94-142 at the federal level—participating cities and towns and regional school districts have turned over the responsibility for special education to a collaborative, which sets up and staffs the classes.

The collaboratives were originally created at the request of the state's Board of Education because of "increasing special education costs," and many have provided effective teaching over the years. By their continued existence, however, they may well be helping to retard the integration of children with disabilities in regular classrooms and may even have a negative effect.

A 1991 "Comprehensive Report on the Mainstreaming of Children with Special Needs" by the State Board of Education makes the following points:

♦ "More students than ever before are being placed in special education settings where opportunities to interact with their nondisabled peers are limited."

♦ An analysis of the data indicates that "students with mild to moderate needs and served in resource rooms are spending more rather than less time separated from their nondisabled peers during the school day."

♦ "Clearly, the data shows that not enough is being done to integrate students with mild, moderate, and intensive special needs into regular education settings. Therefore, students are being 'pulled out' [to resource rooms] or separated from their peers to receive special education services."

A letter from a special educator working for one of the collaboratives, who asked not to be identified by name, declares that "Despite increasing rhetoric, Massachusetts has not made uniform progress toward mainstreaming or integration of children with significant handicaps. According to a recent report by the State Board of Education, the rate of children placed in separate special classes in public schools increased by 120 percent over the last sixteen years. The rate of children placed in private day schools has increased 345 percent since 1974.

"The state is increasingly vocal about its commitment to integration, but policy has not yet become practice."

It may well be, as some advocates have suggested, that certain educators and administrators are finding it difficult to readjust their thinking to the historically recent concepts of integrating and including students with disabilities in the educational mainstream. There may even be some with a vested interest in perpetuating existing infrastructures, as more than one irate parent has concluded. Whatever the reason for the foot-dragging, "many students with disabilities are prohibited from attending regular schools and classrooms or programs with peers who are not disabled," in the words of a resolution reaffirmed by The Association for Persons with Severe Handicaps at its 1991 conference.

Declaring that "education is for all students, not 'regular' and 'special' education as separate and distinct entities," TASH—which is philosophically in the forefront of advocacy organizations concerned with disabilities—called for "the necessary support" for students and teachers "so separate schools and separate classrooms can be a thing of the past."

If there is to be substantial movement toward integrated schools and classrooms in the immediate future, it will require teacher-student, and educator-parent, partnership. The legal basis for such collaboration has been there since 1975; Robert R. Davila, Assistant Secretary, Office of Special Education and Rehabilitation Services (OSERS) in the U.S. Department of Education, has underscored that "PL 94-142 enables parents to be key participants in the process of making decisions about their child's education." The perspective and the goal are clear, he added: "Increasingly we will be judged on how well we are able to prepare young people with disabilities to compete in the mainstream of society."

In that regard he noted that "at OSERS we are very aware of the special challenges faced by people from minority backgrounds who have disabilities" and called—among other proposals—for "improving outreach to minority communities" and "increasing the sensitivity of professionals."

"Each Tribe Is Different"

Nowhere is this more important than for those—individuals and service-provider agencies as well—who seek to serve Native American communities in the Southwest. In the 1980 United States Census, American Indians were found to have disabling conditions at a disproportionately high rate compared to the general population. The indication is that they have not been receiving adequate help: according to the United Cerebral Palsy Associations' *Word from Washington,* because of the "lack of leadership demonstrated by the Bureau of Indian Affairs in providing services," a number of amendments to the 1991 reauthorization bill for the "Infants and Toddlers Act" sought to improve assistance to that community.

For those who seek to help, however, a Native American parent-professional who works with tribes and communities in the Southwest has a caveat: given that there are still more than 250 American Indian languages, each representing a different culture, the greatest mistake would be to take the same approach to all of them. Each tribe and community has its unique heritage and a unique attitude toward disability and people with disabilities:

> If you go to a tribe, you need to view how it looks at people, how they feel someone with a disability fits into their society. And *each tribe is different:* you can't generalize. One tribe may feel that everyone has a place and a function within that society, that whether you're disabled or not you fulfill that role.
>
> But that's not true in all tribes. Another may feel that a child with a disability means that that child, or that family, or even the tribe, has done something wrong, and that the disability is a punishment, the result of an external force. But again, even there you can't generalize. Even where a disability is considered a punishment for wrongdoing, in some tribes that person would remain part of the tribe, and in others they might expel him.

This man's own son is six and has autism. In his tribe, he adds, everyone has a place in the community: "Even a child with a limited mental capacity can learn what the useful herbs are and go out to gather them. And that gives him value to the community."

For that reason a tribe might reject outright an offer by an outside case worker to take a child with a disability and place him or her in a school where he or she might be trained and educated. Another tribe might choose to reject other services offered. And a family in a third might not respond for some time to an offer of help, the parent-professional says, but that should not necessarily be taken as a refusal of the offer, because depending on the tribe's traditions the decision might have to be made by the disabled child's family's clan or even the entire tribe.

"A Major Challenge"

Professor Ruth Cook, who teaches in a California area with a culturally diverse population, comments that for professionals working with minority groups, "it is a major challenge to understand family needs plus all the cultural systems."

She tells of asking a Japanese family that was in need of help for their child if they had contacted a group she'd told them might aid them. The mother's answer was, "I'd like to, but I'm waiting." For what? Although the mother's English was quite adequate, Professor Cook says, she was hesitant "because I don't have enough English to express my feelings yet."

There may have been an additional reason for the reluctance: since certain Asian cultures have negative attitudes toward failure, parents from those groups are often reluctant even to admit that their children *have* a disability.

"It takes a long time to build trust in communities that have populations culturally and linguistically different from the service providers," says Justine Strickland, director of the East River Child Development Center and former chair of the Interagency Coordinating Council of New York State. "Often families in these communities are reluctant to use services for their own cultural reasons, and also because they feel alienated when they attempt to access the system and none of the significant providers is representative of their cultural or linguistic background."

Sometimes that creates barriers at precisely the moment when the provider is attempting to break them down. It may be the not unusual situation in which interviewer and client use the same English words but are not speaking the same substantive language. Words like "family" and "services" and even "disability" may have different meanings to two people from different cultural backgrounds.

One approach to dealing with the problem on the part of health care and parent advocacy agencies and groups is to try to recruit more men and women from diverse ethnic and cultural groups to their boards and professional staffs. That is particularly important because of the overrepresentation of minority children in special education and the underrepresentation of minority professionals in the field. One of the catalytic agencies in parent education, the Technical Assistance for Parent Programs (TAPP), which is funded by OSERS, has created a select committee to examine the problem, with representatives from underserved American Indian, Hispanic, Asian, and African-American constituencies.

"I Will Persist"

That committee will seek to develop guidelines for working with families from minority communities, but it is clear that each community will require its own approach—actually approaches—based on such additional factors as economic status, culture, and geography. In parts of California, Professor Cook points out, a major inhibiting factor in working with families from below the border recently arrived in this country is "the great immigration fear": "People are afraid to ask for services for their children with special needs because they're not citizens, or because a brother or a cousin or someone else living in the same house is not, and they are afraid to call the attention of the authorities—any authorities—to themselves."

But again it would be a mistake to generalize. Two young Mexican-born mothers, neither of whom speaks more than a few words of English, did overcome their fears and approach the child care system—because their babies' needs were so great. They have different perceptions, however, about how they are being treated.

Juana Lopez feels that some Mexican-Americans who were born here did discriminate against her because of her lack of English, and possibly because her baby was born in Mexico. On a number of occasions, she says, service providers were brusque and "not too polite to me." She has a friend with the same background who is always reluctant to call the van service that takes her child to the doctor because the driver is so unpleasant to her—or so the friend feels.

But Veronica Peña says that generally she has received very fair treatment despite the same language barrier: "If no one speaks Spanish when I telephone, they either get an interpreter right then or call me back with one." Even if she were to run up against what she felt was prejudice or discrimination, she says, she's determined: "I will do the best I can to get what my daughter needs. And that means I will persist. Whether I speak half and half, or no matter how I speak, I will persist—and she *will* receive services."

The Problem: "Poverty Rather than Color"

When members of a racial, cultural, or ethnic minority have difficulty accessing the system and getting the services their children need, it is not an unfair assumption that they are victims of a double discrimination—that in some cases their disabilities and their minority backgrounds are both being viewed as birth defects, doubly relegating them to second-class status.

But while Professor Cook agrees that "it is difficult for minority peoples and people of color to connect with the system," she feels that "it is a function of poverty and lack of education, rather than color or race."

In practical terms, that may often be a meaningless distinction, since an estimated 40 percent of all children of color are poor. The question was therefore put to several African-American parent/professionals: Do black families suffer from discrimination in obtaining special education services for their children; and if they do, is it because they're black, or because of their poverty and lack of education, or both?

In San Jose, California, Florene Poyadue, PHP executive director, felt that

> As far as people of color or minorities not getting as much help as whites, I think that centers basically around what I call SEEOG—Socio-Economic, Educational, Occupational, and Geographic status.
>
> I think color has very little to do with getting help. If more Caucasians are getting services for their children, or getting their kids integrated into regular schools, it's because they have a better SEEOG base from which to work. If people in the inner city get less, it's not because they're blacks or Hispanics, but because of their SEEOG—and because the way funds are allocated, even their geography is against them.

The Parent Coordinator for the Department of Special Services of an urban community with a large African-American and Hispanic population in northern New Jersey was in essential agreement:

Neither color nor minority status is the basic factor in getting help. But being more affluent and better educated does make a difference, because parents who are more knowledgeable, who have done their homework, are better equipped to fight for services for their children.

There is no difference in willingness to fight for their children between white and minority parents—black, Hispanic, or Asian in this community; the difference is on the economic level.

Especially with minority parents, they often don't know enough to fight for services that aren't offered—and there isn't enough time for them to get educated about their rights and about what they should ask for for their children. Not that the schools refuse to give them their rights, but they don't know that there are more things the school system can do, so they just say, "OK, whatever you can do."

To give an example of what knowledge means, one mother who knew the law brought in documentation that her son needed occupational or physical therapy three times a week instead of the once a week the child study team had recommended—so it was written into the IEP. If the mother hadn't made an issue of it, and backed it up, the increase would not have been written into the IEP, even though the child study team knew that the boy would benefit.

Virginia Richardson, PACER Manager of Parent Training, agrees only in part. If "research shows that African-Americans do not use resources for persons with disabilities to the fullest extent," she says, "this is an issue not only of access to information but of trust that the system will serve their children in a fair and respectful way." She adds:

I believe that many factors impact the special education process, and that one factor is sometimes race.

Who is in special education and why is sometimes easy to determine, and at other times much more complex. For children who have visible disabilities and needs that are apparent, the process may be fairly straightforward. But for children with invisible disabilities—i.e., learning disabilities, high-functioning mental handicaps, and emotional and behavioral disorders—the process is more complex.

I seldom encounter African-American parents who believe their child needs special education but is not receiving services. I encounter many parents who have expressed the belief that their child is receiving more emotional and behavioral services than are needed, or parents who are fearful their child will be placed in EBD [emotional and behavioral disorders] or EMH [educable mentally handicapped] classes when they are not needed. I find this sentiment cuts across all socioeconomic and educational lines.

A May 1992 report by the New York State Board of Education on a single Long Island school district indicated that many minority parents may well be justified in such fears. The report noted that black students in the Huntington Union Free School District constituted 38.8 percent of all children in special education, though they were only 13.9 percent of the total school population. Similarly, according to the Puerto Rican Legal Defense and Education Fund, 13 percent of the students in the district were Hispanic children, but they were 20 percent of the special education students. A lawyer for the fund was quoted by *The New York Times* as declaring that the state's report gave a local picture of a national tendency.

Why this overrepresentation of minority youngsters in special education? According to Virginia Richardson,

> During workshops and individual discussions with African-American parents in response to questions, more time is usually spent on issues of assessment and ways of assuring that the child is *not* placed in special education if [it is] not needed. I believe these are valid concerns. Many of the standardized tests are not normed on groups that include African-American children. Observation and interpretation of behavior is made by teams of professionals that often lack input from African-Americans.
>
> I don't believe race is a factor in special education in overt ways, and I feel many African-American children are served well by the system. But many parents feel race is still a factor in the process, and I agree.

Virginia Richardson meets with a support group of African-American parents, she says, but there are no PACER training sessions directed at special groups. "At PACER we are concerned that all parents receive the help needed so their sons and daughters can reach their full potential. Good trainers simply adjust to the people they're training."

Florene Poyadue, at PHP, also makes certain adjustments:

> I don't change our parent training programs for black parents of children with special needs. I don't care if they're white, pink, black, or green, I don't change programs for skin colors. But I do change programs for parents who have less than a sixth-grade education.

A Lesson in "How-To"

One little girl who benefited from PHP's lessons and guidance is eight-year-old Wendy Terry, of San Jose. According to her mother, Lana, she is one of only sixty cases in the United States of children with Russell-Silver Dwarf syndrome. She is only forty-five inches tall; she went through certain aspects of puberty at age five; she has at least half a dozen severe and distinct physical problems; she needs to be fed nightly through a G-tube.

A year and a half ago Wendy was in a special day class. Now she's in a regular second-grade class with "pullouts" to resource rooms for speech therapy and phys ed. Here's how Lana "integrated" her daughter:

> I was just not happy with the day class, and her teacher there felt that Wendy should at least try to mainstream. But when I asked for a regular class, they told me she was too immature. I told *them* that that was because she was in with kids who were immature—they were her role models, so to speak.
>
> When I kept asking, the resource specialist wasn't real happy. She kept saying, "She's going to need hours of 'pullout' every day, and I think it's wrong." And I kept answering, "Well, I want to try it. If it doesn't work, I'll bring her back. But I want to try it."
>
> Then they tried to scare me with the idea that Wendy couldn't survive in a regular class—with the work, with the

other kids who were bigger. They felt the other kids would tease her about the G-tube, and that she might get hurt because of that and because she was so small.

That kept up even after I began looking for the right place for Wendy. Against the school's and the psychologist's wishes, I went around to all the schools in my district until I found a teacher who was willing to take her—and as it happens that school has a wonderful program. And that teacher said, "Let's go for it." And the new principal knew Wendy real well from before, so he was for trying it too. So I pulled her out of her special class and put her into the regular class.

Of course there have been problems. But last year, when the kids did start to tease her about the G-tube, the teacher waited until Wendy was out of the room for one of her services; then she sat all the kids down and explained that this was part of Wendy and not something to tease her about. And it stopped. And this year, no one has teased her at all.

There have been problems with the new school's resource specialist. She didn't like that I asked for and got additional "pullout" for Wendy for reading—the only subject she's been having trouble with. But since the old resource specialist has seen the change in Wendy in the new class, she's said to me, "Yes, this is where Wendy should be."

I don't know where I got the guts to tackle the system the way I did. Mostly from talking to the people at PHP—I've taken their classes on IEP and advocacy training. And when I was trying to decide, I asked them, "What are the consequences? How can I go about it without offending anybody too much?"

So they helped me a lot, and showed me the right way to do things. And I did it.

13

"Their Dreams Can Expand"

Assistive Technology: The Equalizer

Some equipment now available for classroom use has already demonstrated that children with autism or mental retardation, or with severe or multiple physical disabilities, or who are nonverbal, or children who are vision- or hearing-impaired, can be successfully brought into regular classrooms and be effectively integrated there, educationally and socially. With the proliferation of computers in schoolrooms everywhere, for children with disabilities assistive communication technology may be, in the not-too-distant future, the "open sesame" to full inclusion.

Andrea Veith is an example of technology's potential. She is ten, has cerebral palsy, and is legally blind. Because her verbal skills are only "survival-minimal," as her mother Michelle describes them, in the classroom her computer became her voice. Actually she has had her choice of voices and is now on her third. Her first was very "computery" and difficult to understand. For her second there were a number of choices, including a woman's voice that was "so boring-sounding" that they chose a man's voice instead.

Then they found a little girl's voice, much more understandable and acceptable in every way. It came out of the computer, of course, like the others, but the first day Andrea used it, the other kids in the class came home from school and told their parents, "Guess what? Andrea can talk now."

Her computer is portable, so last year she decided to perform in the second-grade talent show. She "pulled up" (programmed) a song, Michelle Veith says, walked out on the stage with the computer, and did her number—"I'd like to Give the World a Song and Furnish It with Love"—to great applause.

The reason Andrea was confident she could do it, her mother adds, is that she sings "Happy Birthday" at parties with the computer voice. The other kids love it, and "it sure makes Andrea feel like part of the group." That's probably as good a working definition of inclusion as there is.

Such communication devices, along with hearing aids, wheelchairs, and some prostheses, are all referred to as *adaptive* or *assistive technology,* and *assistive communication devices* are also often referred to as *augmentative* or *alternative communication systems.* One major difference between such systems and the ordinary personal computer is their "output"—not just the images on the monitor but voice or braille or a combination of all three.

What is most fascinating, even mind-boggling, to parents and others exposed to the technology for the first time is the variety of input devices specifically designed for children or adults with any of a variety of disabilities.

To turn on the system, for example, there are switches that can be activated by a movement of the head (or chin), by the tongue, by winking, by wrinkling the forehead, by a toe on the foot switch on the floor, by the sound of the user's voice, or by sipping and puffing on a straw attached to a special switch.

In addition to using a foot switch, someone without the use of his or her hands can also use a keyboard on the floor. There are also keyboards for one-handed typists, and membrane keyboards—flat surfaces—for those without sufficient strength in their hands to depress the keys.

There are systems that can be operated by tapping a single key, or by one finger; or by a light attached to the forehead—to light up the word or symbol desired; or combined with a scanning system, which keeps moving across the monitor until the user makes his or her choice. There is a system that instructs the computer to carry out specific commands based solely on where the eye is focused.

There is a computer operated without a keyboard: a screen is plugged into the back of the computer and then attached to the front of the monitor with Velcro. It has software for word processing and other programs—or just for fun. One little girl with mental retardation was shown how to use it: "Like magic, there were suddenly figures on the monitor. The kid's attention was frozen to the screen," special education teacher Mary Pulaski recalled.

"I'd Die If I Couldn't Talk"

Yet it is not what communication technology does or how it does what it does that is so "miraculous" to parents, but what using it means to the children and their families. Roger Vu is fourteen and a half and was born in Thailand. Until he was thirteen he was Xatau Vu, but then he decided to choose an "American" name for himself. As a result of a "high fever" when he was five months old, his mother, Me Vu, says, he has difficulty walking, cannot hold anything heavy, cannot swallow, and doesn't speak. Roger was to all intents and purposes a nonexistent personality, she says, until he connected with a computer-plus-voice synthesizer. "That was the first time we ever knew how he felt," Me Vu adds.

Once he had acquired a deep masculine voice, the floodgates were opened. It was not just that Roger could ask his mother "How are you?" and talk about what he'd studied in school that day. More, it was the locked-in dreams emerging: Roger wants to become a doctor, he wants to go on a mission to the moon, and "Whatever he decides," Me Vu says, "I'll support him." Roger says, "I'd rather die if I couldn't talk any more."

Alicia Ober calls what happened to her daughter, Patty, when she got her system "a miracle." The little girl, born prematurely, has cerebral palsy and limited vision, and she could communicate only in a limited way by pointing to objects on a picture-board— until she got a "talking computer." Says her mother:

> Because she is nontalking, even her father and I were sometimes afraid that she might also be nonthinking. Only now do we know how frustrating it was for her to be *full* of thoughts and feelings—and to have them locked inside her. Now they're coming out—and to me it's just as much of a miracle as her surviving in the first place.

But there are limits to the "miracle." Even with the new "voice" she can't get her thoughts and feelings out like people actually talking.

Educators and others involved with computers find that they must constantly inject that same note of caution for parents introduced to technology's "magic" and the "miraculous" differences it makes in their children's lives. That "magic" can enhance the quality of their lives; it can often give them a limited mastery over their environment. It can reveal and augment their capabilities—but it cannot cure their disabilities or their birth defects.

To quote one educator, "It takes more than a thousand dollars' worth of equipment to make a life." Or in the sobering words of another: "We value the fact that a child with Down syndrome now has language and can even write a story or a poem—that's important to him or her, to the families and teachers and friends. But the child still has Down syndrome."

Despite that essential caveat—that technology is only an added tool, albeit a super-tool, nevertheless assistive technology, by helping children with mental, emotional, or physical problems to "see," to "hear," to "talk," to communicate, to learn, to move about, to participate, does have the potential to become not only an educator but a liberator, a socializer, and an equalizer.

In the words of Jacquelyn Brand, regarded as a pioneer in adapting and popularizing technology for children with disabilities: "Too many families where a child has a disability still lack awareness of what technology can do. They don't realize how incredibly helpful and effective technology can be in empowering their kids."

A Product of the Eighties

It is difficult to believe that the adaptation of computer technology for people with disabilities really began only in the 1980s, considering how quickly and widely it has spread since then. In 1980–81, Johns Hopkins University undertook a nationwide search for technical aids specifically designed for the use of individuals with special needs, and got more than 8,000 entries, which resulted in hundreds of inventions, many of which have since become standard equipment. One of those inventions, for example, was the tracking system that allows the user capable of no more than eye movement to activate a computer just by looking at it.

Taking it a step further, by March 1983 the Council for Exceptional Children was already exploring the use of adapted computers in special education. The 1986 "Infants and Toddlers Act" included a Part G, which promoted the use of technology in educating students with disabilities, and in 1988 Congress passed what is known as the "Tech Act"—Public Law 100-407, the Technology-Related Assistance for Individuals with Disabilities Act. That law defines assistive technology as "any item, piece of equipment, or product system, whether acquired off the shelf, modified, or customized to increase, maintain, or improve the functional capabilities of individuals with disabilities."

One aim of the "Tech Act" is to help each state, with a three-year grant of $500,000 a year, to develop a program of consumer-driven assistive technology services. It is left to the individual states to decide how best to do so, with the active involvement of consumers (including parents) as partners in decision making.

Providing technical assistance and information to the states in developing their programs is a group known as RESNA. Formerly the Rehabilitation Engineering Society of America, it is now the Association for the Advancement of Rehabilitation and Technology, working under contract to the National Institute on Disability and Rehabilitative Research.

Where to Find the Right Devices

For the average parents who might want to find assistive equipment for their child, there is almost too much going on. Not only are new devices becoming available regularly, but the multiplicity of merchandisers adds to the difficulty of choosing. Most rehabilitation specialists and special educators are still unfamiliar with the technology themselves, and teachers who use computers constantly in regular education classrooms are seldom knowledgeable about adaptive devices. In fact, some research suggests that billions of dollars worth of such equipment is already sitting in school storerooms. A resource specialist in a computer center says she even found a resource room full of specialized software, none of it being used. "I got the idea," Jennifer Lemmons says, "that the aids running the program thought it just wasn't worth the effort. I think they'd given up; or maybe they were burned out. Or maybe they just don't have the right kind of software that would work with the kids they have there now."

For those parents and educators who have a pretty good idea of what they're looking for, or simply want to get a general idea of what's available, *Exceptional Parent* publishes an annual Computer Technology Issue, which is a valuable source of resources.

United Cerebral Palsy affiliates can also prove to be extremely helpful. By January 1991 sixty-five affiliates had assisted more than 29,000 individuals with technology-related services. An excellent resource to help parents determine what works for their youngsters is the UCP Tech Tots program, parent-run "libraries" that lend families of infants, toddlers, and preschoolers adapted toys, adaptive switches, and computers for home use, first showing them how the equipment they are getting works.

One of the confusing aspects of choosing is that there is often more than one solution—different combinations of hardware and software—to the same problem. With all the competing claims, experience has shown that not all of the equipment is equally suitable or equally effective for any one person. Families can see and test some of the equipment in one of the computer resource centers affiliated with the Alliance for Technological Access (ATA). These centers are geared to assist students, parents, and school professionals in finding individualized solutions to specific school-related problems. By 1991 there were forty-six such centers in thirty-five states (See Appendix B). Jacquelyn (Jackie) Brand, one of ATA's founders, has predicted that by the middle of the decade "there will certainly be centers in every state, and multiple centers in many of them. These centers will have created a very parent- and consumer-driven approach to services."

The centers are not just a different kind of computer store, she says. "One of the major roles of our centers is to help families see the tremendous power of technology in a context away from the medical model, the model where health care people are in charge. Technology can give parents back the responsibility and the joy of making decisions for their children with special needs, just as they make them for their other children."

"To Be Everything She Could Be"

ATA started with a single center in the middle eighties, the Berkeley (California) Disabled Children's Computer Group (DCCG), which still exists. Actually, Jackie Brand says,

> I didn't plan to start a network, or even a center. My goal was really to figure out ways that our daughter, Shoshana, could take advantage of the technology that was then available to get into a regular classroom—in order for her to be everything she could be. It took three years to put together the right technology for her, the different pieces she needed in order to be able to use the computer to do her reading and spelling and math. I had to become a semiexpert just to figure out a few answers for my own kid.
>
> My daughter has cerebral palsy and cortical blindness. She started in a special class; now she's a sophomore in a regular high school. Technology was the key.
>
> One group least aware of how technology could help their kids are the families of children with cognitive delays or limitations. The myth of technology is that you have to excel cognitively to use it. It's as if you can't drive a car unless you're a mechanic.
>
> You don't need to understand the guts of a computer in order to use it and exploit its power. Kids who are struggling with reading and never get the joy of knowing what a story is sit down at a computer, switch it on, and it talks back to them. They now have the pleasure of reading—just by listening.

DCCG in Berkeley is an interactive computer center full of hardware and software. These are some of the people you might find there:

◆ A girl about seventeen in ninth grade who is nonverbal and cannot use any part of her body. Her hands have only involuntary motion. But she can move her chin; the computer system she uses has a scanning device that she stops by lowering her chin when it hits the letter she wants. It is slow—seems like forever; but eventually Onna's synthesized voice will say, "Hello, how are you?" or "I made a blue dress." Turns out she made the dress with her chin-switch also.

✦ A Native American girl with mental retardation and self-abusive tendencies: "You never know when she's going to smack herself on the back," resource specialist Jennifer Lemmons says. She never smiles and she never talks, just grunts.

"But she got on a program," Jennifer recalls. "which matches objects with numbers, and after a while when the apples appeared on the screen she started to count, very very softly. The teacher who comes with her was astounded: 'Linda doesn't talk. They won't give her a speech therapist because they think she's so out of it.'

"People at the school wouldn't believe the teacher, so the next week we videotaped Linda counting out loud along with the computer—so softly we had to turn the volume way up—and then turning and looking her teacher right in the eye, something she never did. She doesn't seem to be aware that she's done something special—but maybe that counting will get her a speech teacher."

✦ A little girl with microcephaly, poor motor skills, and learning problems. Her computer helps her with letter recognition, math, and matching objects. And she has lots of friends in her first-grade class, because she's teaching everyone how to use her equipment.

✦ Eleven-year-old Jonathan Cool, who was born with Down syndrome, and was brought to DCCG for testing because he was unable to communicate except through grunts and gestures. His computer is not only a verbal communicator, but "an interactive tool," his mother, Carole, says:

> Where Jonathan shows real delight is when he sees an immediate result of what he's doing. Whether he uses a joystick or presses a key and sees some concrete action resulting, that's something he's very much aware of. In the last year, in fact, he's become aware of the power of communication; he's really seeing that he can communicate his needs to people. It used to be a guessing game and still is at home, because we can't afford to buy the voice synthesizer.

Aside from his new ability to communicate, what is equally important to his family is that Jonathan, who had previously been entirely in special education settings, went into a regular third-grade classroom a year ago. Carole Cool explains that

Right now Jonathan is in an integrated classroom with a computer that has a voice feedback—but it isn't portable. If he had one of the mobile devices in his IEP, then they would be responsible for seeing that it was available in the classroom. That's what his teacher and I are working on now.

In August 1990 the Office of Special Education Programs (OSEP) of the U.S. Department of Education made it clear in a policy statement that assistive technology can be considered special education or related services, or supplementary services required to help a student with special needs stay in regular classrooms.

Technology: Part of the IEP

As with any other aspect of special education, therefore, where assistive devices can be shown to aid in the child's basic education and/or integration in regular education, they should be incorporated into the child's IEP.

Despite the fact that personal computers can be found in countless classrooms across the country, only a limited number of school districts have begun to provide the assistive devices that would turn them into communication systems for children with special needs. Even when parents are knowledgeable enough to ask, says Helen Miller, who is a computer resource specialist at the Berkeley DCCG center, "some schools tell them: 'We'd love to help, but we just don't have the money.' If that happens—or even before it happens—one important role of the ATA centers is to work with families to help them strategize about incorporating technology into their child's IEP."

In 1990, through its fund-raising arm, the Foundation for Technology Access, ATA created what it calls CompuCid—the Computer Classroom Integration Demonstration project—to answer the key question: How can computer systems aid in the integration of students with disabilities into regular public school classrooms?

There is a very good reason for such studies: since court decisions have indicated that "We can't afford it" is not a valid reason for denying children with special needs the services they demonstrably need, some schools have been putting parents off with such other excuses as "he/she doesn't need it," "it wouldn't be of any benefit," or "he/she couldn't use it."

When that happens, families can request an assistive technology evaluation, just as they would any other service they're convinced their child needs. Some schools are already providing the evaluation. Others, which do not feel that they have anyone with the requisite assistive technology expertise, are having such testing provided by outside sources, including local ATA centers. Says Helen Miller:

> Many parents come to our centers to get an evaluation, and then ask for a letter describing what the child did, how she or he did it, and what devices were used for her or him to do it.
>
> To find out, the first question we ask is: "What is your son or daughter interested in? What does he or she like to do?" Often that takes parents aback. They're so used to being asked what their kids can't do, or what they don't want to do, or what they won't do.
>
> Then we let the kids look at different kinds of software in action, just to get them interested. And then we let them *try* some of the different kinds, a whole variety of software, just to see what works the best for them. But this is under special conditions; to see how the system works in the child's natural environment, we will lend the family equipment and software to try out at home. And we have had some instances where it didn't work out. When that happens, we may tell them to try it again a little longer, or something else. Or we may tell them to try again next year: kids change, mature.
>
> When it does work, schools are often ready to accept not just our final evaluation but in some cases, where the school hasn't sent the parents but they've come on their own, the evidence that technology can meet the child's special needs. It indicates a seriousness and determination on the family's part: these are not just parents saying, "Gee, I'd really like my kid to have a computer," but parents who have gone out and researched it and have good reason to believe in it.

It is seldom a matter of simply adding a device to the computers the school system may already have. It may require a complete system for input and output. In some cases, children with severe or multiple disabilities may require a team—not only a computer specialist but an occupational therapist and/or physical therapist to help train the child to control his or her muscles or head or facial movements before he or she can operate the system.

"It took us two years to find the right switch placement for one child," Helen Miller remembers. "We tried all sorts of placements on various parts of his body, but always after about five minutes he'd get so tired he couldn't use the technology." Eventually he got a puff-and-sip switch.

One additional mission of the ATA computer centers, therefore, is to provide enough resources, support, and information for educators (including both regular and resource teachers), rehabilitation specialists, speech teachers, and therapists to help the child use the available technology effectively. If someone comes in with a special problem—a child who is blind, for example—the center will add a specialist with special knowledge in that area to the team. When the fatigue factors are especially difficult—but solvable—the team will generally include vision, occupational, and physical therapists, as well as knowledgeable staff members, and the parents.

When the right kind of technology is provided by the school system, it is not merely an educational tool; it can change the quality of the child's life. When Portia Ann Lemmons was four, she entered regular preschool. "It really scared me." her mother says, because Portia Ann was born with cerebral palsy and spastic quadriplegia. "I'd heard about mainstreaming," Jennifer Lemmons adds, "but she was in a wheelchair and I didn't want the other kids to tease her. But it worked out fine."

Portia Ann had trouble writing, so in fifth grade, when she was ten, the school provided her with a word processor—nothing special, the kind that can be bought at any computer store—to speed up her ability to take notes. She does that now with a laptop, which can be connected to the printer. Aside from how it's helped Portia Ann's education, Jennifer says,

the computer seemed to be an esteem builder. She seemed to have more confidence. She's never said it, but I think now that she's in high school she just assumes that everybody knows how important it is to her. She's a risk taker now; she's talking about moving away from her father and me and moving in with a friend. But to tell the truth, we'd have some trouble with it; it just goes with parenthood.

No others in class have the device she uses, because she is just one of the two disabled students in her school. Technology is a good social icebreaker, because she knows something about something that the other kids don't. They come over to her, and they say, "You're lucky that you have that computer, and you're lucky that you get to drive a power wheelchair." And she answers, "No I'm not." The other kids ask to use her wheelchair, and sometimes they play with her joystick and make her jerk around.

She says that they are not always nice to her, but I think even if she were able-bodied that might be true: that's the way kids are. I tell her that maybe the fact that they are that way is an indication that they accept her. Maybe that's their way of being friendly.

Bobby Fliegel is another teenager to whom the computer has become "a major part of his life," his mother says. He was born with cerebral palsy and lives in an area whose school district has a real commitment to inclusion.

After his parents had psyched themselves up for a battle with the school administration to get Bobby into a regular kindergarten group, they found out that the school had been planning to do exactly that—to provide the same placement they'd picked for his nondisabled twin. In second grade they gave Bobby a computer of his own.

"When he's not at school," Sarah Fliegel says, "he spends more than 50 percent of his time working or playing at the computer. What other teenagers do for recreation with their bodies, he does on the computer." And Bobby, who has a sense of humor, adds from his wheelchair that when he was asked to write an essay on "putting your best foot forward," he wrote: "Whatever I do, I put my best wheel forward."

He was very fortunate in another way. When the Fliegels decided that Bobby's progress would be enhanced if he had an identical computer for use at home, they asked if they could purchase it through the school to save money. The school answered that they couldn't legally do that and instead offered to lend Bobby the second computer for as long as he remains in the school system.

"It Doesn't Come Cheap"

It is seldom that easy for parents to get assistive technology systems for home use. Jonathan Cool's parents were able to duplicate some of his communications system for use at home, but not all— "It was not financially manageable for us to get it all," Carole Cool says. "We got what we could; the rest was much too expensive."

Families who want to buy a computer-plus-software for home use, but have a limited budget, should look to the possibility of buying devices that are not identical with the school's but are compatible with them and often cheaper. It may be possible to walk into a computer store and buy items off the shelf, but the specialized software necessary is probably not available. There are many stores with lots of different possible systems for accomplishing the same purpose. How do you decide?

There is one key consideration, DCCG computer specialist Helen Miller cautions:

> When parents come in to our center and see the wonders our equipment can do, they get excited and ask, "What kind of machine should I buy?" and I ask them, "Whom are you going to buy it for?" Regular technology is broadly oriented, for anyone's use, while adaptive technology takes into consideration the special needs of the individual for whom it is put together. Adaptive technology is only a machine and some software unless you make something more of it by relating it to the end user.

Assistive communication technology "doesn't come cheap," she adds. It may run into the thousands of dollars for the computer and the special input and output devices the child may need to adapt it to his or her use. Given the fact that most local education is financed from property taxes, it is not surprising for parents to be told these days that there are "no funds" for the technology that they know would make such an enormous difference in their child's life.

One possible exception worth exploring for parents of children with severe visual impairments is specialized adaptive equipment, interactive communication systems that would enable them to read computer screens, as well as printed or written materials, and respond. This equipment may be available through the state's commission for the blind and visually impaired or, in some cases, the state rehabilitation agency.

The American Foundation for the Blind has a low-interest loan program (with funds partially supplied by the Xerox Corporation) to help blind and legally blind people buy a computer system that translates printed materials into synthetic speech. There are a number of conditions, however; for information and an application, contact AFB's hotline at (800) 232-5463 or (212) 620-2147; or write Sheron Rice, National Technology Center, American Foundation for the Blind, New York, NY 10011.

While wheelchairs are often financed by insurance companies and Medicaid as a "medical necessity," the insurers generally refuse to pay for assistive communication systems, devices, or services, because they consider them to be only "educationally necessary." That made one parent comment bitterly when he was turned down, "They will finance technology to get the kid to school, but not those things that will make it *worthwhile* for him to get there."

Some families have been successful in having the child's physician certify that augmentative communication devices are "medically necessary" for a nonverbal child on the grounds that otherwise the child is unable to communicate his or her symptoms, reactions to medication, medical needs, and so on. Even when this has been challenged, states have been compelled to provide funding for augmentative communication devices precisely as a "medical necessity" for persons who have no other way of communicating. In fact, in a number of states, "speech services" are mandatory for eligible individuals twenty-one years of age or younger who have severe speech impairments and because of other involvements cannot use sign language.

Especially in smaller communities, parents have sometimes found such local groups as the United Way, Rotary, Kiwanis, Elks, Lions, Masons, and Shriners, as well as churches and corporations, to be generous in providing prostheses and wheelchairs, including motorized wheelchairs, for children with physical disabilities. It may be that one or other of these groups might be willing to provide funds for the purchase of communication technology as well.

Local affiliates of national groups aiding children may be able to suggest additional sources of help, including United Cerebral Palsy Associations, The ARC (formerly the Association for Retarded Citizens), Muscular Dystrophy Association, Spina Bifida

Association, National Easter Seals Society, and the Telephone Pioneers of America. (See Appendix B for others.)

The state affiliates of ATA may also have suggestions for finding funding sources for home systems. Jackie Brand remarks:

> One important role of our centers is to work with families to find resources. There are a lot of them out there, and more all the time, but it still takes a highly motivated family to find them.
>
> It will help if there is a real breakthrough in the schools. Right now there is little occurring in most school systems relative to the needs of the children. The first priority for parents is therefore to get assistive technology into the classrooms, because that's where a majority of the kids will have access to it, and where educators and parents can see what it can do.

Transition Planning

That breakthrough may already be taking place. Families of preschool and grade-school youngsters are by and large still at the stage of struggling to prove that technology is a tool that will "make a difference in their kid's life," as one specialist puts it. When those youngsters are teenagers, however, it becomes a tool that is theirs by right, because it has the full force of a federal mandate behind it.

The beginnings of that right can be found in the Carl Perkins Vocational Education Act of 1984 (PL 98-524), which provided that students with disabilities had to receive a vocational assessment and special vocational services, as well as career and transition counseling. Not only were the student and family to be apprised of any special vocational training that was available, but the student's IEP had to incorporate the necessary training in work skills. Ideally, the transition program team was to include not only school personnel but representatives of vocational rehabilitation agencies and of the business community. The program was to be based on the realities of employment in the community, meaning the chances of actually getting a job as a result of the training.

A major advance was registered in 1988, when Congress changed the name of the law to the "Carl D. Perkins Vocational and Applied Technology Act." The intent of the renaming was clear: technology was to be part of transition planning.

To deal with still another area, one that had been left somewhat vague in earlier legislation, the 1990 Individuals with Disabilities Education Act (IDEA) required that when as students with disabilities were concerned, transition plans had to become part of their IEPs no later than age sixteen or when they reached the ninth grade. When appropriate the planning must begin at age fourteen or even younger.

Another important contribution was IDEA's defining "transition services" in part as "an outcome-oriented process . . . including post-secondary education, vocational training, integrated employment (including supported employment), continuing and adult education, adult services, independent living, or community participation . . . based upon the student's needs . . . preferences, and interests." A far cry, even if only in concept and not yet in widespread practice, from the days within recent memory when the law required only that students with disabilities be given classroom space until they could be "aged out" of the educational system legally.

Technology now has to be included in the transitional IEP when the need has been demonstrated. Like other elements of the IEPs, the fact that such services do not yet exist in the school or the system, or that "there are no funds for them," may not be used as excuses by school personnel for omitting technology from the IEP. Such services have to be provided to the student and at no cost to the family.

Should families find problems arising when they ask for such services, each state now has a federally funded Parent Training and Information (PTI) center, which is designed to provide not only training and information but support for students and their families. To find the nearest PTI center, parents can telephone either the National Parent Network on Disabilities at (703) 684-6763 or the Technical Assistance for Parent Projects at (617) 482-2915 (or See Appendix B).

Sometimes parents discover that the program for technology inclusion already exists in their states, but that their school system hasn't caught up. A report by the National Conference of State Legislatures in 1991 indicated that not only had some states had transition planning before it was required by federal legislation, but that they had already worked out some innovative programs.

To prepare the student "for the changes and demands of life

after school," the report declares, "some schools are offering up to five paid community work experiences as part of their program prior to graduation. Innovative programs offer skills training in natural rather then simulated environments, including the home, and work places such as grocery stores, offices, and restaurants."

To a great extent, the options that have been hitherto offered to high school graduates (or dropouts) with disabilities have been sheltered workshops, sheltered workshops, sheltered workshops—and an occasional entry-level dead-end job in a fast-food restaurant. Given results-oriented skills training, real-life pre-graduation work experiences, and a number of programs geared to provide support for people with disabilities on the job, it is no longer unrealistic for many young men and women, even those with severe or multiple disabilities, to hope for competitive employment. Says Ed Roberts, president of the World Institute on Disability:

> Very few people want to work in sheltered workshops just because there's no pressure there. Given the option, would you like to earn a dollar an hour, or six bucks an hour? The kind of thing they do in workshops—assembling one widget after another—is part of the old system: very patronizing, and with very low expectations of the people who work in them.
>
> Unfortunately, today people with disabilities are viewed by some of the others around them as hopeless, helpless, people to feel sorry for. When you grow up facing that kind of attitude, you wind up with a lot of frustrations and very low expectations.

It isn't only that young people with disabilities who want employment are shunted off into nowhere jobs. Many who are intellectually equipped for success in higher education tell of running into high school vocational counselors who tried to dissuade them from "dreaming the impossible dream." One administrator told the boy's mother, "it would be just setting him up for another failure."

> We were told by the director for the blind that our son's expectations were too high. People like that carry the sick attitude that a blind person shouldn't reach too high. But that experience only made my son a fighter, and he's going to show them who is reaching too high.

Perhaps it was an honest belief by the director that he was "sparing" the boy from heartbreak, but he failed to include determination and motivation in the equation. At last report that young man—with his family's support—had successfully graduated from high school and had gone on to become a nuclear engineering student at a state university. So much for the "reaching-too-high" stereotype.

In fact, a 1990 survey by the National Association of Developmental Disability Councils found that 90 percent of the adults with disabilities surveyed said they were ready, willing, and able to work. But in recent years between a half and two-thirds of them have been unable to find work.

Ed Roberts feels that to the extent that that is the result of prejudice and discrimination, there is hope that the Americans with Disabilities Act will prove to be an effective instrument in changing attitudes and creating new opportunities for employment and community living.

When that begins to happen, Jackie Brand wants people with disabilities to be ready to seize those opportunities. "Technology is now so pervasive in society," she says, "that it will either enlarge the gap between people with disabilities and the rest of society, or begin to close it. Right now we're at the crossroads."

"Dreams and Visions"

Parents must start by dealing with some of their fears first, she believes:

> I think technology is still extremely intimidating to most people. But families with disabled children cannot afford to be intimidated by it, because it has too much to offer. Families don't have to be technical experts—it is not all that frightening when you get some guidance.
>
> Parents have to understand that assistive technology will have such broad applications that they can really begin to hope—because it is going to challenge the limitations that have been placed on our kids. It is going to shatter those ceilings that we were told they couldn't pass through, that have held them down.
>
> Once kids begin to get hold of this stuff, their own ex-

pectations of themselves, their dreams and visions, can begin to expand. You're talking about a whole different quality of life.

When you help them break through those limitations, a whole world opens up for them. And there's no question it will happen: parents will go to the ends of the earth to find the tools that will make a difference in their kid's life.

Before the advent of assistive communication technology, what would have been the odds against Nicole Anderson's even *beginning* to "break through those limitations?" Born with so many disabling conditions, mental and physical, that she needed the services of more than seventy-five different professionals by the time she was six years old, Nicole had a special communication problem: she talked at home but never outside it.

At preschool, when Nicole was four, the staff therefore decided to try something as an experiment, a way to communicate without Nicole at first using her own voice. The "experiment" is actually quite common today: press a picture on the device, and the computer "talks" the word for you. There were no overnight "miracles": she continued to use that device for about a year and a half while she was growing with it. Among other things, her mother, Maria, says, she learned to use it as a protective device: "When the other kids began to bug her, she might be afraid to tell them to stop, so she got the computer to do it for her."

If there were no "miracles," there were some notable milestones for Nicole: When she first began to talk along with the machine. When after a while she began to *answer* it. And when one day her teachers and her mother realized that she was really talking, even if only in four-to-six-word sentences.

Nicole is in school full-time now—half the day in a resource room with children who have physical problems, the other half in a regular classroom. At that rate, who is there to say what "dreams and visions" she may one day make real?

14
....

"Children with Disabilities are Vulnerable"
The Child's Sexuality and the Parents' Role

After all is said and done, after parents do all they can to help shape and encourage their child's independence, almost every parent reaches a point at which he or she must confront the child's sexuality. Will anybody want to go out with my child? Can my child marry or ever have a family? Can he or she express sexual urges and needs as everybody else does? Sexuality, in its broadest sense, is loving and caring and intimacy. It is related to the full range of personal relationships, and our physical and emotional lives.

Sexuality is a part of every person's life. The youngest infants are sexual beings who delight in their own bodies and respond with great pleasure to the closeness and caresses of parents and siblings. As they continue to grow and to learn, children begin to develop a richer sexual identity that encompasses not only the physical attributes of their gender, but a broader appreciation of human relationships, including the right of each individual to healthy, nonexploitative sexual expression.

Dwight M. Goodey, a Seattle, Washington, father of an eighteen-year-old son with Down syndrome, presents the challenge for all parents.

Now that community living is an accepted goal for the handicapped, the need for more information and advice on sexuality is pressing. Although this is also a problem with normal children, it is particularly important that the handicapped be given the information and support in this area to ensure that they will not be exploited, but can achieve the maximum personal satisfaction. However, even though we consider ourselves well informed, we are not satisfied with our efforts in this respect and suspect that most parents are in need of assistance and do not know how to obtain advice that they consider satisfactory and adequate. Numerous sources have been investigated, but we still do not know how to keep our child from getting hurt because of her naivete and inexperience.

The Sexless Child

It is not easy to come of age today in America, and it is particularly difficult for youngsters with disabilities. If they are thought not to have sexual needs or desires, or if the idea that they do is intolerable to the larger society, information about sexuality will become increasingly restricted for them. Why tell them what they need not know or must not find out? Children from whom sexual information is kept secret, who are discouraged from asking questions, scolded for experimentation, shamed for being found out, and denied both the privacy and the social opportunities to explore their natural sexuality, will probably suffer more than normal adolescents under the same circumstances. In sum, to deny the sexuality of young people because they have disabilities is to burden them further. It is not a kindness to structure their lives to close off the entire area of sexuality; it is handicapping them in addition to whatever disabilities they may have.

A good way to stress this critical point is to quote an article from the special issue of *Coping,* the magazine of the Maine Association of Handicapped Persons, May 1984, which was devoted to the issue of sexuality. Listen to Annabel, a woman who described herself as having a great capacity for compassion, passion, understanding, sensitivity, and love: "And my heart often aches to share these qualities within myself with another human being . . . but I cannot walk, I use a wheelchair, I am handicapped." She goes on to say, "How do I get the idea across that

I'm a person with a sexual identity? That I have a warm, tender, caring side of me that I want to share with another human being? The anger and frustration build and build to the point of utter discouragement and painfully felt sadness."

She goes on to say that she was treated as a sexless child. Now twenty-eight, a beautiful, bright, sensitive woman who was born with cerebral palsy, Annabel was throughout her childhood assured that she would marry and have children and be sexually fulfilled (but not to worry about it now, "when you marry your husband will tell you everything you need to know"). Still single, without any friends or lovers, she feels betrayed and despondent most of the time.

Sexuality and Self-Esteem

Sexuality and self-esteem are intimately connected. For those whose learning skills will never carry them into law, medicine, music, or science; for those whose uncooperative bodies will never accept discipline or grace, success and satisfaction in personal relationships are particularly vital in giving a great sense of self-esteem and self-worth. There is little left for one who has cause to feel permanently outside the circle of things that matter. More than their "normal" peers, adolescents with mental or physical disabilities need to understand that with or without arithmetic or the ability to drive a car, they are important and valued members of the larger society and, among a smaller group, considered attractive, interesting, and desirable individuals.

To this end, *information* is a first and most powerful ally. It is a sad and dangerous mistake to protest that youngsters with disabilities have enough to do to learn to read and do arithmetic.

Education for sexuality is especially important for such youngsters, who may be less adept at separating fact from nonsense in the highly charged sexual messages in the media and other unreliable sources of sex information.

How to Begin

For all children, special needs or not, many sexual feelings and attitudes are determined before the age of five, whether or not parents make any special effort to transmit values or to explain particular aspects of sexuality. Children learn by seeing what happens and noticing what does not occur, by hearing what is said and noting what is left unspoken.

Parents can do their preschool children a considerable service by always using the correct words for bodily parts and functions. Males have penises; females have vaginas; the toilet is used for urinating or for making bowel movements. It is no kindness to any child, least of all one who already has cause to feel different, apart, or inferior, to send him or her out in the world with a babyish and embarrassing substitute for a proper sexual vocabulary.

If one accepts the relationship between sexuality and the adjustment of the teenager who has some disability to other aspects of his or her life, then parents, teachers, and other involved individuals cannot disregard sexuality. They need to integrate sexual health as a necessary ingredient in the youngster's life.

Some beginning thoughts for helping parents to learn about, and accept, their child's sexuality (as suggested by our colleagues Ted and Sandra Cole):

+ The presence of physical deformities or a limited mental capacity does not mean the absence of desire.
+ Inability to move does not mean inability to please.
+ Urinary incontinence does not mean genital incompetence.
+ Absence of sensation does not mean absence of feeling.
+ Loss of genitals does not mean loss of sexuality.

These are important concepts for all parents to take seriously. It's critical that you appreciate that knowledge is not harmful, but ignorance often is.

Educating Your Child about Sexuality

Roberta Van DeWalker, an Iowa mother, perhaps sums up most parents' feelings on the subject: "I'm going to admit that I'm scared to death to think ahead to the time when Jenny will reach puberty and all the things that are involved with that. . . . Maybe you can tell me how to tell a blind, mentally retarded girl about menstruation."

No one said it would be easy. Yet parents need to accept the idea that it's just as important for children with disabilities to have a sexual education as anybody else. You need to be askable in this area as well. If you are askable, your children will ask questions, and it's your responsibility to tell them the truth, using correct terminology and explicit details. There is nothing dirty or insidious about menstruation, and it is the parent's job not to make it *seem* dirty by not informing their children. There is no value for any child in being shocked or startled by natural experiences. Rather they should be prepared to recognize these experiences as normal aspects of sexual development.

Children's true need is for knowledge, not for suppression disguised as protection, and for as much freedom and independence as their impairments permit. Children who have disabilities must be taught about love, conception, contraception, and sexually transmitted diseases. They must also learn to take chances and play the odds as everyone else does.

Certainly, the idea of letting such a child "take chances" and "play the odds" stirs up all kinds of fears and protectiveness in the parent. Often, and understandably, a parent discourages a teenager with a disability from dating or going to school dances or parties for fear the child will be hurt or rebuffed. But the child denied an opportunity to try, to get dressed up and go out and take a chance, to risk getting hurt and feeling heartbroken, is also denied a major part of living, one that none of us would ever agree to do without.

Sexual Thoughts

All sexual thoughts, impulses, dreams, turn-ons, are normal. Although behavior can be abnormal, thoughts cannot be. If parents help their children realize this, it can be enormously therapeutic, even liberating, to the child. If children feel guilty about thoughts, they'll have them over and over again, until they become obsessions. If they realize that sexual thoughts and turn-ons often emerge from the unconscious and are OK, the thoughts and turn-ons pass, and nothing happens.

Masturbation

The mother of an eighteen-year-old who has Down syndrome says:

> I chose not to take a teacher's advice to smack my son's hand whenever he would touch himself (or his privates). I handled it differently. I would remind him to do it in the privacy of his bedroom and it worked! Whenever he feels the need to do this, he will go there. I have not been embarrassed by him at all in the presence of others.

It is counterproductive for a child to be punished for or made to feel guilty about masturbating. One can live a healthy, normal life without ever masturbating, but it is a normal and healthy expression for anyone, whether or not he or she has a disability or impairment.

In relatively well adjusted children, masturbating is self-limiting. It is done for the satisfaction of sexual urges. In maladjusted children, masturbation can be used as a way of coping with anxiety (it becomes a symptom), just as overeating can become compulsive if it's used as a way of relieving anxiety instead of satisfying hunger and occasionally enjoying a favorite food.

Parents must, however, recognize that there is no physical harm in masturbating (provided that no intrusive objects are used or inserted, of course). Even if it's compulsive, it can be remediated; in any case, it is far less harmful than compulsive eating.

Children usually discover on their own that the genitals give pleasure. It may be necessary, however, to help adolescents who have serious coordination disabilities to discover appropriate means of masturbation, perhaps even the use of vibrators or other creative ways. Some persons with mental retardation used to be taught how to use lubrication to facilitate masturbation.

On Appropriate Sexual Behavior in Public

Exposing oneself, touching, groping, fondling others, even playing with little kids (this is especially important for older boys with mental retardation) are not appropriate behaviors, and parents need to inform the child of this explicitly. They'll get in trouble. It's saddening how behavior that is accepted among "normal" youngsters is judged to be dangerous among those with some sort of physical or mental disability, for example, playing with younger children.

Parents must also encourage appropriate sexual skills. You don't hug and kiss everybody (only your parents, close relatives). Parents should not hesitate in taking leadership in facilitating friendships.

Fertility

Do not assume that just because you tell a child not to have sex, or don't talk about sex at all, that he or she won't. No, that message to teenagers—not to have sex—doesn't work. An unfortunate example illustrates this point: Susan, a sixteen-year-old girl with mental retardation, asks at the dinner table whether you have to be married in order to have a baby. The response: "Of course, dear, and this is not the kind of conversation we have while eating." Susan was having sexual intercourse with a neighborhood youth, and she wondered about the possible connection between intercourse and having a baby. She was "reassured" by her boyfriend and then by her parents. In a couple of months' time she was pregnant.

What *does* work is this message: "If you're not going to listen to me and abstain from sexual intercourse, at least use birth control." Contraceptive information is essential as the child is growing up. An unplanned or unwanted pregnancy can mean exceptional hardship for *anyone*, but particularly for someone with a disability.

There are those for whom the question of unwanted pregnancy is especially dire: older adolescents and adults at risk and those who can't take care of themselves. There is no reason not to consider sterilization as an alternative. Discuss it tactfully with the person you are worried about and a sympathetic professional in this field. Under some circumstances sterilization is legal for adults in every state. Write to the Association for Voluntary Surgical Contraception for details.

Homosexuality

About five percent of the population is exclusively homosexual and probably another five percent is bisexual. There is every reason to believe that these figures hold true for children with special needs as well.

The facts: We don't know why people are homosexual; they just are. People's sexual orientation is probably determined by the time they are five years old. No one is seduced into homosexuality or chooses to become one. (The only thing we know "for sure" about homosexuals is that they probably had heterosexual parents.)

On the other hand, having homosexual thoughts and desires, and some homosexual experiences, does not mean the person is homosexual. Probably the best definition of a homosexual is a person who in his or her adulthood derives erotic gratification almost exclusively from members of the same sex.

Children need to be taught that being approached by a homosexual, or even a few homoerotic experiences, does not mean they are homosexual. But if as adults they do appear to be homosexual, they should be permitted and even encouraged to live their sex lives in this manner. It's cruel to forbid this manner of gratification. It can provide a healthy alternative to loneliness, even despair.

Sexual Abuse

From a Cuyahoga Falls, Ohio, mother:

> I know from experience that learning disabled boys and girls are very vulnerable because of their impaired view of the world. Last year Todd was approached (while he was playing video games) by a man who wanted to pay him for posing for nude photographs. He asked my son if he wanted to get into "films." Although we had discussed this situation with our boys, I guess I thought it would never happen. Todd handled the whole thing just right; he left. And it didn't seem to bother him one bit, although I was a basket case for a week.

And from Karyn DeHaas, Bartlesville, Oklahoma, whose six-year-old daughter was born with muscular dystrophy: "I worry that she could be taken advantage of sexually when she gets older. Because of her weakness, there would be no way for her to fight back."

Although the fact is that a large number of children with disabilities are sexually abused and molested as they are growing up, they can be protected, not by being kept at home but by being taught to protect themselves.

How? Children who can be taught to go to the bathroom by themselves can also be taught the distinction between private and public places, that all sexual behavior (for example, masturbation) must be done in private (bathroom, own bedroom), and that public places are where people can see you.

It stands to reason that a child must also be taught to respect the privacy of other childen as well. They can be told that no one is allowed to touch their private parts (or to force them to do so to others), not even someone they know. The only exception is when a parent, doctor, or nurse needs to clean or examine them. They have a right to say no, and if someone forces them and they can't get away, they *must* tell their parents right away. It's not their fault if it happens.

Giving advance information does not scare children. It simply prepares and provides, in a sense, rehearsal behavior for them. Every person, even one with severe or multiple disabilities, is capable of some variety of intimate physical expression. The sexuality of such a person might not conform to a parent's or society's view of sex as genital contact leading to orgasm. Special people need special creative ideas and attitudes, and it is cruel to compound their difficulties because we might not be comfortable with the notion that they are indeed able and anxious to express sensual, sexual feelings. A great many families must grapple with these concepts, and it is a rare family that has not been touched by this dilemma in some fashion.

A Special Note for the Nineties

Let's face it. The sexual "scene" is becoming increasingly hazardous, and this makes things especially difficult for young people with disabilities. Sexual abuse, teenage pregnancy, sexually transmitted diseases—to say nothing of AIDS—are at their highest levels ever. All the more reason to be sure that your child is at least informed.

All of Sol Gordon's children's books—*Did the Sun Shine Before You Were Born?*, ages 4–7 (up to 10 for children with developmental disabilities); *Girls Are Girls and Boys are Boys—So What's the Difference*, ages 7–11; *Better Safe than Sorry—A Family Guide for Sexual Assault Prevention*, ages 5–12; and *Facts About Sex for Today's Youth*, ages 10–13, plus unsophisticated teenagers and young adults; and for teens, *Seduction Lines Heard 'Round the World and Answers You Can Give*—are now available from Prometheus Books, 700 East Amherst St., Buffalo, NY 14215. A new paperback edition of *Raising a Child Conservatively in a Sexually Permissive World* is distributed by Fireside Press. Also worthwhile: *Changes in You for Boys* and *Changes in You for Girls* by P.C. Siegel (1991; Family Life Education Association, P.O. Box 7466, Richmond, VA 23221).

For additional information on some of the areas discussed, contact one of the following organizations:

Coalition on Sexuality and Disability
122 East 23rd St.
New York, NY 10010
(212) 242-3900

Association for Voluntary Surgical Sterilization
79 Madison Ave., 7th floor
New York, NY 10016
(212) 561-8000

SIECUS (Sex Information and Education Council of the U.S.)
130 West 42nd St., Suite 2500
New York, NY 10036
(212) 819-9770

15

······

"The Right to be Involved in the IEP"
How to Get Involved

A report to Congress by the General Accounting Office once characterized the Individualized Education Program as "the most important tool in helping school districts achieve PL 94-142's goal of a free appropriate education for each handicapped child."

If the IEP did nothing more than to individualize each child with a disability and force school systems to look at each child as a child and not categorically as "a handicap," that would have been an important enough step. But it does much more.

The IEP does not guarantee results. But it is a written agreement, binding on the school system, that does guarantee the provision of the services, programs, equipment, and facilities, both educational and supportive, that are itemized in it. As well, it embodies the concept that school systems and local education agencies are accountable for at least *trying* to produce specific results. The IEP spells out (or should) both general goals and intermediate objectives within precise time frames, and that aspect gives parents milestones (or perhaps only yardstones or even inchstones) by which to monitor progress regularly and frequently and to assess the program's effectiveness.

It gives parents leverage they never had before. That is why parent and advocacy organizations resisted so vigorously when, among other "amendments," the Reagan administration proposed that the requirement for written IEPs be discontinued. Instead, parents won out, and that proposal was dropped.

The IEP gives parents leverage, provided they know they have it. Sue Allen found out by accident. Her son is permanently disabled as the result of a head injury.

> Eric was in Special Education for two years before I found out what an IEP even was. On impulse, I refused to sign an IEP, not realizing that I was enforcing my rights. After I refused, I found out what an IEP was, and what an important part it plays in the education of my child.

By law, the school or education agency is required to produce an IEP in writing within thirty days after the child has been evaluated and found to have a disability and to be in need of special educational services. In those systems in which parents are routinely involved in preliminary discussions and in the development of the program, they almost never have any problem signing it ("except maybe the paperwork, when a three-year-old has a file three inches thick").

When Parents Are Not Involved

But difficulties have frequently developed when the parents' first involvement was being one day handed a sheaf of papers they had not seen before and told to "sign here." One New York state school even simplified the process further for a girl with Prader-Willi syndrome: they asked her mother to sign blank IEP sheets, which the school people would then "fill in" later.

Other schools have had other, equally "time-saving," techniques. When a little girl was sick with pneumonia and the family had to miss the IEP discussions, the school simply went ahead on its own and sent the completed IEP along "for your signature." Some systems have had a regular procedure of not bothering to schedule IEP discussions after the initial one ("to save paperwork," one administrator said); instead they simply mailed updated (and sometimes unchanged) IEPs to the parents to be signed.

In such instances, parents need to be aware of their rights

stemming from PL 94-142 and the regulations spelling them out. The advice given by PACER, the Minneapolis advocacy group, is that if they receive an IEP in the mail with instructions to "sign and return," parents who want input in the program should (1) write *No* on the IEP, (2) not sign it, (3) make a duplicate copy for themselves before returning the original, (4) file a complaint, in writing, about the procedure with the state's complaint system.

PACER describes one parent's experience with one such pre-packaged IEP:

> Bob reports they developed the IEP without inviting him. The social worker brought it to his shop for his signature. Bob said, "No way. You were supposed to include me. Set the meeting. I'll be there; together we'll plan the IEP."

Bob went to the IEP meeting and demonstrated that he knew why he was there. When some of the proposals in the "completed" IEP seemed inappropriate for his son, he insisted they be corrected. They were. It may not be entirely due to Bob's insistence on participating, but his son, an adopted ten-year-old with learning disabilities who couldn't read two years ago, now reads at the fourth-grade level.

Conferences Don't Necessarily Mean Involvement

Being invited to a conference or a "staffing," though, doesn't always do it, parents find. It is not at all unusual to walk into the conference room and find that, as far as the others present are concerned, the session is pro forma: the IEP is lying there on the table, neatly typed. Any questions the parents might have before signing are made to seem almost like an intrusion: "Most parents here [an Idaho community] are not invited to IEP meetings until all of the information and programs have been developed and discussed. Then they are invited into a roomful of experts who are asking them to sign a document."

Parents who were aware of the intent of PL 94-142—that parents be involved *at every step* of the program's development—and balked at this procedure did not always find the going easy.

When PL 94-142 first went into effect, the Livingston family, with
a child who had autism, were

> presented with our son's IEP already typed up and ready for
> our signature; we were asked to approve it and sign it. Of
> course we didn't. We asked them to allow us the right to be
> involved in the IEP development.
>
> This demand caused some friction between the adminis-
> trators and us. It was hard for us not to seem pushy; yet we
> stuck to our guns, not signing a prewritten IEP for our son.
> And in recent years, we have always been asked to help de-
> velop the IEP.

There is no law that the IEP must be signed at the conference
either. Parents have the right to take it home for up to ten days
to study it, though some knowledgeable parents have had to educate less-informed school staff of that fact. And there is no reason
why parents can't get help in studying it during those ten days—
from other parents, disability organizations, advocacy groups, and,
especially, the youngster's therapists—any or all of whom may
have valuable ideas to contribute.

Parents Can Make Changes

Parents' changes may be relatively minor but they may also be
quite substantial. On occasion parents have returned the IEP un-
signed for the school staff to make changes, because on studying
it carefully they have realized its inadequacies. And it is not only
the first IEP, when the child is entering school, that can be inadequate: a member of the board of the National Association of
Parents of the Visually Impaired, who has two children, both of
whom are legally blind, has never had any problems with the IEPs
until recently, but

> in the past two or three years, we have found our local school
> system doing the IEPs without knowing our children or having
> any expertise in visual impairment. Believe me, you need a
> watchful eye.

One of the problems parents find with the IEP is what one
calls "stilted language," which may actually be precise professional

terminology, but which parents may need to have translated into parent English. They should not hesitate to ask for that kind of interpretation if necessary. It is important that the parent understand the IEP completely, before agreeing to its provisions, because it is crucial to the child's education and future.

One mother took advantage of the fact that the IEP does not become a valid document unless and until the parent signs it. She didn't sign it until three months after it had been written, because she insisted she didn't understand it fully. During that time she visited the school, watched her child's speech therapist and classroom teacher, took extensive notes, and then invited the director of Special Services to come see what she had seen. Only then did she sign the IEP, with changes.

Some parents have complained that they were made to feel like intruders when they suggested such classroom visits. But PL 94-142 and the implementing regulations make it clear that parents have a right to be present in the classroom, when they feel there is good reason for it. Parents are not "intruders": in fact, the right to be there is theirs by law from the earliest stages of the IEP process, actually the pre-IEP process, which determines which remedial aid is needed.

The Evaluation Procedure

The determination of whether any child requires special educational services is made, or should be made, through a full assessment or evaluation. There are a number of legal provisions to make certain that this procedure is fair, thorough, and accurate, but perhaps the most important safeguard is the parent's right to be present and to monitor the process.

The procedure is supposed to guarantee the fairness of the evaluation; there is a proviso, for example, that the tests will not be biased against any child because of racial or cultural factors, especially if the language spoken in the child's home is not English. Nor is there supposed to be any discrimination because of the nature of the child's disability: whatever special materials, aids, or equipment are necessary must be provided so that the evaluation gives a true picture of the child's abilities as well as inabilities.

For that reason, no child is given a single IQ test these days.

There are a great number of intelligence, psychological, and other tests to choose from, and it is a good idea for parents to ask what each of the intended tests is designed to show, why it is being given, what the results are supposed to mean, how they will be interpreted, and how they will be used in the planning of the child's program. These explanations, too, must be given in language the parent can understand, and not in psychologists' or educators' jargon.

There are a number of ways parents can ensure the fairness and accuracy of the tests. Diane Crutcher, formerly the executive director of the National Down Syndrome Congress, not only requested that she and her husband see and approve the tests to be given to their daughter Mindie in advance, but that they be allowed to observe the actual testing without their daughter's knowledge. They also asked that they be given a copy of each test as it was being administered, so that they could follow their daughter's progress and make their own notes for the follow-up conference.

Other requests were that Mindie be tested only in the mornings, with the tests spread over several days, and that they be allowed to cancel the tests any day Mindie was not feeling well. Their final request was that Mindie and the person administering the tests be given a chance to get to know each other in advance, rather than wait until test time.

Admittedly that is a fairly substantial set of demands. But the parents felt they had good reasons: to get Mindie the chance to be tested, they had pursued the local school system to grant her permission to enter that school, but ran up against the proverbial brick wall, since "all kids with Down syndrome are only trainable." They simply wanted to be sure that Mindie had a chance to put her best foot forward. (She did and has managed to do very well, with help, in a regular public school.)

If Parents Object to Testing

It is important that parents not take the validity of the testing procedure for granted. Even with all the safeguards in place, there is still the possibility of error. That's what happened to Barbara Levitz's son, who was also born with Down syndrome.

Inept testing by an inexperienced and "uncomfortable" psychologist proved a devastating experience to us. The picture presented was that of a child with an intelligence score at least twenty points below his actual functional level, and descriptive data totally unlike our son.

Fortunately, we were successful in having school personnel begin to look at our child on the basis of his individual needs, rather than on an outdated stereotypical generalization about children with Down syndrome.

Parents may also want to challenge the assessment if they feel that it was incomplete or superficial. It is too easy to write off a child as "emotionally disturbed," for example, without taking enough time to probe for an underlying mental or physical disability that preceded and may be responsible for the emotional problems. It is too easy to write off a child as having mental retardation when the problem may be a learning disability or even a hearing impairment that has gone undetected up to that point.

If Need be, Get an Independent Evaluation

The parents' challenge may not be enough to change the school's position. In that case, many parents feel that their disagreement with the school's assessment needs professional substantiation. And that is possible, because parents are legally permitted to get an independent evaluation of the child, though they may have to pay for that testing themselves. But although the outside assessment must be made part of the child's record, parents are often surprised and unhappy to learn that the school is not required to *accept* the evaluation in place of its own, a major reason for later parent appeals to even higher authority.

One Denver couple found their indepenent evaluation rejected by their son's school even though it was based entirely on the school's *own* tests. They weren't surprised, like a great many other parents who seek such outside assessments, for it was based on a history of negative experiences with the school: "We have been consulted and involved in our son's IEP," they say, "but it is sometimes a facade. We are asked to comment, but our comments are not taken seriously."

Another parent who sought an outside evaluation as a protective measure was Wendy D., whose daughter was born with spina bifida. She took the little girl

> to an outside agency for an independent educational assessment when she was five-and-a-half years old, to ensure that we got accurate information about her educational needs, rather than a reflection of what the school district had to offer in the way of programming. Making sure that our daughter gets an appropriate education is an ongoing and constant concern, something we feel we need to keep on top of at all times.

The law provides that the results of all tests be confidential, but accessible to the parents. Not only do parents have the right to see such results and to have them explained, but since 1974 they have also had the right to see *all* the school's records on the child (though that may require a request in writing).

Parents' Right to See Records

In fact, the school is technically required to provide all parents a yearly listing of records it keeps on its students, not only official documents but all notes or comments that may be in a student's file, and to indicate where they are kept. Parents also have the right to have all entries explained to them, to challenge them, and to ask that any inaccurate information be corrected or removed. They may also request copies of all records, which the school must supply at the cost of copying.

Parent have found that not all schools are aware of these rights. Others are not especially happy about parents having them. Debbie Stevenson recalls that

> at the first IEP meeting, the principal of the elementary school got up and walked out of the meeting. He was a little steamed because I knew everything that was in Trent's personal file.

Parents as Part of Assessment Team

Debbie Stevenson's son has cerebral palsy, and she has always been involved in his IEP meetings because she feels she has a unique contribution to make: information and observations about him that only she can provide. There are certain aspects of the child's makeup and personality that may not show up in any of the testing, or that the unreal, out-of-the-ordinary experience of being tested may distort, and parents can help to put into perspective.

Many schools recognize this and automatically invite parents in to discuss and explain the assessment results and to become part of the assessment team. If they do not, parents should *ask* for an opportunity to participate.

Sherry Cullison has taken even greater initiatives. Her son is now eleven, with learning disabilities, visual discrepancies, and other deficits. He is in a special class for the communicatively handicapped. She feels she is "an educated and supportive parent, after eight years of long hard hours and hundreds of dollars spent." Some of those hours and dollars are an investment in outside experts, who are also an integral part of her son's team.

I start assessments with the public school system, and then I advise with independent professionals. After completion of both, I arrange for both teams to meet, for informing and working together for my son's goals and objectives.

I am now consulted, because of my insistence and because of the meetings I arrange with the professionals and educators before the IEP meetings. In these meetings, after I am given the assessment results, we discuss the next steps and decision making. My IEP meetings are simply a carryover from these meetings.

Seeing Proposed IEP in Advance of the Conference

Even when parents are fortunate enough to have so extended an opportunity to discuss and analyze the child's assessment—and there is some question as to how many do—that may well be the last involvement they have in the IEP process until the staffing conference itself, at which, for the first time, they see the program they are expected to accept.

The assumption seems to be that the discussions around the child's assessment provide the parent with all of the information and background necessary to pass judgment on the IEP. But, as Nancy L. points out, "the time of the initial evaluation is a very traumatic time!"

With her own experience as a guide, she has therefore been teaching other parents to ask their children's schools for the following:

> Before the IEP meeting is held, they should request that a draft of the IEP be mailed to them so they can look at it ahead of time. As it is now, parents spend all their time listening, trying to grasp what is being told them, and there is little or no time or opportunity for their input. School districts should take much more responsibility for training parents for these conferences.

There is no reason schools should not be willing to go along with that suggestion, particularly if enough parents ask that it be done: all it requires is a little more lead time. But even if that isn't done, and parents do not get to see the IEP until the conference itself, there is no reason to feel rushed into approving it without an opportunity for a more careful, unhurried, and unharried analysis. There is no reason not to take the plan home and check it through.

One aspect of the proposed IEP worth considering is whether it takes into account any of the outside evaluations that parents go to such great lengths to arrange. Parents have also suggested a number of other questions to bear in mind, not all of which, of course, will apply to any one IEP.

An IEP Checklist

Goals and Objectives

◆ Are the goals and objectives specifically tailored to your child's needs and abilities, or are they vaguely worded all-purpose formulas that might fit *any* child?

◆ Are they specific enough, and their time frames precise enough, that you can monitor progress and keep track of whether the schedule is actually being met?

◆ Do they promote your child's growth as a human being, or are they too limited?

◆ Do they take into account *your* goals and objectives for the child, as well as the quality of life *you* want for your child, in addition to the educators' professional projections?

◆ Is there a timetable, preferably in writing, for reevaluation of the program and possible revisions? *Treat your child's IEP as an experiment. If the approach increases the student's skills, continue the plan. If the approach produces limited increases in skills, reevaluate and try another strategy. Avoid feeling guilty, but also avoid blaming the educational staff when an approach does not produce the desired results.*

Program Details

◆ Is the program content actually individualized, as intended, or are the details "standard" for all children with the same disability, focusing on the label and the disability rather than on the child?

◆ Do they fit the program to the child or force the child to fit into the programs the school already has available?

◆ A closely related question: Is the program based on the child's needs or the school's budget?

◆ Does it stess functional and problem-solving skills? Does it give enough attention to remedying what are among the most important problems of virtually all children with special needs: inadequate social skills?

◆ How realistic is the program in terms of helping to prepare your child for life in the world outside and after school?

◆ Does the school have any other program options than those

included? Are there other schools, in the district or else-where, that might have more suitable program possibilities?
◆ Does it incorporate any suggestions you or the child's therapists have made?
◆ Have the members of the school's team checked out additional or alternative programs you may have learned about from other parents or disability groups? (One mother had seen a special reading program work wonders for a neighbor's boy and proposed that it be added to her son's IEP (he has dyslexia) in the sixth grade. "But they would not do it. Then his seventh grade teacher added it to his IEP, and they went along with it without any problem because the teacher put it there.")
◆ Does the program detail and itemize any special resources, aids, and equipment to be used or supplied? (A Lancaster, Ohio, father whose son, diagnosed as having a learning disability, needed to use a calculator for math tests, eventually discovered that he had the right to insist that the item be incorporated in the IEP. It was.)

Related Services

◆ Are all of the supportive and supplementary services the child needs, including necessary therapies, spelled out?
◆ Are the related services being provided on the basis of what the child needs, or what is "available?" This may be one of the most vital questions for parents to ask: even though the courts have consistently held that "lack of funds" is not a valid reason for withholding necessary supportive services, there is a gray area surrounding "how much" of such services. In one large southern city, the school system "will not write on the IEP the amount of services my daughter needs but insists on putting in only what they can provide."
◆ Is the time for such specialized instruction as special physical education specified? (The danger is that otherwise, in practice, the child will receive only a token half-hour or so a week.)
◆ If transportation is included as a related service, as it should be where necessary, is the maximum permissible travel time specified? (Parents sometimes do the child's chauffeuring because they discover too late that otherwise the child

spends up to an hour and a half, each way, on the school bus daily.)

Placement

+ Which came first: program or placement? Was the placement made because it suits your child or because "all our blind/CP/MR children go there?"
+ Is the "least restrictive environment" written into the IEP actually the least restrictive in which your child can function? Is there a time frame for progressing toward a less restrictive setting, with steps you can monitor regularly?
+ Does the program specify the way the child's day is to be divided between the regular classroom, special classes, resource room, and other settings?
+ If the placement is not in the neighborhood school, is it as close to home as possible?
+ Have you been given an opportunity to check out the proposed placement, as well as possible alternatives, beforehand (for the size and arrangement of the class, what subjects are being taught, the methods and materials used, the pupil-teacher ratio, the atmosphere: tense or relaxed, busy, or apathetic)? Are you convinced that the setting is right for your child?

Even if the result of the parents' detailed examination of the proposed IEP is to leave it unchanged, they have had an opportunity to raise any questions they may have with the school's IEP team before agreeing to the program. There is of course the possibility that in some systems parents will be made to feel that they are "intruding" in matters beyond their experience and capacity. But more and more parents are being made to feel welcome: other parents have paved the way.

The principle is quite simple: parent participation can only serve to improve the IEP. The "team" is more effective if parents are on it: they add a special—in fact an essential—dimension.

16

"We Have Become Knowledgeable"
Some Negotiating Tips from Parents

Patricia McGhghy is now able to go to IEP conferences and say no when she disagrees with the school's suggestions ("knowing that they are just that: suggestions"). She even takes along her own list of the items *she* wants to discuss. But she still remembers her first IEP meeting: "I felt like a mouse that had just walked into a roomful of cats. And I was very close to tears when I left."

This kind of feeling is so widespread among parents—and for some every time, not just the first time—that Nancy L., the mother who suggested that the IEP be sent to parents in advance of the conference, has been

> trying to teach professionals how overwhelming those meetings are to a parent: three to six professionals and one or two parents. It's hard for a parent to avoid that "ganged-up-on" feeling in these conferences. I urge parents to take along a spouse or a friend, who can also be an extra set of ears.

> Mary McAllister, who has two children with mental disabilities, is also convinced that it's wise for two people to attend the IEP conferences, staffings, testing-result sessions, and so on, to

"give the parent some moral support, and if the parent can't remember exactly what was said about a certain issue, hopefully the second person might remember." A small cassette recorder "might remember" even better, but the law recognizes the need for "moral support." Parents can take anyone they choose, and there is no requirement that that second person be a relative or a friend.

Experts as Advocates

It is a rare set of circumstances when parents feel that the input they need is not just "moral" and that they have to take a lawyer along (though it does happen), but many do bring professional support of another kind: physicians, therapists, or others who have been working with the child and can provide some additional expertise. "It is very helpful at the IEP to have my son's private home therapist there to explain what she has been doing and to help prepare my son's program," says one parent; and another: "We never hesitate to call in outside professionals from the medical clinic or assessment team to explain a specific question regarding our daughter's needs."

Al and June Lindley used to feel not only outnumbered, but powerless in the face of the phalanx of school people marshaled against them at their daughter's IEP meetings (Wendy has a number of disabilities) until they had an idea.

In the past, we were overrun by "experts" challenging our wishes. This time we invited about a dozen persons who had come into contact with Wendy in both a professional and personal way. And this group, our *own* panel of "experts," did the talking for us. As a result, Wendy actually got more than we had been prepared to request.

Lois Berg, whose twelve-year-old daughter has finally been diagnosed as having ADHD (attention deficit hyperactivity disorder), regularly felt "not just outnumbered, but intimidated" each time she came into the IEP staffing:

Not only were there some people there that I had never seen before, but a few just sat there and never said a word, so I wondered why they were there at all. Then I got an idea: I can bring anyone I want, right? In that case, they bring ten people, I bring ten, including some of my good friends. I only had to do that twice; now the only people there—on both sides of the table—are people who really have something to contribute.

Other Parents or Advocates

Successful advocates may not always be easy to find on an individual basis. But another possible source, and one especially qualified, is a parents' or advocacy group. PACER, the Minneapolis parent advocacy group, will assign an advocate to go along with a parent if there appear to be serious problems that the parent doesn't feel competent to handle alone. One such PACER advocate, a parent reports, "was marvelous: attended meetings with us, IEP conferences, etc., and provided us with a lot of moral support."

In some circumstances, the advocate to take is the child himself or herself, whose presence may provide the strongest arguments of all, provided, of course, that hearing a discussion of his or her problems is not going to have a negative effect on the youngster. The child's presence serves as a living reminder that the IEP is not about a file folder, not about "a collection of symptoms or a skin-covered container of behaviors," but about a human being, kid-type.

Even though not all parents will agree with her, one parent strongly in favor of the student's participation is a California mother, whose eighteen-year-old son has a learning disability; she feels that any youngsters who can should

> attend all conferences with doctors and professionals. Explain their handicap to them as early as they can comprehend. Don't exclude them; let them attend IEP meetings as soon as you and the teacher think they can handle it. Explain to them their rights and also the teacher's rights. Teach them to be self-advocates; let them be independent. Don't be overly protective.

Are the Right School People There?

If there are likely to be any special problems with the IEP, it is not enough for the parents to have the right people there advocating for the child; it is equally important that the right people be there to represent the school or the school district.

In passing PL 94-142, Congress was quite explicit in stipulating that among those present at the IEP conference there should be at least one school representative with the authority to make a commitment of whatever resources might be needed to implement the plan and that there should be another there who is knowledgeable about any classroom problems that might be likely to occur and competent to suggest methods for coping with them.

If the school's only real decision makers are not present, then any discussions about changes may end in nothing more than a bureaucratic game: *passing the buck.* That's when the school people "have to check on this," or "get the principal's OK on that," or "let you know whether we can find the funds for that in the budget."

It is not that the administrator or principal can't play the same game: when there is no one higher in the school or district hierarchy to pass the buck to, it is passed to another agency: "That problem is medical, not educational."

Games Systems Sometimes Play

Buck-passing is just one of a number of bureaucratic games experienced parents have learned to deal with in the course of negotiating a child's IEP. Each represents another way of *accomplishing* "no" without flatly *saying* "no": even the most stubborn of school systems does not want to be seen—and shown to be—flouting PL 94-142 openly: too much flak.

From the game player's point of view, the "game's" greatest virtue is that inexperienced parents don't always recognize "no" when they're hearing it, and by the time they realize that "no" was what they got, they're already outside the door—next case. Sometimes, fortunately, other parents who have been through the mill will serve as an "early warning system," to alert newer parents to the games and to suggest from their own experiences ways of handling them.

Games come in assorted shapes and formats:

The Money Game

The money game is easily the most popular and widely used—its key phrase is "can't afford"—chiefly because there is always some measure of truth in it: "They" seldom *do* provide sufficient funding for special educational services. "The occupational therapist and the physical therapist employed by our district work only part-time," one parent reports, "although everyone agrees"—everyone but the budget-makers, that is—"that there is more than enough work to justify a full-time person for each position."

It should be no surprise that on the theory that supportive and related services are the easiest targets, they are usually the first to go. Here is one version of the game reported by the mother of an adopted boy with cerebral palsy, from an Ohio school district:

> I would like my son seen daily by the occupational therapist. However, they don't have time to do so. There are many other things I would like included that are not possible because of the lack of manpower or availability.
>
> We have been told that the school doesn't have, and can't afford, certain services. Money seems to be a very big issue at our school, and everything usually boils down to "We don't have the money."

At a time when school budgets are being cut back, that may sound not unreasonable, except that it is illegal: even before PL 94-142 the courts had ruled that schools could not eliminate necessary services for children with disabilities simply because they were costly and there wasn't enough money to go around. Often those who supposedly "can't afford" such services are really just taking the path of least resistance: cut programs with the fewest children involved.

But the principle that the courts have set down is that if any school system doesn't have enough money to provide all the services all the children—disabled or not—should have, then the available funds have to be so apportioned that no child is entirely excluded from the services he or she needs. The child who needs more is to get a fair share, even if that fair share is more costly than the nondisabled child's "fair share."

The money game sometimes shows up in disguise. Two variants are the "fairness" game and the "grateful" game.

The Fairness Game

"Is it fair to spend three times as much of our limited school budget on your child as on any other student?" And another version: "Is it fair to deprive so many children of *their* share of physical education just so that your child can get an hour of special physical education every day?"

The *real* unfairness, of course, is in the school's juxtaposing the needs of the child with an impairment against those of the rest of the children. If funds must be found for special physical education, the real fight ought to be, *has* to be, for a larger school budget, with parents and administrators on the *same* side.

The Grateful Game

The grateful game comes right out of the nineteenth century, or even earlier: One school told a mother who wanted some help for her child, who had a severe physical disability, "to be glad I'm getting what I am." In other schools it has shown up as an administrator's telling a parent about "how much we've done for your child," or "how can you ask for more, when it's already costing the taxpayers so much?"

Back before PL 94-142, when parents had no legal ammunition, children with special needs did often have to rely on a school's benevolence. But today a "free appropriate public education" is their right and their due, both as a matter of public policy and of law.

The Blame-the-Victim Game

Blaming the victim is undoubtedly the meanest game of all, whether the victim is the child or the parent or both. Parents who seek the school's help in dealing with specific problems may be told that their "interference" is only "creating" or "worsening" the problem. Or, as an excuse for not providing services to Kevin Salvi, who has a learning disability, the implication was that Lori Salvi and her husband *were* the problem:

> They initially suggested that perhaps there was a problem at home that caused or explained our son's behavior. We assured them that if there was, we were totally unaware of it and insisted that he be tested. In reviewing the evaluation results with us, they told us there was no indication of an educational problem. Hint, hint: maybe a home problem?
>
> What we were unaware of then was that a thirty-eight-point difference on the WISC-R between his verbal and performance scores was very significant. In our trust in the wisdom of the school, we just assumed that they were correct.

Other parents have been told that a child's learning disability or emotional problems would disappear if the *parents* had therapy, which prompted one Texas mother to comment dryly that "I often disregard the advice of professional educators when they infer parental guilt and practice psychology without a license."

Janie Wurzel used to run across a situation in which the people representing the school were attempting to get out of their responsibilities by fastening the blame on her son, who is profoundly deaf. That was in the beginning, before she learned how to deal with the game successfully.

> Instead of saying the services weren't available, the administrators would just say, "Your son isn't ready." It would be *his* fault that he couldn't utilize the services that were available.
>
> We have now become very knowledgeable in negotiating our son's IEP. In the past few years, we just stopped signing the IEPs unless we were fully consulted. It usually takes a few meetings to get the message across.

The Intimidation Game

There are many educators who protest that intimidation exists only in the minds of parents and is the product of their own anxieties. An honest assessment would have to confirm that there is a certain amount of truth in that suggestion.

One parent comments that "many parents are defensive and frightened by their Committee on the Handicapped even before they go to the board *for the first time*" because they do not know what to expect.

But the fears cannot be dismissed out of hand as imaginary: not all are unfounded. Jean Tierney, who says she has taken "hundreds of pages of notes" on her dealings with school authorities in trying to get an "appropriate education" for her daughter who has a learning disability, wonders

> about all the parents who are intimidated by the school, and there are a lot who are! I've had a paper stuck under my nose and was asked to sign it, about an IEP meeting that never took place. I was also asked to sign an IEP that I totally disagreed with; of course I refused.

Fancied or real, there is no question that parents, especially inexperienced parents, *are* feeling intimidated. Nancy Wilson, parent and author, reports:

> Because I am on the board of a local ACLD [Association for Children and Adults with Learning Disabilities] group, I sometimes get calls from younger parents who are having problems with their local school districts. They indicate they would make more of a "case" when they disagree with local educational practices, but they're afraid of their school.
> Parents really do fear retaliation, especially if they have other children at school, and most of them do. Whether this fear is justified or not, they wonder how the teachers and administrators will treat their children, if they—the parents—are labeled "troublemakers."

If parents' fears of retaliation are unwarranted, it may say something about perceptions of the education system and its personnel that these feelings seem nevertheless to be so widespread. In that case, it should not be impossible for the system, through the people who represent it at IEP meetings and other negotiations, to put such imaginary fears to rest, simply by the welcoming way they react to parents' suggestions and objections.

As for the way parents can cope with real intimidation, where it does exist, it should be noted that there are two distinct points of view. One is "a most helpful piece of advice" that Barbara Abel, the parent of a daughter with a learning disability, says she got in regard to dealing with school officials, which was "Don't anger the alligators until you are safely across the river."

The other viewpoint is from Jean Tierney:

> Do not let the school personnel intimidate you, and they will surely try. First, find out all you can about the services that are available in the area. Also, find out about 94-142 and the local laws. Then be prepared to fight for your child. Sometimes there would not have been an IEP meeting if I had not insisted on having one. If you can't communicate with the school itself, find an advocate to help you.

The Jargon Game

In some situations, there may be a question of whether the jargon game is deliberate or whether some professionals have just become trapped by their own habits. "Jargon" begins as a positive— as a search for language precise enough to provide an exact description of situations and processes, a special, often technical language in which professionals in any discipline communicate with one another.

But when an IEP is written in such jargon—"teacherese," or "educatorese"—it often comes across to "noninitiated" parents as "all mumbo-jumbo" and "vague, disguised language," which tends to render the program meaningless to them. No matter how commonly used and run-of-the-mill words like *cognitive* and *affective* may be to professionals, to a great many parents they do not qualify as understandable English. Parents whose primary language is other than English should insist on the presence of an interpreter (their own or the school's) to translate the proposals for them and make them understandable in the parents' language.

There have been two approaches to dealing with jargon, and each has had its advocates among disability organizations and parents. The first approach is to learn the special terms used by professionals. The Orton Dyslexia Society, for example, hoped that "parents will . . . learn the jargon used by professionals, in order to understand what is being said about the child, and what is being recommended for the child." The Association for Children and Adults with Learning Disabilities, as do other disability groups, at one time offered a six-page "glossary of terms" in one of its pamphlets for parents.

The other approach was to refuse to play the game. As the National Society for Children and Adults with Autism put it, "Insist on a translation of professional terms. Professionals can be intimidating and may seem impatient, so you may need to persist in asking for clarification, until you receive an explanation you understand."

The Expert Game

Jargon may also be part of the expert game. That's when two professionals use "teacherese" to discuss the child and the IEP right across the head of the parent sitting at the same conference table, knowing full well that they are excluding the parent. Sometimes it is even a deliberate put-down, a form of snobbery ("look what I know that you don't"), but often it is simple thoughtlessness. Deliberate or not, it has the effects of reducing parent participation in the planning process.

But that's only one aspect of the expert game, which may be one of the most common games of all if parents' reports are an accurate indication. A Houston mother's description is typical of the way it is usually encountered: when she attempted to take an active role in suggesting programs for her child, "the staff became defensive. They insisted they were the professionals and knew more about my child than I did."

Such put-downs come from an attitude that professional credentials are the only expertise that counts, far outweighing parents' twenty-four-hours-a-day, seven-days-a-week responsibility and observations: you may be the primary caregiver, mother, but we know the child far better than you do. Despite PL 94-142's specific encouragement of parental involvement in the IEP process, one attitude study found that many education professionals feel that parents should content themselves with being "passive observers," not participants: present at the IEP conference (if unavoidable), to be seen but not heard except as suppliers of information on request.

The Case for Confrontation

When parents do insist on making a contribution, school staff often seem to have the ability to listen without hearing. For a parent, that presents a serious communication problem: how do I get through?

Sometimes parents become so frustrated at being ignored that they see no other way to attract administrators' attention than through direct confrontation. And as a negotiating technique, it has been known to produce some positive results. From Stephanie Nankervis, who besides being the parent of a boy born with Down syndrome was executive director of the Wyandotte, Michigan, ARC:

> Several times I have disagreed with educators about services which I felt were essential for my son's education. Sometimes my requests would result in an emotional scene, where it was parents versus the administration in a real battle.
>
> There have been small compromises on our part, but overall the services were eventually provided. And over the years we have gained a mutual respect for each other and can problem-solve without being so emotionally charged.

The Case Against Confrontation

The Houston mother faced by staff people insisting they knew more about her child's needs than she did eventually attained the same results in a different way. Her method can be summed up in two words: *patience* and *persistence*. She chose not to make an issue of the staff's attitudes—the point, she decided, was not her ego, but the child's education—and chose "to ignore the educators' less-than-professional attitude toward me as a parent."

The result is that she is "now treated with respect. We work out any differences before the formal meetings, so that when we come together with our son at the final session, it is just a pleasant formalization of our mutually agreed-upon IEP."

Perhaps because the IEP process has so important a bearing not only on education, but on the life and future of the child with a disability, there is nothing parents feel more strongly about than "the right way" to deal with the negotiations. The two approaches cited are therefore worth a further look.

Compromise or Confrontation?

Some parents feel it necessary to make compromises: "There are lots of programs I'd like to see available, but they are unrealistic here in the woods where we live." And another: "I was not inclined to sign the IEP without the speech therapy but knew that if I did not sign it, my daughter's placement in a special education classroom would be further delayed."

Others, in contrast, feel they do their children more good in the long run by being insistent and assertive: "While there has occasionally been discussion about the 'lack of availability' of some service, or 'we can't do that,' I know how to work through such roadblocks."

This clear divergence in parents' attitudes goes beyond the IEP process and negotiating methods to the system itself. Here are two descriptions of the public education system today. Question: which is the accurate one? This?

> No problems with the school system. Parents must work together with the school. School system is genuinely concerned with doing the best for the child. School principal has been extremely helpful all the way. Child is progressing well, has come a long way, with the help of his parents and the school system.

Or this?

> There are well-meaning, hard-working people within the system who have helped my children, but the system itself *sucks*. Decisions are made strictly on the basis of what's available. I guess my strongest feeling re the system is distrust. I have learned that what "they" suggest is not necessarily what my sons need.

Which is accurate? Both, depending on the situation and the people.

Negotiate? Stand fast? Or both? Certainly, the parental consensus seems to be that some compromises will almost always be necessary. No one, certainly not a parent dealing with his or her child's school system, deliberately goes looking for a fight. That is, unless there is no alternative.

In other words, as one parent aptly puts it, "I'm open to compromise, but insistent": not necessarily confrontational, but *very* insistent.

Parents should work out beforehand, preferably with the best advice and counsel available, those minimal, essential requests on which they are *not* prepared to compromise, on which the law stipulates that they do not need to compromise: programs and services without which the IEP becomes simply more meaningless paperwork.

17
....

"School and Parents Working Together"
How to Become Your Child's Advocate

A strange thing sometimes happens to the IEP on its way from the conference room to the classroom: it seems to lose a considerable something in the implementation. Janice Pestrue, whose eight-year-old is blind, discovered that the "something lost" was on occasion an essential service:

> Just because something is in the IEP does not automatically mean that it will get done. Our transportation issue is an example: if the majority of students who ride the handicappers' bus do not have school, our system feels that it is not necessary to provide transportation for the two or three who do.

In that particular school system, she feels that it represents an attitude that school is not *that* necessary for children with inconvenient problems.

But even in the best of systems, there are good reasons for parents to follow up the program outlined in the IEP very closely. For one thing, "parents have to monitor to see that the goals are covered every year," Janice Pestrue says. For another, as Joan

Simon, whose daughter has autism, points out, "Programs may look good on paper but not work well in reality."

That's why most parents come to feel, sometimes after unexpectedly negative experiences, that even when the IEP is signed and done, it still may not *get* done. And that's why they eventually learn that the end of the IEP planning and negotiating process is actually the beginning of the real IEP process: making it happen.

Actually, provisions for follow-up and liaison with parents are, or should be, discussed during the IEP conference: how often the child's progress will be assessed, whether and how parents will get the evaluation reports, how often conferences will be scheduled, and what role parents are to play as part of the child's "team" in implementing the IEP.

A Year-Long Process

Clearly such continued involvement necessitates not waiting for the end of the year or term (with the possibility of a wasted year or term) to assess progress. To make sure that programs are really working and producing results, Joan Simon feels that a parent "must become a very knowledgeable assertive watchdog: one must always monitor programs to make sure the teachers and other professionals know what they are doing."

Lori Salvi, whose son has learning disabilities, starts her follow-up right at the beginning of the school year. Because she and her husband have learned that some special education staff may not be very knowledgeable in some of the specific areas in which their son needs strengthening, her "scenario" calls for her to meet with her son's teachers when school starts to brief them on just what to anticipate from him: that in certain respects he can function quite well, but that there may be some problems in other areas, specifically thus and such. If the teachers have not had any previous experience with a child like him, she says, "they look at us like we have two heads." After all, the boy is bright, handsome, personable, and very verbal, not the stereotype of a "handicap." But, she adds, "by January, what an enlightenment! Most of them usually say, 'You know, your son *is* learning-disabled.' "

The real point of the briefing, though, is not the enlightenment and education of the teacher, but the enlightenment and education of the child to be taught by the teacher. The preterm briefing is designed to help the teacher (and the school) achieve results with the child. Another mother, June Ravitch, whose son is brain-injured, knows exactly what results *she* is looking for, only some of which can be spelled out in the IEP. Her checklist of goals can serve as a possible model for other parents.

- Is it easier for him to learn now than it was a few months ago?
- Have his language comprehension and output improved and become more sophisticated?
- Is he improving academically to any significant degree?
- Is he becoming more independent?
- In general, is his behavior becoming more appropriate?

School-Parent Partnership

The achievement of such academic and behavioral goals and objectives, whether spelled out specifically in the IEP or not (though most can and should be), obviously requires close liaison between school and parents. The school day is only a small part of any child's learning day. Parents often are and should be very much aware of the role *they* play in implementing the IEP at home.

Teaching doesn't stop at school. Like the child, the parents need to be educated on what the child is learning in order to carry it on at home. I try very hard to have excellent communications with the people who are working with my son. I feel that you have to, in order to aid your child's progress.

"Public education cannot fill the gaps by itself," another parent comments, "nor do it all." This is not meant as a rap against the educational system, she adds: "Education for our child has, on the whole been extremely good, but education must be reinforced at home." And Lori Salvi perhaps sums it up best, in line not only with parents' but with educators' thinking: "It can't be just school or just parents; it has to be both working together."

It is easier, of course, for parents to work with teachers who want to work with parents, and it is almost a rule of thumb, parents suggest, that it is the good teachers (and other school staff) who will be most cooperative, who will not feel threatened by the idea of such parent partners.

When the partnership works well, the benefits to the child can exceed anyone's expectations. A Minnesota mother was seriously considering placing her son in a foster home—"his behavior was beyond repair"—when the school's teacher of children with emotional problems initiated daily contact with her. Working together, they succeeded so well that a year later the boy "is responding very well and is a member of our family once again. My son is so lucky," the mother says.

Teachers Who are "Pure Magic" . . . or Anything But

It doesn't take long for parents to recognize when their children are "lucky" and which teacher it is who brings special qualities into the classroom. As an Illinois mother sees it,

> I think most teachers of the handicapped are as special as the children they teach. Some are better than others, but the love and concern that get them into such a classroom are admirable, and I am really grateful for the type of personality that can see the humanity and love in the handicapped kid and then give their all to try to improve them in the skills of which they are capable.

Many special education teachers come into teaching with considerable background, some after having worked with children who have special needs in some other capacity. Parents often recall with profound gratitude a skilled and dedicated educator who expected more of such a child than the parents did and proved to be right.

Those whose child is entrusted to a teacher with such qualities often describe them in language similar to Joan Simon's:

> The joy of the system is observing a teacher who is pure magic with my child: a teacher who knows her craft, who understands

a child's strengths and weaknesses; a teacher who gives a child knowledge, love, and self-esteem.

Unfortunately, she adds, not all teachers are magic.

> The heartbreak is the opposite: a teacher or other professional who is completely inadequate to deal with handicapped children but who tries to hide that inadequacy with educational jargon and deprecating remarks about the child's potential.

Some parents feel so strongly the need to avoid such "inadequate" teachers that they make strenuous efforts to see that the child is placed with a good teacher, even to the point of hunting up another school to ensure it. But usually that isn't possible.

Among the less than adequate, or worse, cited by parents was the Ohio teacher who implied that it was the parents, not their child, who were the problem, because they were refusing to accept the fact that nothing could be done to help her advance: the little girl, who had a learning disability, was simply a "below-average child." When Shirley Heckman reported that a physician had discovered that the reason her son might not be hearing the spelling words was that he had a 98 percent hearing loss in one ear, the classroom teacher shrugged it off: "Well, he hears with the other ear, doesn't he?" And one high school special education teacher insisted that "children would rather graduate than learn how to read," when an Idaho widow was looking for help for her daughter, who had dyslexia.

And there is the "educator" cited by the Georgia mother of three children with learning disabilities, who

> learned from a friend's child that our son was being used by the teacher as a "bad example." He stopped trying completely. It has taken five years to undo the damage to his self-image that the public school teachers inflicted on him. Can you imagine trying to do schoolwork and being called lazy, stupid, etc., etc.?

Such attitudes, it should be pointed out, are not always the result of incompetence or a temperament not suited to teaching. They may reflect less-than-adequate training.

More Training Needed

The situation used to be much worse before PL 94-142: a classroom teacher with no special training had legitimate reasons to be upset when a child with special needs was suddenly "mainstreamed" into the class without warning. The greatest worry seems to have been that that kind of child required too much time and attention at the expense of the other children, though at least one study found that such extra time amounted to only about a minute and a half per fifty-minute period.

But there was also concern about what special help the child might need: how to cope with seizures and similar emergencies. It was not unusual to find untrained and inexperienced teachers actually frightened to work with a blind child or a child with cerebral palsy or spina bifida.

Time, and experiences with such children in regular classes, have dispelled many, though not all, of the fears teachers used to have. Yet a good many classroom teachers who must deal with children who have serious disabilities in regular classes are still not being given adequate advance preparation. Even now parents feel that, just in case, materials and courses on children with disabilities, not only on dealing with the children, but on understanding the pressures parents of such children face every day, ought to be incorporated into all education curricula. Many teaching institutions have already begun to do so.

The "Special Child": an Egg

One interesting approach to helping future special educators "walk a mile in the parents' shoes" is a sensitization assignment given to her students by the late Professor Nickie Berson at New Jersey's Kean College. Students were asked to adopt a raw egg as their "special child" and to take it everywhere with them for a week, no further away than arm's length, and to make sure nothing happened to it.

"During this week," one student wrote afterward, "I found out to some extent what it feels like to have a handicapped child. I never thought I would be conscious of my child twenty-four hours a day. I had to keep an eye on the egg constantly to protect it from accidents, or to protect it from other people who might hurt it."

Some students actually named their eggs. Most reported that they had found it difficult to relax during that week: "I lived on pins and needles"; "It was easy to see the deep emotional strain a handicapped child must put on his parents"; "I was afraid something bad would happen to my child. A lifetime of living in this manner must take its toll on the parents of a handicapped child. My heart goes out to the parents."

Parents Teaching Teachers

Another approach to helping teachers already entrusted with working with children who have special needs is used by some parent advocacy groups. Iowa Pilot Parents, for one, has been running workshops to help teachers appreciate the problems a youngster with a disability might be expected to encounter in a regular classroom. (Many parent groups have adopted the same approach to sensitizing local physicians or medical students.)

The concept of parents teaching teachers is not all that rare; many parents find themselves doing so on more than one occasion on a one-to-one basis. That education is limited, however, to providing useful information about the child and his or her disability. Parents have no illusions about their reach: the basic responsibility for teacher preparation still devolves on the school systems or the local education agencies. In fact, where there is not enough staff with special education training, PL 94-142 requires a commitment to inservice training for any regular classroom teachers working with children who have special needs. The better school systems do so as a matter of course.

"Let's Work Together"

Whether it has a scientific basis or not, parents also tend to rate systems as a whole by the degree to which they welcome parent involvement as part of the child's educational team. Take, for instance, the New Jersey district in which Martha T. lives. Her twelve-year-old daughter is profoundly deaf.

We have always received all the help we needed. Teachers were and are great; services are super. The most helpful person was the head of the team, who became superintendent of schools. The team itself has always been good to and for us. If you approach the school with a "let's work together" attitude, things usually work out. They want the input of the parent. It makes their job easier.

A number of school systems welcome such involvement. In La Grange, Illinois, the Department of Special Education's Parents as Effective Partners (PEP) program trains parents in home behavior management and in teaching techniques. In North Carolina public schools, a similar strategy is implemented in the "parents as coteachers" approach, with parent volunteers helping out in understaffed preschool programs.

Establishing Communication

It may be more than coincidence that in schools that are responsive to parents and welcome their participation, the quality of education tends to be higher. At least two dozen studies have shown that parent involvement does improve student achievement measurably.

Parents are understandably delighted when the school takes the initiative in developing a good working relationship in connection with the child's education, but they are not hesitant about taking the first steps themselves. "I try very hard to have excellent communication with the people who were and are working with my son," says Karen Ruschill, whose son had not yet been clearly classified at age five. "I feel you have to in order to aid your child's progress."

Barbara Levitz, whose son was born with Down syndrome, is among those who cite some very good reasons for parents to seek such close working relationships with the school. "Teachers, therapists, and professional staff constantly change as the child moves through the educational process," she points out. "The parent remains the one constant person working with and for that child." And from their side, schools should recognize what an asset parents can be to the team. "Parents have the greatest vested interest in how well the child develops. As parents, instinctively and through experience, we are very well aware of the individual needs, strengths, and weaknesses of our children."

Levitz's son is now twelve. Because of her experiences during "seven excellent years" with her school district, she has given the matter of parent-school relations and cooperation considerable thought, and her ideas might well serve as a model for the school-parent partnership.

It is imperative for parents to establish a relationship with school supervisors and administrative personnel on the basis that "we are all working together for the child." Decisions need to be made jointly as a cooperative effort in a friendly atmosphere at all levels, from teacher conferences up to high-level official meetings. Good results by teachers and staff should be praised, not overlooked or taken for granted by the parents. Parents should be open to compromise, as long as it does not affect the level of service, and as an indication of willingness to be open to the ideas of personnel who may very well be on the right track.

But parents should also be prepared to stand firm when necessary. They must not feel that professionals "hold all the cards" and feel defensive and beholden to professional decisions. As long as parents are knowledgeable about available programs and services and can proceed with a cooperative attitude—assertive but not obnoxious—an effective parent-professional relationship can be established.

The parent who is armed with a good knowledge of the laws and parents' rights, does not misuse this information, and has an understanding of the process can be very effective in securing good programs and services.

How to Deal with Uncooperative Schools

Unfortunately, it is not always up to the parent whether relations with the school system are harmonious and cooperative. Despite PL 94-142, there are still systems that deny youngsters with disabilities basic services: An Idaho junior high refused at one point to do an IEP altogether for a teenager who had dyslexia, saying it was a "waste of time: because Susan is a girl, the school's thinking is that she can get married soon, have babies, and doesn't need to know how to read!"

There are still schools that stonewall on services and then try the intimidation game: "I was told that if I was not satisfied, the school system could place my son on a home-study program that would mean one hour of tutoring a day. Or they could possibly find placement in a residential facility for him."

Although some parents have met such lack of cooperation head-on because they felt it was the only way they could get services for their child, "adversary relationships are a strain for everyone," Barbara Levitz points out, and the consensus seems to be to try to negotiate differences first. "We have found that you get more with honey than with vinegar," Diane Crutcher comments, "and we are trying to work *with* those professionals interacting in our daughter's life, rather than against them."

And as Barb Crawford, whose daughter has cerebral palsy—and an IQ in the gifted range—puts it:

> I am trying to be my child's strongest advocate (who cares more than I?) while watching carefully not to rock boats or step on toes. I feel I have gained the overall respect of the professionals who deal with my daughter. I am very verbal about what I want and try hard to be reasonable. So far they respect my wishes. Knowing the law and your rights is crucial for dealing constructively with the system.

Parents as Advocates

"In order for a handicapped child to get what he/she needs," a Minnesota couple comments, "not just from the schools but from society as a whole, it is necessary for parents to devote a portion of their lives to being advocates for our kids. Learn to be assertive. Keep asking until you get an answer."

For a good many parents, though, assertiveness doesn't come easily. Being a parent, even a concerned or desperate parent, does not necessarily qualify you to be an advocate. A woman who had just adopted a seven-year-old with cerebral palsy wrote to PACER, the Minneapolis parent advocacy coalition: "I'm very concerned about what the district will be able, or willing, to offer in the way of services that are really geared to his individual needs. I guess what I'm really asking for is some help, I know the laws, but I'm a little frightened at the thought of having to stand up to others to make sure our boy receives what he's entitled to."

That isn't unusual, PACER answered; a lot of parents have the same anxieties. "Consider the fact, however, that standing up and advocating for anything in this world involves risks, and as advocates for our handicapped students we must be willing to accept this role. We should be assertive for our children's needs: should calmly, firmly, and politely stand up for ourselves and our children without violating the rights of others."

Assertiveness, Not Aggressiveness: Advocacy Training

Some parents feel reluctant to stand up to bureaucracies because they confuse assertiveness with aggressiveness. But they are not the same: you can advocate for your child without insulting others or trying to force them to accept your beliefs or demands, by accepting their right to disagree with you. You're looking for compromises, not confrontation; harmony, not hassles.

Parents are often surprised to discover that advocacy can be studied and mastered, that assertiveness is less a matter of temperament than of techniques and skills that can be learned and taught. More parents than not do need some help in learning how to be assertive effectively, and many parent and disability groups are now providing assertiveness training for parents. (If there is no such group or training program within reach, there is a very good self-training manual available, with some interesting and on-target exercises, called *Parents Are to Be Seen AND Heard,* by Geraldine Ponte Markel and Judith Greenbaum, published by Impact Publishers.)

Since 1975 and Public Law 94-142, parent advocacy groups have sprung up in most larger cities and many smaller communities, with most providing some sort of advocacy training. If the parent grapevine or other local contacts do not produce a name, many of the groups listed in Appendix B provide exactly that kind of training. (If it turns out that there is no parent organization in the area, probably the best guide to starting one is *How to Organize an Effective Parent/Advocacy Group and Move Bureaucrats,* published by the Coordinating Council for Handicapped Children, 20 E. Jackson Boulevard, Room 900, Chicago, IL 60604.)

The model for many groups is PACER, 4826 Chicago Ave. South, Minneapolis, MN 55417, one of the most effective groups providing parent assertiveness training. PACER came into being in 1976, a direct result of PL 94-142, as an informal parent and advocate coalition, primarily to inform parents of their rights under the new law. As it has grown and developed through the years, PACER has undertaken workshops and training programs to "professionalize" parents at least to the degree that they can begin to deal with credentialed professionals on behalf of their children pretty much as equals.

Professionalizing parents isn't only a matter of teaching assertiveness and advocacy techniques, but providing parents with a broader perspective by focusing not only on the needs of their own children, but on the larger issues involved as well. That entails helping parents to understand that sometimes the only way to gain a specific program or service for their child is to band together with other parents to get or create that program or service for all similarly deprived children. (But parents sometimes have mixed emotions when a program they've fought so hard for comes into being, because it may well be in time to help younger children, but not their own, who have already outgrown that particular need.)

PACER: Fostering Mutual Respect and Cooperation

As PACER has evolved, a number of systems in Minnesota, originally skeptical or even hostile, have come to welcome its efforts, largely because its philosophy as an organization is the same as that it teaches parents to practice as individuals. "At the present time," says Paula Goldberg, PACER co-director,

> many school districts rely on PACER and encourage parents to attend our workshops. That is because we view ourselves as an advocacy organization, not in an adversary relationship

to schools. We tend to resolve conflicts. We communicate with parents and the schools, and try to improve communication between parents and school staffs. We feel that we have gained the respect of the education community.

An illustration of this respect: One mother told PACER that what she had found most useful in her training program was the information "that parents had rights! I didn't know we had input and could influence district programs." With this new knowledge and confidence, she proceeded to write letters to the district and stand up to the principal who had said her child could never learn, and then she began a campaign against the miserable classroom setting in which her child and other youngsters with disabilities were being taught.

Not only did she get her child transferred to another district for more appropriate programming, but her persistence also brought about "a better setting for the whole class: they were moved out of the junior high dungeon where they had been."

And there was an epilogue worth noting: "The social worker gave credit to parent involvement as making the difference in programming that teachers had not been able to bring about." There's an important point there: parents should never assume that all "pros," or systems, are hostile to change and determined to maintain the status quo. Though they may not be able to say so, school personnel often welcome parent assertiveness. In this case, they were as frustrated about teaching conditions as were the parents who finally "brought about changes the teachers had been wanting" but had been unable to effect themselves.

Educators as Advocates

In fact, teachers, particularly special educators, have often become advocates, not only for a single child but for a whole group they feel is getting less than the "appropriate education" promised by the law. Sometimes living up to their professional ethic even compels them to put jobs and careers on the line.

As far back as the early 1980s, a Kentucky special educator named Pamela McCoun, feeling "strongly about the issue of professional advocacy" and disturbed over "the inconsistency between what a school system is supposed to be and do and what it actually is and does," found it necessary to file a grievance through the teachers' union over the inappropriate classroom she had been given. She got a new one.

Rebecca Cole, a speech and language pathologist in Texas, was not so fortunate. Unable to get her school to correct "grave deficiencies" in its policies and programs, she and two colleagues resigned. There were a federal investigation and statewide publicity—and they had to battle to keep their teaching certificates. She lost ten thousand dollars in back salary and had to relocate, and her chances of getting another teaching position were lessened. Yet, she said, "Without hesitation I would follow the same course of action again."

Parents as Professionals

One other reason parents should not assume that the professionals with whom they deal are unsympathetic is that an increasing number of parents have gone from being advocates for their own children into professional jobs, as teachers, special educators, social workers, and therapists.

It is obvious that they bring a special point of view to their new responsibilities. Typical of this group is Stephanie Nankervis, the parent who became the executive director of an ARC affiliate in Michigan. The mother of a child with mental retardation, she went back to college to get an M.A. in the field of special education for youngsters who are mentally impaired. Being a working parent in the field gives her great personal satisfaction, she says.

"It provides me with a chance to advocate for services from a different vantage point than other professionals. And it convinces me that parents and parent groups must advocate together and create positive change for the future of their children."

There are a great many other parents who, although they do not become professionals, come to feel the same sense of commitment to all children with special needs as a result of their own experiences. But at the same time that they are advocating for all such children, they find themselves still involved in the often lonely advocacy of a single family for a single child.

Advocacy: "Speaking for the Child"

There is a spirited mother like that named Marge Mann, who learned a great deal about advocacy from the people at PACER, "a literal lifeline," in Minneapolis, before she moved to Milwaukee. Once there, she found herself involved in bitter battles with the school system to prevent inappropriate placements for her son, who had developmental delays.

Perhaps nothing could better express the credo of all parent advocates than some excerpts from a letter Marge Mann wrote at one point to the school authorities:

> Wisconsin seemed to be a place where things were in place for handicapped education, and I welcomed that. Do you know why? Because I am so tired of fighting for the things my son needs.
>
> I don't enjoy demanding, threatening, and insisting. I would like to be just quietly absorbed into a system that is doing all it is supposed to do and all that it can do for handicapped children.
>
> What happened to me did happen. And if it happened to me, what about the other parents and guardians of handicapped children? What is happening to those parents, and ultimately their children, who don't know what the law says, and who might not be as vocal and persistent as I am? I am, in all honesty, scared to death for them, because they are a part of me, even though I don't know them.
>
> PL 94-142, headache though it may sometimes be to school administrators, is a Bible to me, is a lifeline to my son for his years in education. I believe that the vision, unrealistic though it may sound, of PL 94-142 is to be able to meet the educational needs of every handicapped child somehow in every school district in every Somewhere, USA.
>
> I have spent a lot of time, a lot of tears, and a lot of energy working with the law because I believe in it. And because I have to be involved in the educational process for all of our children; and especially for my disabled son, because he cannot represent himself.
>
> I have to speak *for* him, because he cannot speak for himself.

18

"We Have Had to Use Every Strategy"

Due Process and Advocacy Techniques

The "due process" procedure provided by PL 94–142 was long overdue. Incorporating it in the law still did not put parents on an equal footing with school authorities, but by opening up the arena in which decisions about the education of children with disabilities could be made and providing parents with rights and recourses they had never had before, it helped to create a new atmosphere for parent-educator negotiations.

What Congress did in 1975, at the urging of parents and advocacy groups, was to shuffle what had been a stacked deck: previously, local school principals or administrators were virtually a law unto themselves in respect to admitting and providing programs for a child with special needs, except for whatever procedures were specified in state laws.

The "due process" procedure written into PL 94–142 to unstack the deck consisted of five separate appeals steps:

- ◆ An independent evaluation of the child
- ◆ An impartial hearing before a neutral hearing officer who could not be an employee of the affected school district

(the "fair hearing" modeled on procedures in other government agencies)

+ An administrative appeal against that hearing officer's decision, to the state commissioner or department of education
+ A complaint to the federal Office of Civil Rights
+ The right to a final appeal to the courts, as a civil action

Due Process as Leverage

Experience has indicated that it is better to have due process and not need it than to need it and not have it, because it can be costly, complex, and time- consuming, and in the end there is no guarantee that parents can win. But because capricious and arbitrary, or simply stubborn, school authorities can no longer be certain that they will win at higher levels, the right to due process has given parents considerable leverage and authority in pre–due process meetings and in informal negotiations generally.

In this sense, due process serves primarily as a catalyst affecting relationships and attitudes between parents and the school system. Since 1975, relatively few parents have gone the full due-process route, but a great many parents have learned to use it without using it, paradoxical as that may seem.

A Michigan father, who happens to be an attorney and so was familiar with PL 94–142's provisions as well as the provisions of the state's education statutes, provides an apt illustration. His daughter has a hearing impairment, and he found that there were eight children in her special education class, one more than the state permitted. More important, he felt, was the fact that there was no teacher's aide assigned to the class.

When I raised the two matters, the school administrator argued that "they couldn't afford them." I refused to sign the IEP and told them that we'd just have to have a hearing. I also indicated that I would be fully satisfied if there were a teacher's aide: I'd just forget that there was one child too many in the class. The result was that they agreed to hire an aide, and I signed the IEP the same day.

Another father learned at an IEP review session that the school had decided, without consulting him, that some of the services his child was getting were unnecessary and was planning to terminate them. He wasted no time: next session he brought along a Legal Aid attorney, and the school authorities immediately changed their minds.

Negotiations Avoid the Need for Due Process

Without due process as an invisible presence at the session, it is not likely that, on the merits of the case alone, this kind of informal-formal session would have won the restoration of services, if in fact any such session would have occurred before PL 94–142. If in fact any such services would have been provided at all.

The effectiveness, from the parents' standpoint, of such informal premeetings undoubtedly accounts to some extent for the relatively small number of parents who have ever begun formal procedures. In the last school year for which statistics are available, 1979–1980, the U.S. Department of Education reported that there were only twenty-six hundred hearings and appeals concerning either evaluation conclusions or IEPs nationwide, certainly not a very great number, considering the well over 4 million disabled youngsters in the public school system. There is no indication that the number of hearings has increased substantially since then.

It is possible, of course, as some parts of the education establishment suggest, that the low number of hearings and appeals is a reflection of parent satisfaction with the workings of Public Law 94–142. But education and parent advocates also offer a number of additional, less positive reasons that parents sometimes fail to take advantage of the procedure.

Other Reasons Due Process is Not Used

Schools are supposed to describe it, but—out of a desire not to encourage use of the procedure?—the description is often superficial, sometimes nothing more than a printed brochure or a duplicated sheet, with no real explanation for parents of the procedure's significance. Some schools do even less. When PACER, the parent advocacy group, held an information meeting in a small Minnesota community, one parent was "absolutely astounded" to learn that there was such a thing as PL 94–142 "with all its far-reaching effects." Once she understood her new powers, "that very precious law led us all the way through a due process hearing for our son, which gave him the right to an appropriate education."

Another reason for shying away from the process is fear. Even when parents do know the procedure is available to them, some are too intimidated to use it. They may worry about retaliation against brothers and sisters at the school; but not infrequently the worry is about the student whose education is already at issue. Nancy Wilson ran into that kind of situation with her teenager, who has a learning disability:

> He was closed out of a DHO [diversified health occupations] vocational program because the instructor said she didn't like special students, and she'd never had any in her course. Yes, I know we had a perfect case for a lawsuit, but my husband reasoned that if we forced her to take him, she could still flunk him out in about three weeks.

Costs, Financial and Psychic

Still another reason parents shy away from pressing on to court action is the financial costs. For some parents in the low-income brackets, there is a possibility of obtaining free or low-cost legal assistance, but for middle-class parents the cost of a lawsuit can be substantial. This situation was largely eased by legislation passed by Congress in 1986, entitling parents who go to court under PL 94–142 to reimbursement for attorney's fees if they win their suits. In introducing his bill, then-Senator Lowell

Weicker, Jr., now governor of Connecticut, a notable advocate for children with disabilities, declared that he did "not believe that it was ever the intent of Congress to exclude from the broad coverage of the Constitution and our civil rights statutes the claims of handicapped children seeking an education."

Another, invisible cost that weary parents often find themselves weighing in the balance might be termed the *human erosion factor:* the psychic energy parents have to expend year after year, the internal wear and tear that comes from dealing with stubborn and tireless bureaucracies in the school systems: we against so *many.* "No matter what," says a Kentucky couple who adopted two children with developmental special needs, "we will be there. No matter what, we will work as hard as we can to do the right thing." But

> there are times that we only hope that we can make it through only one more school year without a fight, one school year without struggling to keep what we have and get things better, one school year where everybody will just do what is "right." No matter how naive this belief is, we continue to hope that one day it will come true.

Finally, there is always a strong possibility that after the expenditure of all that money and time and energy, in the end parents still may not win. The odds are no better than fifty-fifty: In Massachusetts, where the results of fair hearings were once analyzed on a case-by-case basis, it turned out that parents and authorities each won the decision a little bit less than half the time, with the small remaining number of cases ending in a negotiated compromise.

The Best Advice: Negotiate First

For any and all of these reasons, most parent advocacy groups advise parents to try to work out their differences with school authorities informally first, if at all possible. Joan Simon would not hesitate to resort to due process, she says, but only after she had explored the possibility of getting the problem resolved through what she calls "the informal network." But she does her homework first:

> I have spent a lot of time studying "the system." I've learned who makes the ultimate decisions and searched for people who can influence them. I've found this cheaper and easier than going "due process" through 94–142.

By taking the process of problem resolution one informal step at a time, nowadays there is a very good possibility of finding someone somewhere inside the system with whom the parent can reach some kind of understanding that helps the child. It should not be at all surprising that a great many educators are as strong advocates for children with disabilities as parents are, including the many educators and other school professionals who are themselves parents of such youngsters.

But those particular school educators and professionals are by no means the only people parents can negotiate with successfully. It takes time and energy, but parents can climb the ladder, even informally, from classroom or special education teacher, to administrator or director of special education, to principal, and even on to state levels; if they do not lose heart, somewhere along the line there is a very good chance parents can find some sort of resolution or compromise that meets the child's needs, in part if not entirely. "When it becomes apparent that the problem cannot be solved at the building level," a Minnesota couple is "not hesitant to contact administrative special education within the district."

And another mother, in order "to find a school where my older daughter could be accepted as a regular kid who happened to be in a wheelchair, while still receiving services because of her handicap," had to go all the way to the top of the special education hierarchy.

And still another won her appeal without going to a "fair hearing" by writing to the state commissioner of education and sending him copies of all her correspondence with the school district. When the commissioner's legal advisor looked at the supporting papers, including cassette tapes of the parents' meetings with authorities (a good idea in difficult situations: "that way no information could be changed"), the attorney upheld the parents' claims completely.

When Due Process is the Only Recourse

If parents have been up and down the "informal network" without getting any of the help they consider vital, or if relationships with the school have deteriorated beyond the point of amicable negotiations, then each family must decide for itself whether the problem is *so* critical, the effect on the child's education *so* basic, that they *must* go to due process. A Kentucky couple with two adopted youngsters have faced that situation more than once and have developed their philosophy perhaps further than most parents.

> The *Rules for Radicals* [by Saul Alinsky] is our guide to dealing with the educational system. If you understand that they are not very competent when they are serving "difficult-to-serve children," and do not understand why you want what you want, and do not have a history of doing the "right" thing for children with developmental special needs, then you can appreciate their position, and work from there for what you want for your child.
>
> We have had to work hard to get what we wanted from the school system, but that is to be expected. We have had to go to a number of due-process hearings. We have had to bring the consultants to tell the local district what to do. We have had to use every strategy that we could think of using to get what we wanted for our children.

It may stem from a generalized dissatisfaction with "the system," but it is a specific grievance that generally prompts parents to act. A decade after Public Law 94–142, parents can still find themselves faced at a critical moment with a school's inappropriate placement of their child, or inappropriate programming, or (and this is most frequent) its refusal to provide necessary related services. In such situations, formal appeals may be the only recourse. One illustration: a couple who finally found it necessary to go to a "fair hearing" simply to get physiotherapy for their child. He now gets such therapy three times a week.

Before formally initiating action under any of the due-process procedures, parents should check out their own state's special appeals procedure: PL 94–142 mandates that each state have one. It is also a good last resort to send the school a letter indicating that the action is being considered; putting it in writing, even informally, may just do the trick: it's the parents' version of the letter from a lawyer.

Due Process: The Procedure

If it becomes clear that the school still won't budge, a formal request for either an independent evaluation of the situation or a fair hearing should be made by registered letter, to both state and local education officials, specifying the complaint in detail and including information about the school system or district and the school personnel involved in whatever actions or decisions are being appealed.

An independent evaluation is usually sought when a school has refused to consider special education services for a child, either arbitrarily or on the basis of an assessment by its own staff or professionals. But as indicated earlier, such an outside evaluation may not change anything, since the school does not have to accept or act on its findings or recommendations.

If the parents request a *fair hearing,* it must be held within forty-five days, at a time and place convenient to the parents.

Parents should use that time *to prepare for the hearing.* The school is required to make available to the parent a complete set of the records, documents, evaluations, and reports—even informal comments—that it has kept about the child and may not introduce at the hearing any records that have not been made available to the parents at least five days in advance. The school must supply copies of all these documents either free of charge or at a nominal cost. The documents must also include copies of all the child's IEPs, including any the parents refused to sign, as well as the school district's overall plan for special education.

Parents should also look over any notes, letters, and cassette tapes (parents should ask permission to tape every session with authorities and school personnel whenever a problem seems to be developing), plus any other records that might be helpful in winning the case.

This is the time also for parents to decide whom to take to the hearing. The law provides that they may have with them at that time anyone they choose—a relative, a friend, the child, expert witnesses (therapists who might have made an independent assessment, for example), or an advocate—someone who can speak for the family, whether volunteer or professional.

Taking Along an Advocate

Even if the problem appears simple, open and shut, the parents should consider finding and taking with them someone with previous experience as an advocate in such hearings. Fair hearings seldom remain simple: being a parent, even a highly motivated and determined parent, is not necessarily the best preparation for the task.

The school is supposed to inform the parent about any legal or advocacy help available to him or her. Some parent groups seem to feel that an attorney is needed as an advocate at this stage, but there are also other kinds of advocates who could be appropriate and supportive. A knowledgeable parent from a local parent or advocacy group can be extremely helpful (and can give needed moral support). Another possibility, especially if the child has mental retardation, is the citizen advocate.

Citizen Advocates

The Arc, formerly National Association for Retarded Citizens, has been the leader through the years in developing citizen advocacy programs for persons with developmental disabilities throughout the United States. Other groups are now also taking this one-to-one approach, in which volunteer advocates acquire the skills necessary to defend the rights and interests of a child or adult with disabilities.

In some areas, such volunteer programs have been incorporated into the state's protection and advocacy (P & A) system, under contract to the state. As the result of a 1975 law, each state has been mandated to set up a P & A agency, to advocate for and protect the rights of all developmentally disabled persons.

Though their actual effectiveness may now be hampered by minimal funding, these agencies do deal, with considerable success, with the problems of children with special needs receiving improper, inadequate, or inappropriate services. The particular emphasis of the agency varies from state to state. Some may become involved in class advocacy, when an entire group of children may be having the same problem, but by preference P & A agencies focus chiefly on individual cases.

They have the right to file lawsuits against offending institutions and systems but do so in fewer than 10 percent of all cases. Their primary effort is directed toward negotiation and compromise with school authorities. But if it comes to it, P & A representatives will also attend and advocate for the child at the hearing.

Parents' Rights at the Hearing

Parents have some say in whom the *school* shall have at the hearing. The school must produce any of its personnel whom the parent requests, so that they may be questioned at the hearing. The parent is of course also permitted to offer witnesses, even the child, if advisable.

The parent may decide whether the hearing shall be public or private and may also request a verbatim record be made, as a protection. It is relevant to note, though it may surprise and dishearten parents seeking a hearing, that although the hearing officer may not be an employee of the school district under challenge, he or she *may* be someone employed elsewhere in the state's school system.

The hearing officer is required to render a decision, with a copy by registered mail to the parent, within forty-five days. If the parent chooses to appeal the ruling, the next step is taken.

An *administrative appeal,* in most but not all states, is an appeal within the framework of the educational system, and is directed to the state Department of Education (elsewhere the appeal goes directly to administrative law courts). An internal appeal may involve meeting with the state commissioner or the commissioner's representative. There appears to be no consensus among parents about whether they should have an advocate or an attorney with them at this point. It would seem to depend generally on the ability of the parent or a volunteer advocate to present the case.

If the ruling is again unfavorable, and the parents feel that the situation represents discrimination against the child, which is forbidden under the provisions of Section 504 of the 1973 Vocational Rehabilitation Act, they have the following options:

◆ *A complaint to the federal Office of Civil Rights,* either in the Office of Education or in the Department of Health and Human Services. A complaint to either of these agencies should result in an investigation of the charges. But instead, they may hire an attorney and file

◆ *a civil suit* in either state or federal courts. This may be either an individual action or—if there are other parents and children involved in the same kind of situation, and particularly if there appears to be discrimination against all children with similar disabilities—it can be joined with others as part of a *class action.*

There have been a number of very successful individual suits, in both state and federal courts. In one landmark case, a North Carolina judge awarded more than thirty thousand dollars, plus the cost of a year's private education, to the parents of a youngster with dyslexia, because the school personnel had failed to recognize his disability and remediate it.

Class Action Suits

What often brings parents to the stage of filing a class action suit is discovering other parents (and children) in the same boat. A Tulsa, Oklahoma, mother "was told frequently that the school system couldn't afford to educate and transport" her daughter, who had severe multiple disabilities. It turned out that she was far from being the only one with such a complaint. "The Deaf/ Blind Multihandicapped Parents' Group in our state made it possible for me to meet and discuss my problems with other parents, to get legal advice, etc. Class action suits by our parents' groups achieved the services needed."

There have been a number of other notable class action suits filed on behalf of entire groups of youngsters with special needs denied an appropriate education. In one concerning the requirement that such youngsters be educated in the "least restrictive environment" possible, a Denver advocacy group filed a federal civil rights complaint on behalf of a number of children being educated in a segregated facility.

Many such suits are coordinated by the parent-oriented disability agencies in the community. "Preschool would have been very difficult for us," a New York City mother reports, "had it not been for United Cerebral Palsy's ability to find funding for such programs through class action at the Family Court level. We would have had great difficulty doing this on our own."

Finding a Lawyer

Some parents have encountered difficulty finding the right lawyer to handle a lawsuit for them. Other parents may have some suggestions or know of an attorney with such experience; if not, the best bet is to contact the relevant national or state disability agency and the state's P & A system. The address of the National Association of Protection and Advocacy Systems:
900 Second St. NW, Suite 211
Washington, DC 20002
(202) 408-9514

Other possible sources of information and/or assistance:
American Bar Association Center
on Children and the Law
1800 M St. NW, Suite 300
Washington, DC 20036
(202) 331-2250

Children's Defense Fund
122 C St. NW
Washington, DC 20001
(202) 628-8787

American Civil Liberties Union
132 West 43 St.
New York, NY 10036
(212) 944-9800

One legal source worth checking, if there is such an institution in the area, is the law school or legal department of the local

university; they may even be able to assign a student to help
prepare the case without a fee. Cost is often an important consideration, of course, and many parents seek out the local Legal
Aid Society for that reason. But cutbacks in government funding
have severely curtailed the amount of help Legal Aid can give.

Even if parents can afford to hire a private attorney, and one
with experience in this area, it may still take a considerable amount
of time before they meet with success if the school system chooses
to stonewall. That's what happened to Nancy Binder, when she
decided to fight an inappropriate placement for her son, who is
hearing impaired but mentally gifted.

Even after the family was able to find an attorney who would
take on the case, even after they found other parents in the same
situation and others began to threaten action, even after the Bind-
ers threatened to sue because of a series of obstacles and broken
agreements, it took the arrival of a new school superintendent to
break down the bureaucrats' obstinacy and straighten things out.
But all that took nearly two years, while her son was growing up
unplaced.

Other Avenues for Advocacy

Henry and Gale Hedgecock found a way to make things happen
a lot more quickly, but they had to go outside educational channels
to do so. Their son was one of those who was dumped between
the cracks as a result of certain agency "interpretations" of PL 94–
142 immediately after it was passed. The state Commission for
the Blind stopped providing orientation and mobility training for
their son, Craig, who had a visual impairment, on the ground that
it was now the schools' responsibility, and the local school system
also failed to provide it: another of those "not my table" situations.

Craig and other youngsters like him went for an entire year
without the training, and no help in sight, until the Hedgecocks
took their story to their local newspaper. The paper did a three-
day front-page series on the problem; within months there were
a qualified instructor and a program.

Such advocacy strategies can often be far more immediately
effective than going through due process. In another instance, Al
and June Lindley had had some tough battles getting even thirty
minutes a day of "bedside school" for their daughter Wendy, who

has multiple disabilities, while she was in the hospital, so they anticipated even greater problems when she was sent home. Shortly before Wendy was to be discharged, the Lindleys decided to "go public" with Wendy's story. Among other things, they publicly challenged their congressman to do something about the cuts then being recommended for PL 94–142 by the federal government. Three major television stations and twelve radio stations picked up the story.

Five months later, when the congressman failed to meet with them, Wendy's father and brother picketed his office. "What happened surprised everybody": not only did all the major television stations and eighteen radio stations send reporters to cover "the story," but the family received several invitations to do talk shows about Public Law 94–142.

Today Wendy is in special classes, and "we have had no major problems with the school system since Wendy was discharged from the hospital. Since challenging Congressman X, we have been most successful in working through the system."

Political Advocacy

The Lindley case is unusual in that members of Congress don't normally have to be challenged; they are much more likely to help *do* the challenging. Most have a local office and a local telephone listing, with staff aides to deal with constituents. And members of Congress are themselves often in their districts to serve the voters. There is probably nothing more effective than a phone call from a member of Congress (or any other legislator at the national, state, or local level for that matter) in cutting through a school system's red tape quickly: instant persuasion, instant placement, too, as in the case of a retardation center that had no room for a little boy with spina bifida, until a congressman called.

Where parents feel that the situation is one that doesn't affect only a single little boy or girl, but is a matter of national policy, and want to reach beyond their own representatives, or when parent groups want to do so, it is possible for them to make their views known directly to the White House. To do that, they should telephone the Office of Public Liaison there at (202) 456-1111 and ask to speak to the specific person in the Office of Policy Development who deals with the area of special concern to them.

This avenue is open to all persons on all political issues, of course. Parents organized in parent groups have not only helped to make their views on policy known at every level (local, state, and federal) but have helped to *change* policies, to make them more responsive to the needs of children with disabilities. An especially valuable guide to getting the maximum benefit from "parent power" is a presentation by a mother named Susan Duffy at a Montana symposium on early education and the exceptional child in the mid-eighties. She called her presentation "Being a Mom Is a Political Experience."

> If there is anything that parents of children with handicaps learn rapidly, it is that services for our children are subject to change due to lack of money, ignorance of their necessity, or the whims of those in positions of authority. Although it is a pain in the neck to continually have to reinvent the wheel and reeducate the public, it is an ongoing process.
>
> Becoming the parent of a child with handicaps is, for those reasons, one of the most rapid boosts toward assertiveness that one can receive. It becomes a matter of survival, your own and your child's.
>
> Three adages come to mind:
>
> + The squeaky wheel gets the grease.
> + You catch more flies with honey than with vinegar.
> + Don't get mad, get organized!
>
> Saul Alinsky, a famous and unorthodox labor organizer, once said, "You don't have to have the majority of the people for you; you just have to have the majority of the people not against you." Most people are apolitical or apathetic about causes, and, for the most part, that's OK. You cannot convince everyone of the righteousness of your cause anyway. The people you have to convince are those who have the power to make the changes you want to have made.
>
> When organizing for a cause—new services, expansion or upgrading of existing services, etc.—several points should be kept in mind:
>
> 1. Exactly what do you want and why? If you can't get what you want, what are you willing to settle for?
> 2. Who has the power to give you what you want? How do

they feel about the issue? What are their reservations and why? What part, if any, do they support?

3. Has the cause been fought before? If so, by whom? When and why did they lose?

4. What factual information supports your cause? What factual information needs to be overcome?

5. What groups beside your own have reason (you may have to think up the reason for them) to support your cause? What groups will fight the cause and why?

All of these questions will need to be answered before you can effectively wave your banners. Once you are fairly sure of the answers, you are ready to go public. The following suggestions are some ways of going about it.

1. Have a fact sheet to hand out that explains what you want, why you want it, and why people should support it. Families of handicapped children are constantly accused of wanting more (we do, of course) and of not being grateful for what our children have already been given. (Parents of regular kids are not asked to be grateful for the existence of public schools and extracurricular activities, but that is another issue.) Your job is to show people that what helps our kids helps the community at large, too.

2. Write a letter outlining your cause, your reasoning, and your proposed solution and send copies to every community organization you can think of, asking them to endorse your cause. Add a separate cover letter to each that explains why you feel that group has a personal stake in the issue. For instance, veterans' groups might have a stake because Vietnam veterans have an unusually high rate of children born with birth defects, churches support the causes of less fortunate people in general, Planned Parenthood and Right to Life groups both promote stability in families, medical people spend a lot of time and effort keeping handicapped children alive, the Chamber of Commerce promotes community services to businesses considering relocation to their area, etc. You can usually make a connection if you think about it. Look in the Yellow Pages, find out what groups exist, and write to all of them. You are not asking their members to go out and beat the streets for you; you are asking only for their

endorsement—but accumulated endorsements from a cross section of the community add up to strength.

3. Figure out who the best speakers are in your group and offer their services. Most local groups have monthly meetings or luncheons and would be happy to have your speaker fill their programming slot. Just making the offer may help you in some cases.

4. Write short, reasoned letters to the editor of your newspaper. Go in and talk to the editor about your goal. He or she may be happy to write an editorial on the subject if you suggest it; editorial writers are often stuck for topics of local interest. (Don't ask for an editorial if the writer seems hostile to your case, of course.)

5. Most local television and radio stations have local talk shows. They may run at peculiar times, but they are free to your group. Broadcast media in Montana have just as much air time to fill as do stations in New York City but have fewer people and causes competing for their time. Broadcast media are required by law to present a certain amount of "public service" programming, and your group qualifies as such, thus helping them out, too. So go in and ask. If you will be holding a meeting, particularly if there might be good "visuals" involved, notify the television news people. They are particularly hard up for news on weekends.

6. While in the process of launching your campaign publicly, make personal contact with the people who have the power to change the situation. Make these contacts by appointment so that the time you have will be uninterrupted. Because persons in authority are more comfortable on their own turf, try to arrange your meeting at their offices or on neutral ground, perhaps in a restaurant over coffee. If there are several people who need to be convinced—a school board, for example—make your contacts individually. People in groups feel less personally responsible for what is being discussed.

7. When you meet, be prepared. Have your facts and figures ready. Know the answers to questions you are likely to be asked. Be straightforward and nonthreatening. It is easier for people to agree with a person they can like and with whom they can feel something in common. Hidden agendas and veiled threats make people nervous. Tears

and shouting make people nervous and embarrassed. Be
pleasant, businesslike, and informed. Remember that having a child like one of ours is one of the worst things
other people can imagine happening in their own lives,
and they are uncomfortable with their own feelings. You
need to show them that as people and parents you are
more like them than different. Do not play to pity. Play
to logic, community responsibility, and basic goodness
(it's in there somewhere).

8. After you have spoken individually with the persons in
authority, identify who is for you, who is against you, and
who is wavering. Consolidate your positive support. Do
your best to resolve the problems the waverers have with
your cause. Find out if your group and a waverer have
any mutually respected friend and have that person speak
with the waverer in your behalf. If you have a nondramatic
opportunity for the waverer to meet your child, take it.
Most of our kids are doing a lot better than most people
think they are, but it takes a parent to point out how well
the child is doing because the public has a hard time
getting past the face of the situation.

9. Keep plugging until you get what you want. It may take
a while, but you need to remain visible. It is much easier
for persons in authority to ride out short campaigns than
ongoing efforts, especially if you are continuing to educate
the public as you go along.

10. When you win, don't celebrate your victory as a battle
that has been won by your group over another. Make it
a celebration of the community, of a cause that everyone
had a stake in but wasn't aware of until you came along.
Go back and say thank you to everyone who helped you
out in any way. Thank them personally, through letters
and in the newspaper. And always remember that those
filling positions of authority change from time to time,
and the new people will have to be reeducated. It is much
easier to do this on a continuing basis than by having to
launch a whole new campaign because you let it go by
inaction.

It is not only a program, but a philosophy that had its origins
in Susan Duffy's own experiences. There seemed no problem
getting educational services, when her daughter Keough, who has

both physical and mental impairments, was accepted at the age of twenty-two months—"the youngest they've taken so far"—into a local preschool program. The family "decided to let the school system ride for a while": after all, the little girl was already *in*.

But that turned out to be "a very big mistake." The preschool program was soon phased out, and "we had to run a political campaign for a year to get it going again." Since then, she says, "I've learned to keep my ear to the ground for distant early warning signals. When you're a parent, you haven't got the luxury of assuming that people of good will will prevail."

19
....

"They Need to Learn to Survive"
How to Help Your Child Become Independent (or More Independent)

Except possibly for the parents of children with the most severe or multiple disabilities, there isn't a parent anywhere who doesn't dream or hope or fantasize about a time when the child with special needs can be independent, or at least as independent as possible.

That dream almost always focuses on schooling. On the frontier, where very few people could read and write, an astute psychologist once pointed out that there was no such thing as a "learning disability." But here and now, say *independence*, and nearly everyone equates that with *education*, except the parents of older children, and the young people themselves.

Bebe Antell, whose son, now a young adult, has learning disabilities, and who is herself a learning disabilities resources specialist, makes the point that "we all tend sometimes to be overly anxious about our child's academic progress. My fantasy was, 'If only he could learn to read, everything else would be easy.' But when he learned to read at age ten, it still wasn't easy."

She concludes, "How you feel about yourself, and how you relate to others, and how you perform in life, are more important than academic skills for a disabled youngster." Or, as some put it, not only can children with disabilities be "educated" without becoming independent, but they can become reasonably independent without being very "educated."

For that reason, many older parents who are still involved with their young adult children—as well as young adults with disabilities themselves—have come to feel that such skills as getting along with people, budgeting, shopping, dating, and using public transportation are more important to living than a knowledge of the ABCs. The centrality of the school system in the lives of children with special needs makes it essential, therefore, that such "survival skills" and socialization skills be incorporated in IEPs throughout—from age three to age twenty-one, or until the young man or woman leaves the school system.

Growing Up

By the high school level, the student with special needs has already "aged out" of the more sheltered environment of grade school and younger schooldays into a universe that can be as painful as it is rewarding. Even more than for other young people, for such students the high school years are a rite of passage. Parents may hear and see and agonize, but there are a growing number of situations for their children, especially with peers, in which they can no longer run interference. The price of adulthood: each young man and woman must learn to "make it" socially, as best he or she can, alone. Here are some thoughts that may help young people do so:

In our society you score no points for having a problem. Every person who has a disability has to struggle to make it.

- Nobody can make you feel inferior without your consent.
- If *you* have an *interest* (hobbies, work, talents, passions) someone will be interested in *you*.
- If you are bored, you are boring to be with.
- If you do not have a sense of humor, watch people who have one carefully.
- Join an advocacy group for people with disabilities.
- Do not dwell on the meaning of life. Life is not a meaning. Life is an opportunity for any number of meaningful experiences.
- Read. Discover as much as you can about yourself and the

world. For heaven's sake, do not watch more than a couple of hours of television each day.

* Operate on the assumption that the so-called general public is uncomfortable with you. Most people *are* uncomfortable in the presence of people who have a noticeable disability. Somehow convey to them that it is OK to feel uncomfortable. If you announce that they do not have to feel guilty about it, then they will not have to respond by withdrawing from you or having pity on you.

Fantasy and Fear

As exhausting as it is for parents to deal with the daily medical, social, academic, and emotional crises in the child's life, the underlying fear in the back of most parents' minds is that this future adult will never be able to deal with these crises alone. What every parent would like to see, that hope/dream/fantasy again, is that child someday leading a happy and productive life as an adult. What every parent *does* or can do is to help the child "make it" in life to the greatest possible extent.

The mistake parents too often make is to put all their eggs in the school basket. It's natural: the passage of PL 94–142 has helped make school so central in the existence of every child with special needs. It is true that many of the better schools are expanding their efforts on behalf of children with disabilities beyond the "normal" curriculum to include "survival skills," with the parent as an important part of the team. But at best that still leaves a considerable share of the responsibility for preparing the child for a successful adulthood, and at worst, almost all the responsibility, to the parents.

Here are a dozen ways—there are many more, of course—that parents suggest families can contribute to a child's confidence and determination to help him- or herself to achieve some measure (or a greater measure) of future independence.

Accept Your Child

It shouldn't need saying, yet parents and professionals agree that for some families just accepting the child is a real hurdle. Ella

Mae Howell, whose daughter was born with cerebral palsy, puts it very simply: "I used to think of my daughter first of all as being disabled, but now I think of her as just a little girl. If someone I knew had a child like mine, I would advise them to treat the baby like a normal child, a healthy child, as best you can."

It may help to think of it as if it were something written by Gertrude Stein: a child is not a disability; a child is not a "handicap"; a child is a child is a child. "After her surgeries," say the parents of a baby born with spina bifida, "we just wanted to stop focusing on health problems and start enjoying our baby girl."

It may be self-evident that children will never begin to think of themselves as "persons" unless you think of them that way, and not as bundles of symptoms and deficits, but Mrs. Perry Mendell points out how difficult that can sometimes be:

> Sometimes it's easy to get so involved in treating the handicap that you forget there's a child there who thinks and feels just like any other child. And if they're not treated as they might have been were there no handicap, then they will be different from other children not only physically, but also emotionally.

Person first = can do. Disability first = can't do. For children ever to become independent adults or to achieve whatever degree of independence they have the capacity for, they must first believe it is possible to do so. They must believe in themselves. Parents say that the image children have of themselves in those formative years is basically the image they see in their parents' eyes. That's why it is so important, say Elizabeth and Paul Cooney, whose son has a severe seizure disorder and a form of cerebral palsy, to

> try not to think of the things your child can't do, but rather the things he can do. Try to see your child not as a handicapped child, but as a child with handicaps. Try to think of your child as what he or she is, a little person with needs and feelings just like everyone. Most of all he or she is a child and needs your love.

It hardly needs to be said how much of a difference love, demonstrated love, makes in enhancing the child's self-appreciation and self-esteem. *"Dass du mich liebst,"* a German poet once wrote, *"macht mich mir wert."* Roughly paraphrased, the fact that you love your children gives them worth in their own eyes.

The family's attitude is key in another respect, the Colorado mother of a boy with Down syndrome notes. "Acceptance is important because once the child is accepted in the family, he or she will then be accepted in the community and finally in society in general." And community attitudes will have a major impact on the degree of independence the child as adult ever achieves.

Promote Your Child's Self-Esteem

To feel self-esteem, some children need no more than their complete acceptance by the family. For a child with a disability though, more often than not this requires the family's conscious assurance and reassurance, with deliberate emphasis on the child's strengths. If adults will believe almost any praise or even flattery (try it), why shouldn't children, especially your own child?

Some of that positive reinforcement will, or should, also come in school. When a Richmond, Virginia, couple placed their non-reading daughter in a school ready to work with her more intensely, "it made a tremendous difference. Not only did they help her reading, but her self-esteem shot up 200 percent."

But what of youngsters who are not able to do well in their schoolwork, no matter how intensive the teaching? Says the astute mother of an eighteen-year-old girl with learning disabilities:

Find something that the child can do well outside the academic world. Give her an opportunity to do well at that activity. She must find a place where she is secure with being good at *something.*

If it can't be at school, there may be other areas in which to look for ego-bolstering success. One important way to promote self-esteem is to look for opportunities to teach your child something new. Unfortunately, too many parents give up on this because of bad initial experiences, like taking the child to a busy and crowded restaurant with the family, and having the child create a scene. When families react by giving up and telling the child that because he was "bad," restaurants are out for him from then on, they do even more harm to the child's self-image.

The trick is to try it again under controlled circumstances—one parent, no siblings—at a time when the restaurant is relatively quiet. Give yourself an additional edge by explaining to the waitress some of the difficulties she may encounter and why, and that you'd greatly appreciate her patience. And of course tip her well afterward, especially if you want to try it again.

Apply that technique to other activities you think the child might be able to master with a little patience. Perhaps the first time he tried to ride a bike or swim, some people made fun of him. Try a swimming lesson when there is no one else around. There's a complete package right there: security, protection, and measured praise for achievement.

At a minimum, there's the immediate reward: "Look, Ma, I'm swimming!" And in the longer-range context of helping the child to think and believe independence, "Look, Ma, I didn't think I could, but I can!"

Don't Help Too Much

As long as there's no danger, let the child *do,* even if the doing is done badly.

If parents don't allow a child with a disability to try and to learn by doing because in their hearts they don't believe the child can, then after a time the child will also believe he or she can't and will *stop* trying. That is actually stealing the child's independence, because in the end the child will decide there is *nothing* he or she can do or learn to do. That's the way loving parents can themselves handicap such a child even more.

Vicki and Steve Cauley try to encourage their three-and-a-half-year-old daughter, who has cerebral palsy, to do as much as she can, and in fact a bit more:

> We believe in treating Sarah just like other children. We don't baby her or help her out with things she can do for herself, even if it takes a little longer. Obviously there are things she cannot do at this time, but she is asked to try to do them. If it is too difficult for her, we show her how to do it, and let her try again another time.

There are many situations in which it isn't easy to encourage or even to watch. The classic case: a child lying on the floor crying, begging for help to get to her feet, while you tell her she can use a piece of furniture, or her crutch, to do it herself. If that's what's been prescribed, cringe if you must, but don't interfere, a Louisiana mother says.

I learned a long time ago that you have to harden your heart and let the child do for herself, and not run to do everything for her. Take your own personal feelings and set them aside, because you have to go with what is good for your child: the benefit will come later. It's only your present, but it's her future. It's the end results that you're hoping for.

Her daughter has cerebral palsy and hydrocephalus. Ethel Clough, whose daughter was born with Down syndrome, went through the same learning process. "It was very hard to say 'Don't help her; she has to do it on her own,' but it certainly paid off." Not only is her daughter, at twenty-two, working in a nursery school, but, Ms. Clough adds, "She's delightful!"

If parents have any hope that the child will one day be able to venture out into the world, overconcern and overprotection are the worst ways to prepare for that time. For example, although it is important to be prepared to advocate for the child with the school system, parents should also be aware of how much is too much and should assess what they do by how well or badly it prepares and equips the child to handle life situations on his or her own later on. If it isn't clear earlier, it becomes quite apparent as children grow older. Mrs. Ty Malloy, whose fifteen-year-old daughter has a learning disability, notes that when the children were younger

we, in a sense, overprotected our youngsters from uncaring teachers and teasing peers, but we are now, during high school years, pushing them away from us, trying to teach them to stand on their own two feet. As a parent you *want* to say, "I'll take care of that so-and-so," but even though your heart is tearing, you force yourself to state firmly, "*You* can handle that, I know you can."

You give them advice and suggestions on how *they* can solve their problem. We parents silently say a prayer, as we give our children a pat on the back and push them toward a problem on their own.

The earlier and oftener that pat on the back, the better. In fact, don't just pat: *push* your child, gently but firmly, to do *more*.

Expect More of Your Child Than Is "Realistic"

Parents make "miracles" happen by having unrealistically high expectations.

Never underestimate what your child may be capable of accomplishing, and never let pessimistic predictions keep you from exploring "impossible" possibilities. Some parents even believe in setting goals for children to try for—"a man's reach should exceed his grasp," the poet Robert Browning said—and reward their children not only for getting there but for *trying* to get there.

It is true that not all youngsters, regardless of the effort expended by their parents, will be able to exceed the progress and the achievements parents have been told to expect. But so many parents *have* succeeded in helping to extend the child's limits by their encouragement that clearly the effort is always worthwhile, as the Michigan mother of a boy born with a left hemiparesis, who got a lot of pessimistic "words of wisdom from physicians," can testify.

> One doctor told my husband and me not to expect a lot from our son. That was the worst advice! We do not push our son, nor do we place great demands on him, but we do expect him to progress. We continually motivate him to learn new things, use his arm, etc. Our son is so proud of himself when we clap and cheer for a new skill he has achieved. I think the best thing parents can do is always to expect new learning. And never settle for less.

If there is any secret to parents' "miracles," that's it: the family *expects* the child to progress and *shows* it. The best advice ever given her, a California mother recalls, was by a school psychologist: "What you have expected from your daughter has worked thus far. Keep going with it."

It may well be, especially at first, that the beneficiaries of these exercises in confidence building will be the parents as often as the children. A parent's faith, or lack of it, can make a considerable difference in the way the child thinks about independence, as Bebe Antell points out:

> Some of us have little confidence in our children's abilities and don't encourage them to try things on their own. If your

child is afraid of the swimming program you'd like him to attend, and you make no attempt to change his mind, you may be reinforcing his dependency.

If you want an independent son or daughter, you're going to have to work at it. It sometimes helps not only to discuss your child's disability, but to point out also his/her abilities. It also helps to discuss the goals you want for your teenagers, and how you hope they can be accomplished.

The key may be finding the right motivation: concentrating on something the youngster is interested in and wants to do. In the case of Shana Toole, who is fourteen and has a learning disability, the key to improving her self-confidence was her determination to be a cheerleader, despite her coordination problems and her difficulty in learning the cheers. "Like everything else Shana does," her mother says, "cheerleading doesn't come easily or naturally. She must work ten times harder than anyone else to succeed, but she *can* succeed."

And she did. After two years of being cut from the cheerleading squad, in the third year she made it and has in the process learned how to tackle and overcome other obstacles on the road to independence.

That's the positive. Parents can also make a contribution to the child's independence by avoiding the negative: being insistently "realistic" about their abilities and capabilities sometimes translates in the youngsters' minds into being told they *can't* do something before they even try. It is not that parents want to put their youngsters down; the rationale with which parents defend themselves is that letting their children try "the impossible" is merely setting them up for more failures that they don't need.

But life is like this: you *have* to risk failing any time you want to succeed.

Don't Overprotect Your Child

If you overprotect your child, you will often guarantee that the child with a disability will become a handicapped adult.

For many parents, the thought of allowing children, especially when they're still young, to take risks may be very frightening. But the only way children with disabilities can be helped to discover the world and themselves is by being allowed to take a certain amount of risk, as other, "normal" children, who are not under the constantly watchful eyes of their parents, do quite casually. Such risk taking is a critical ingredient of any progress toward independent living, Nancy Jones feels.

> You can't baby them. They have to be made ready for their place in the world independently, and they can't learn if you overprotect them. Fight for their rights, but let them grow and learn too. Let them fall and be hurt, and be there to let them know you understand. We have to help them become strong, for they will need the strength to cope with others.

Fine, some parents might say, in theory. In principle, all parents would agree that if you wrap the child in a protective cocoon and keep him or her there, there is a good chance that he or she will never develop the strength to break out of it. But in practice not everyone applies the principle to real situations. A parent has to accept and integrate the concept into his or her own credo to be as matter-of-fact as the mother of a fifteen-year-old girl with cerebral palsy who loves to climb trees. "She falls down a lot more than normal children," the mother says, "but she gets up and tries again."

Risk-taking is normal for all children, and the Wisconsin mother of two children who are legally blind felt the answer for them was to "just let them be as normal as possible." But her husband was far from convinced, especially when the children were young.

> Their father was just learning to deal with the visual problem, and he did not want to play ball with his son for fear of the boy's getting hurt. He didn't want our son climbing trees, riding a bike and such either, so I took over for a while and taught him to climb trees.
>
> My husband suffered the most during these times, out of fear for his son's health and well-being. But after seeing how happy it made him to do all the things other boys did, my husband let go.
>
> Letting the children go on their own was and will always be the hardest thing. It was only when we started sharing with other parents that my husband knew he wasn't alone in his feelings, and it was okay.

Don't Hide Your Child in a Closet

Whatever your reasoning for minimizing public contact—fear the child will be injured, rebuffed, or mocked—"expose that child to the world," a Catawba, North Carolina, mother says. "Don't shut them up in the house. There's a big world out there, and they need to learn to survive."

And survival is not all they'll learn: if children are treated normally, exposed as much as possible to as many of the same things as other children, then they may never realize while they're growing up that they are supposed to be different. And if you treat your child like any other, says Elizabeth Villani, whose son was born with Down syndrome, others may get the idea, too.

> Take him everywhere with you, to the supermarket, shopping, the beach, picnics, movies, on vacations. We always have. Don't be afraid of people staring at you; many will respond positively when they see the caring interaction between the handicapped child and his family.

A Minnesota couple could very easily have allowed the birth of a baby with spina bifida to turn them in on themselves. Instead they decided immediately that they were going to lead as normal a life as possible and treat the baby as normally as possible. They took her on walks with them, took her shopping in a backpack (and found that everyone oohed and aahed over her), and when she was four months old flew off to Iowa to visit relatives with her and "to show her off."

Parents may feel that hiding the child who is disabled away is merely protecting him or her; that's the reason such parents give for not letting their children play with "normal" children. What they don't realize is that they're only delaying the day when their children will have to deal with the normal world.

There may be parents who will snatch their "normal" babies away as though the disability were contagious (and parents report that they are sometimes asked whether it is). But there's good reason to begin early. Left to themselves, younger children can be marvelously accepting, as a Missouri grandmother who adopted her grandson, a little boy with cerebral palsy, can testify:

> We got a wheelchair to push Ace around town in, and we took him for a walk every day unless it rained. We took him to the

park; that's where most of the children go to play, so this gave him playmates. They'd sit and play with him under the tree, and you know, some of those kids were even jealous.

They told Ace he had it made, and they wished that they could ride in a wheelchair. So Ace said, "You can." So I would give them a ride in it. They thought it was neat.

Don't Let Your Child "Get Away with Murder"

Parents often have real questions about how much they should discipline a child with an impairment; it is also one of the most common areas of disagreement between husband and wife. One parent (and interestingly enough, it appears to be the father as often as the mother) wants to "pamper" the child, so that the other, who feels it is necessary to draw the line at some point, is cast in the role of the family "heavy."

That is also true, of course, in families with only "normal" children. What makes any family work best is agreement between the parents on a consistent course of behavior. Ideally, when it comes to relating to the child with a disability, that means that both can be "pamperers," but both can also be "heavy" when necessary, if "heavy" means enforcing certain rules, and a certain amount of discipline. Too much permissiveness with the one child for reasons the others may be too young or simply unwilling to understand or accept can easily turn all the other children in the family against the child being "coddled." "Sometimes we have a tendency to let Jim 'get away with' more than we should," says Mrs. Albert Steinbrenner, of Fort Recovery, Ohio. "A child who is always given whatever he wants whenever he wants it can make life miserable for the whole family."

But the most important argument against giving in to the youngster all the time—"to stop his/her crying," or "because it's easier on the nerves"—is that in the long run it does the child no good.

Once out in the world, even if at first it is only the world of an early intervention program, the child will discover that he or she can no longer get away with destructive behavior and that tantrums no longer are rewarded by lollipops. It's better for parents to teach those lessons before the world does. Ethel Clough was fortunate; "very open and understanding" counseling from a social worker at her daughter's nursery school helped her to understand that "it's easy to have a 'retarded brat,' but it takes some effort to have "a nice young gal with Down's.' I found out that if I wanted the latter, I needed to discipline exactly double that of my 'normal' children."

What is important is that teaching the child to be "one of the family" is also good training for life, perhaps some day, *away* from the family.

Teach Your Child Household Skills

Do not take for granted that a child with a disability, be it mental or physical, even relatively mild, will automatically "pick up" the mechanics of doing household chores by the usual normal process of watching parents or siblings, or even by being shown the process once or twice.

Even if the child says confidently, "I can do it," take nothing for granted. The simplest of activities—sweeping a floor, making a bed—may not only have to be taught, but demonstrated over and over again. For a harassed parent with too little time—and that means nearly every parent of a child with special needs—this is an excellent area in which to try to involve other siblings, after first educating them about the problem, of course.

With many youngsters who have disabilities, the learning process at home or at school may be spotty; some skills will come more easily than others. Those that come hard may test the patience of even the most understanding parent. The real consolation, and motivation, for parents is that every skill mastered early on is an investment for the day when those children may be living in their own apartments or shared dwellings.

Bebe Antell, whose son is now a young adult, has carefully studied the problem of teaching, and making youngsters responsible for, some household chores at an early age. Her suggestions were developed specifically for children with learning disabilities but can readily apply to others:

Start early, by having your very young child do a simple task with one or two components, such as emptying all the wastebaskets in the house and putting the accumulated rubbish into

an outside can. Once that task is mastered, add another one-
or two-step task.

Many children with learning disabilities have problems organizing themselves and their thoughts, the same as any children, only more so. They need to be shown how to manage
their time to accomplish a chore. The trick is to introduce one
chore at a time, but first to analyze the steps and put them
down on paper in sequence. Show your child the first step
until he masters it; then proceed to the next step until the
entire task is ritualized and becomes automatic.

Remember too that timing and readiness are important
factors in the child's learning anything new. Your twelve-year-
old may not be ready to master the complicated chore of
changing bed linen, but at fourteen the task becomes much
simpler for him. Don't stop assigning household chores just
because you run into problems; but it is important to choose
those which accord with the child's competency at that time.

It hardly need be added that not all children with disabilities,
be they mental or physical, can handle every type of chore. But
before parents decide that just because the teaching process isn't
going well the task is impossible for the child ever to master, it
might be a good idea to try to find out whether adults with similar
disabilities *are* able to do that particular chore or task.

Find out whether your child's school or center has special
teachers with expertise in teaching such skills. If it isn't possible
to get the services of such a professional to help with especially
difficult tasks, you might discuss or read about precisely how such
tasks *are* taught to children with similar problems. Then you can
apply that procedure. (This is not the only area in which parents
of a child with a specific disability discover that teaching the child
begins with teaching themselves!)

Teach Your Child Other "Survival Skills"

"We cannot take it for granted," Ms. Antell points out, "that the
disabled child will ever be able to master the mechanics of independent living on his or her own." Psychologists and therapists
who work with adolescents and young adults with impairments
note that many are often buffaloed by such commonplace situations as shopping in a department store or helping themselves in

a self-service grocery. Many young people never seem to have mastered the basics of grooming and may never have shopped for or learned to care for their own clothing.

But the teaching of "survival skills" must start at a much more elementary level. Some of what must be taught is what others, who don't have to deal with such problems, would shrug off as ordinary "common sense." Okay, many parents say, not a few children with special needs have to be *taught* common sense. And it's not likely they can learn it in the classroom, Lori Salvi, whose son has a learning disability, decided.

> We wanted them [his teachers] to spend their time away from his actual schoolwork and help him build his strengths, problem-solve, organize. My husband once made the remark: "Wonderful, they're going to make a speller out of him. But when will they teach him to come in out of the rain?"

Children with disabilities can of course "pick up" certain living skills in just the way other children do. But their learning is more uneven than that of others. Parents frequently note that thirteen-year-olds with a disability may be able to take apart a household gadget and repair it easily, but be unable to tie shoelaces.

Some parents only discover which of the basic "survival skills" their children have *not* acquired along the way when the time comes to use them: "Haven't you ever seen me do such and so?" But for such children, it is important for parents to understand that just seeing isn't learning. Seeing something done is not the same as understanding how to do it any more than, for others, listening to a foreign language half a dozen times qualifies them to speak it. Complexity is a relative concept.

Once parents understand that certain skills have to be taught, however, even the more complicated may be teachable—perhaps only to a limited extent to youngsters with mental deficits—if approached step by step. A particularly important example, important for independence, is budgeting. For most young people with disabilities attempting to live independently, budgeting available funds is one of the most difficult skills to grasp.

That may well relate to the fact that they have never had to earn money. Money is simply something that magically appears from somewhere, usually the parents' bottomless pockets. Spend it, and there's usually more, even if it is occasionally accompanied by grumbling. But even budgeting can be taught.

The first part of the process, because of those previously bottomless pockets, may be conveying a concept: so much is available, and no more. After that, Bebe Antell believes, "with constant repetition, and with training in the use of budget envelopes and pocket calculators, most young people with a variety of disabilities can be taught to keep their finances in order."

Depending on the precise nature of the child's disability, teaching even less complex skills than budgeting may often require an almost infinite amount of patience. Training in such skills should never be allowed to become a one-parent responsibility, not only because even the most loving parent may run out of patience, but because each member of the family "team" may have something special to contribute. In fact, parents should not be very surprised if a sibling, older *or* younger, makes greater headway than they do in certain areas.

Help Your Child to Use His or Her Leisure Productively

Promote activities that require active participation rather than passive "spectating." It may take considerable effort to wean the child away from the television pacifier, but there are several important reasons why the effort is worth it.

First, on its most basic level, any hobby or special interest is a self-teaching tool, which provides stimulation for the development of the child's physical or mental capacities. Second, no one who must be entertained all the time can be even reasonably independent; everyone needs to find, or be taught, one or more satisfying ways to be alone. Third, and perhaps an even greater boost to independence, hobbies and special interests are very often the best way to make and keep friends: someone who has such interests and the associated skills is interesting to be with and to know. And he or she is likely to be identified not so much as "the kid in the wheelchair" as "the kid with the terrific stamp collection."

Parents and siblings may have to take steps to introduce the child to the hobby, rather than expect the interest just to happen. The microcomputer can become a prime tool: it has already made enormous changes in the learning and leisure-time activities of all children, not just those with disabilities. And, with the special adjunct appliances available for children with any of a variety of disabilities, it may become first a window and then a door to the world.

Parents, though, may still have a special role to play. Because children with special needs, no matter what the problem, are more limited than others in their ability to explore and discover and test, parents will often have to take considerable initiative in finding something to catch the child's interest. It may sometimes take a great deal of persistence and patience until the youngster develops any real enthusiasm and can go it alone.

Organize Social Experiences for Your Child

Although going it alone with a hobby may be a great leap forward for some children, even hobbies are meant to be shared. Yet many—it may not be too far from the truth to say most—parents of children with disabilities would admit to considerable unhappiness because their children cannot find, cannot make, cannot keep friends: sometimes the only friends the child has are his or her parents.

Here again, parents ought not merely to sit back and wait for friendships to happen, the way they do for nondisabled children, *without* parental intervention. Once families understand that there is really no substitute for friends and social experiences, they *should* intervene.

Most parents need to make every effort, no matter how contrived, to organize such experiences *for* their children. Because of their disabilities or the resultant special living circumstances, many of these children have trouble making and keeping friendships on their own. It is therefore critical that parents and/or siblings take a hand in "arranging" social contacts, groups, friends, even a "first date."

However much such intervention may seem to operate against the child's eventual integration into the world of "normals," a beginning must be made somehow, even if it means seeking out parents of similar children, even if it means that your child will be with children more disabled than he/she is and will be expected to be helpful and friendly to someone even more vulnerable than he or she.

This doesn't mean that all social experiences should be limited to contact with other children who have disabilities. Wherever

possible, it would be worthwhile to explore the possibility of a
regular summer camp, clubs, or play groups, provided the parents
can be certain that such experiences will be nonthreatening ones.

Parents do sometimes hesitate to thrust their children into
social situations because they are afraid the children will be rebuffed and hurt by some of the encounters. What they have to
weigh in the balance when deciding whether or not to take the
initiative is whether it is preferable for their son or daughter to
grow up a social isolate.

Certainly, there will be callous people—callous children,
too—out there; yet there are also those who will accept the "different" child, the "different" adult. Parents can increase the odds
for success by guiding children to special clubs or organizations
in which their hobbies or other activities will provide an immediate
community of interests. Parents can also arrange parties in their
own home and make certain that their home becomes an inviting
place for other young people to visit. And they can do one thing
more.

Teach the Child Social Skills

It isn't enough to search out social occasions and experiences for
your child and say, "Go." Many adolescents become isolates because they cannot cope with the simplest social situations. They
don't know how to dance. They don't know how to order from
a menu. They don't know how to ask for a date, or what is expected
of them if they get one. They sometimes lack even the most
rudimentary social skills.

Many have never been given an opportunity to *learn* such
skills. It is often an area that "falls through the cracks": parents
assume that children are learning as they go along or that school
is doing something to enhance such skills. But when her son was
ten, Bebe Antell realized that it wasn't happening.

He was a person with social and emotional needs that needed
gratifying. School had taught him to read, but there was no
curriculum in school to teach social skills. It was vital for
youngsters like him to have friends, or at least other children
with whom to play. But they didn't know how to "play." In
fact, even before they could be taught how to play they nearly

all had to be taught simply how to get along with other children.

Whether it is younger children, who don't know how to get along or play with others, or older children, adolescents who lack the simple social graces, parents should never take for granted that their children will learn either by watching, or by normal interaction with, their peers. Like household and "survival" skills, these abilities are easily grasped by most other children by the time they become teenagers but must frequently be taught to those who have an impairment.

The Long Island mother of a twenty-three-year-old born with expressive aphasia is convinced that this is the one area of life in which she might have done more to prepare her son for independence. As the one who had to make a great many decisions for her son, she feels generally satisfied with her efforts and would, she says, do it all again the same way, with an exception:

I would make one change. I would spend more money on social skills as opposed to academic skills, because in the final analysis these youngsters need to be able to fit into a social world as adults, to become adept at the skills which would help them later on to fit in with so-called "normals" in the social world.

And that, in essence, is what all the ideas and suggestions families have about helping a child with a disability become more independent are about: to help that child "fit into" the world and survive.

20

"Our Ultimate Goal: Full Inclusion"

The Unfinished Magna Cartas

When Public Law 94–142, the Education for All Handicapped Children Act, was passed in 1975 after a long and persistent campaign by parent advocates, it was hailed enthusiastically as the Magna Carta for the education of children with disabilities. Yet well into the nineties, despite a number of major amendments to fill gaps and close loopholes, and the expenditure of more than $70 billion in federal funds, all too often families find they cannot take that education for granted. "My greatest pain is that parents are still having to fight to get what should rightfully be their child's by law," says Florene Poyadue, executive director/CEO of Parents Helping Parents in San Jose, California.

"Things move very slowly, true," she adds, "but families still have to struggle. I'd feel better if they had to struggle and there were no law there. But there *is* a law, and it says that your kid should have certain rights, and they don't."

Others who have been longtime advocates for children's and disability rights across the country feel the same way. Granted that "94–142 was a major piece of legislation and an excellent law, rightly called a 'quiet revolution' for chidren with disabilities," says Paula Goldberg, co-director of Minneapolis's PACER Center.

"But I think we are still having to make sure the law is implemented. There are still cases of school districts where the law is not being followed, and kids are not getting the 'free appropriate public education' the law calls for. In large part that's because the parents still don't know—and are never told about—the rights the law gave them."

Nevertheless, we've come a long way from the exclusionary policies that were not uncommon before 94–142, when Congress found that more than a million children and young people with disabilities were totally excluded from the public schools of this country. In those "dark old days," which parents of an earlier generation still remember with pain, disabled children were frequently at the mercy of the decisions, or whims, of school principals or school boards—with no recourse, no appeal.

One writer called them "benevolent dictatorships" and noted that "school systems reigned supreme then. . . . They dispensed education to some students, excluded others, provided one program and disregarded others." Parents of children with mental retardation or physical disabilities were routinely told their children "didn't belong in school," and "would be much better off at home or in an institution where they could really help them." A parent relates one incident from those days:

> When our son Ken—who is legally blind and has other disabilities—came of kindergarten age, we took him to school to enroll him. The principal had a sympathetic face, but when we finished describing Ken's learning problems, he looked at us dubiously and said, "I've never heard of anything like this. We'll just put him in the kindergarten class and see how he makes out." "What if he doesn't 'make out'?" we asked him. "In that case, you'll just have to take him out of school"; those, of course, were the days before "special classes." "But what do we do with Ken then?" The principal shrugged his shoulders: "I don't know what to tell you."

PL 94–142 did more than unbar the schoolhouse doors and let the children in. It gave certain rights to children with disabilities and their parents or guardians that are worth recalling:

◆ The right to a free appropriate public education, with all necessary supportive services, for all young people between the ages of five and twenty-one, no matter what their disability.

❖ The right to receive this education in the "least restrictive environment" (LRE) possible for each child, to discourage both the practice of segregating children with disabilities from others ("because it's better for them") and the perception of educating the disability rather than the child.

❖ The right to an Individualized Education Program (IEP) for each child, listing specific educational goals and objectives along with a timetable for them, with a proviso that the IEP be reviewed at least once a year. Parent participation in the evolution of the child's IEP has been termed the *core element* of the law.

❖ The right, in the case of parent dissatisfaction with the school's implementation of the law, to an impartial "due process" procedure, a series of steps available for parents to appeal against evaluations, placement decisions, or programs with which they disagreed, or (what turned out to be the most frequent source of action) against failure by the school to provide "related services" necessary for the child to *benefit* from the other rights.

Looking back, it is not surprising that parents felt that the new law was at long last the Magna Carta children with disabilities had needed. The immediate result was that hundreds of thousands of youngsters who had previously been "outcast children" were quickly able to enter "special classes" in public schools throughout the country. Legally it armed parents—previously supplients— with an arsenal of guarantees for the education of their children with special needs alongside the other children in the neighborhood.

It soon turned out however, that 94–142 was not the finish line but the starting gate. There were foot-dragging school systems; there were too many areas left vague or left incomplete or left out.

"It was such breakthrough legislation," says Colleen Wieck, executive director of the Minnesota Developmental Disabilities Council and past president of TASH, The Association for Persons with Severe Handicaps, "that we couldn't anticipate all the ramifications—and so we had to "fix up' what was missing and what was not working quite right.

"Our experiences kept piling up and our understanding kept developing so that we had to add whole new age groups and new categories. And it may be that changing circumstances and services may force us to go back for even more amendments than have already been required up to now."

"A Little Widening and Tooling"

Patricia McGill Smith, the executive director of the National Parent Network on Disabilities (NPND), calls it in part "a little widening and tooling of things that were really necessary from the beginning but didn't get in when the law was first passed. And then when you live with something you learn what has to be strengthened and shored up.

"For example, we wanted to make parents the key component of the child's team from scratch, but the law didn't provide the mechanism for it then. That didn't happen until ten years later in the Infants and Toddlers Act, when the mechanism was provided through the IFSP—the Individualized Family Service Program."

There were a succession of amendments to 94–142. Those added in 1983 provided incentives for preschool, early intervention, and transition programs. In 1986 they lowered the mandatory age for beginning special education as a part of the public school system to three and established the "infants and toddlers" program for children with diagnosed diabilities from birth on.

A landmark change, previously described, amended the 1984 Carl D. Perkins Vocational Training Act in 1990 to incorporate assistive technology as an aid for students with disabilities. That same year, PL 94–142 became IDEA—the Individuals with Disabilities Education Act. Just as the "infants and toddlers" amendments had added services for children at the birth end of the age scale, IDEA now focused on older students with disabilities. The incorporation of assistive devices and other services in transition programs is intended to stretch IDEA's effects well beyond the school years.

"I Don't Want to Sue"

Parents continued to encounter administrators, school boards, and even staff, however, who were ignoring or narrowing down some of these hard-won rights. The result was that disputes once confined to the principal's office sometimes went to "due process," on occasion even going beyond the school system into the legal system.

As a result, court rulings were required to confirm certain rights for children with disabilities that had already appeared to be implicit in the language of the amended PL 94–142. For example, in the *Rowley* case in 1982, the United States Supreme Court had to rule that schools must provide *sufficient* related and support services for children with disabilities actually to *benefit* from their right to an education. In the 1988 *Honig* case the same court decided that a child could not be permanently excluded from the classroom unilaterally by school authorities, even for supposedly "dangerous or disruptive behavior." School personnel were also forbidden by the justices in the 1989 *Timothy W.* decision from barring youngsters on the grounds that they were supposedly "uneducable."

As late as the summer of 1991, a federal judge in New Hampshire had to order a school district to stop threatening to switch a twelve-year-old boy from regular to special education unless his parents medicated him to control his behavior. That same summer Philadelphia officials were urging parents to sue the state of Pennsylvania if they wanted preschool for their children. But one mother said, "I don't want to sue the state—I just want preschool for my son."

"Budget-Busting" or Underfunding?

Such attempts by school boards and local authorities to shift the costs of special education have been a constant since 1975, antedating the current recession, and to a certain extent it is understandable. It is not merely run-of-the-mill grumbling by backward communities about "unanticipated costs," or accusations that parents who press for special education are "budget busters." Such programs have been "grossly underfunded" by the federal government, charged Major Owens, the chairman of the House of Representatives Select Education Subcommittee, at the 1990 hearings on IDEA.

Even before the successful effort by recent administrations to shift the cost of programs dealing with social and educational needs to state and local budgets, "there was never enough money from the federal government," insists Paula Goldberg, "The law has never been fully funded." When Congress passed PL 94–142, "federal support [for special education and related services] was supposed to peak at 40 percent," the American Speech-Language-Hearing Association has declared, but it "has never gone above

12 percent." In fact, in 1990 the share appropriated was only 9 percent.

"Especially now," Paula Goldberg adds, "when local school districts are facing a financial crunch, parent groups are going to have to mobilize their energies to press Congress and the Administration for adequate funding." Also, given the continuing fiscal problems, the danger is that some budget authorities will not be content with shortchanging programs for people with special needs but will actually initiate benefit rollbacks.

Because the medical needs of youngsters with disabilities are often as great, if not greater than, their educational needs, it is hardly necessary to point out how disastrous proposed cutoffs of benefits may be in some cases. "Medical costs for such children are often a very real problem for their families," Florene Poyadue points out. "A local station in California has already done a program about people actually leaving this country with their sick children and going up to Canada for care they couldn't afford here."

Even without health-care rollbacks, not just poor families but even some middle-class families are already suffering under the burden of medical costs. These are families whose youngsters have been rejected for coverage by private health insurance companies because of "pre-existing conditions," including some that "pre-existed" while the child was still a fetus but were only diagnosed later. Such families are a significant segment of the 35,000,000–40,000,000 Americans without health insurance who might hope to benefit from one of the several national health plans now under discussion. It is small wonder that the child disability movement is among the strongest advocates for some such plan.

At a minimum, the plan might contain provisions similar to those in a bill passed by the New York State Legislature in the summer of 1992 (to take effect April 1, 1993). Under its provisions, commercial insurance companies must provide health insurance to anyone who applies—no matter how sick—and are also forbidden to charge higher rates to applicants because of their age, sex, or medical condition.

Training Parents for Advocacy

Parent advocacy advanced PL 94–142,—and was advanced by it. A major unlegislated result of that law has been the vast increase in parent activity, including the development of parent-to-parent networks and parent information, training, and advocacy groups (See Appendix B), not just locally but as part of a nationwide network.

"Before 94–142," says PACER co-director Marge Goldberg, "parents didn't have nearly as great a role as they do now, because the laws didn't give them any authority. And to tell the truth, most weren't equipped for it, because they didn't have nearly enough information. Today, as a result of the existence of parent groups and networks, parents can easily access information and resources and training in advocacy that weren't there ten years ago."

Pointing to the many new laws affecting children with special needs that were a product of the eighties and nineties, Paula Goldberg emphasizes that "the enactment of any new law is just the beginning of a process that leads to its implementation at the community level. Every day we get calls from parents who are hungry for information about IDEA and who are totally unaware of the rights they have. I don't think there will ever be a time we can stop reaching out."

A Harris poll conducted in the eighties confirmed that three out of five parents of children with disabilities said they knew little or nothing about their rights under the special education laws. "One reason we have to keep doing the same things over and over," Patricia Smith says, "is that there are always new children and new families. The problems are always different, but always the same. All new parents go through what others have gone through."

A Canadian mother who says she has "paid her dues" adds, "Sometimes we have to be reminded that someone before us, probably a very scared but 'tough' mother, once pushed for the services we now take for granted. But there are still barriers to remove, obstacles to clear away, paths to plow for my son and other sons and daughters."

Passing on such accumulated experience is a major contribution of the 350 or more grass-roots parent-to-parent programs that have sprung up around the country. Their purpose is to link a parent who has already "been there" with a new family, to help it over the inevitable rough spots. One member of such a group calls it "just paying back for the kind of help *we* got from other parents when we really needed it." And another adds, "We don't duplicate what professionals do; we complement it. We can't do what they do—and they can't do what we do, because parents speak the same language, and that means that mothers who are total strangers one minute become sisters the next."

That often means that parents give parents hope after a purely medical prognosis has left them with very little. "Parents are told over and over again," says Jackie Brand, a cofounder of the Alliance for Technology Access, "to have 'realistic' expectations for their kids. That's one of the biggest disservices professionals can do to families. Because when they say 'realistic,' they really mean 'low,' and that comes across as 'Don't expect your child to achieve.' "

Technology's "Brightest Promises"

From her own experience in dealing with that kind of negative outlook, Brand describes how she found a way to deal with it:

> In my case, it is technology that allows me to have all kinds of "unrealistic" expectations for my kid. Maybe technology is the concrete kind of thing that allows you to throw that kind of pessimism out the window. We can raise the expectations of so many by incorporating assistive aids and devices into the lives of people.
>
> We need to move from a basic general awareness that technology may be valuable to making it available to children and adults who need it so they can find out if it works for them. We have to insist that being provided with assistive technology is part of the civil rights of all people with disabilities who can use it, a matter of right for any person who can benefit from it.

Senator Tom Harkin, chairman of the U.S. Senate Subcommittee on Disability, feels that in recent years such technology "has emerged as a critical support for many people which can assist them in leading lives of dignity, choice, and independence."

Paula Goldberg agrees that such aids and devices "will help young people to become independent. She also believes that

> costs will go down for it so that technology will become more accessible, both in school and at home. I think it will result in employers hiring more young people with physical disabilities or mental problems, so that transition planning in the school years will be more jobs-directed and focus more intensely on life *after* the end of school.

> That means that at the high school level we need to prepare students for the time when they will leave, prepare them in all the necessary ways. Our ultimate goal is the full inclusion of young people in all parts of society, so that when they graduate or leave school they can become part of the community just like other young people—in their work, in housing, in all of the social and other aspects of society.

94-142's "Unfulfilled Dream"

No longer are hundreds of thousands of children and young people excluded from public education, as they were before the enactment of PL 94–142. But neither are they fully included, as those who fought for the passage of the law hoped, perhaps naively, they would be. Before 94-142, children with disabilities often had to say goodbye to their school-going siblings and neighborhood friends at their own front doors; now they may still do so—at the front doors of the schoolhouse, as they are shunted off to special classes and resource rooms, away from the others, bussed off to an entirely different schoolhouse outside their neighborhoods.

But as the decision in *Brown v. Board of Education* relating to students of color has attested, such segregated education is not equal education. Separation from their peers helps to create a lifelong psychological barrier ("I'm different"). Educating children with disabilities for roles as disabled and additionally handicapped adults leaves them educationally and psychologically unprepared to participate in "regular" society.

Speak to leading parent advocates about what heads the agenda for children with special needs and they are virtually unanimous on two points: the ultimate goal is full inclusion in society; and from preschool through transition planning, their education must point toward that goal.

That was what many advocates felt PL 94-142 would automatically accomplish. Patricia Smith, for one, calls full inclusion "the most unfulfilled dream" of the law. She speaks with some authority. The organization she heads, the National Parent Network on Disabilities, founded in 1987, joins parent information, training, and advocacy groups all over the continental United States as well as Alaska and Puerto Rico (see Appendix B).

"Even now there are still educators, politicians, and administrators entrenched in their traditional beliefs and unwilling to 'dream dreams' " she says, "and even parents who do not believe in their hearts that kids with disabilities can be educated alongside other kids—and that's because they haven't experienced it."

She cites her own experience with her daughter, Jane, who was admitted into a regular high school, but only into two special education classrooms—"for safety reasons." Behavior problems resulted; they disappeared when Jane was included in two regular classes, plus vocational training the rest of the school day.

"I wonder why parents who have tasted the fruits of integration still have to fight for it every step of the way," Smith says with some bitterness. "Isn't it time for the walls of segregation to come down and let our children in?"

"Children must have the right, no matter what their disabilities are," Martha Ziegler says, "to be in the regular classroom with peers their own age, and with appropriate support services." Ms. Ziegler is executive director of the Technical Assistance to Parent Programs network, Federation for Children with Special Needs, based in Boston.

"And not only in the classroom," she adds. "In the classroom, on the playground, wherever the other children are. We have to see this from the perspective of preparing them for full inclusion in society. All of us, parents, teachers, and administrators, are working on it, but we're not there yet."

Getting there may still take considerable doing, Colleen Wieck believes. "Public education must fundamentally change," she says, "in order to produce students with disabilities who graduate with the competence to live, work, learn, and enjoy life in the community—with the necessary supports, of course. That is why we have to make sure that the national administration's program for educational reform, AMERICA 2000, when it says 'all children' means our children too."

AMERICA 2000 — "Inclusive Enough?"

In April 1991 President George Bush and U.S. Education Secretary Lamar Alexander announced an ambitious set of goals for education to be achieved by the year 2000. "AMERICA 2000 calls for a revolution in American education," Assistant Education Secretary Robert R. Davila declared that summer. Writing in *OSERS in Print,* he called the initiative "an innovative, far-reaching plan to revitalize the nation's schools, workplaces, and communities" and declared that he and Secretary Alexander were bent on "ensuring that people with disabilities are included in all aspects of the reform movement."

Some in the disability movement were not altogether persuaded, however. In the *Journal of Visual Impairment and Blindness,* Christine E. Pawelski, a national education consultant for the American Foundation for the Blind, pointed out that "the AMERICA 2000 booklet . . . does not even mention the rights of children with disabilities." And "the emphasis on content areas (i.e., reading, writing, and arithmetic) . . . excludes the millions of Americans who will *never* achieve in those areas."

Christopher Button, writing in the United Cerebral Palsy Association's *Word from Washington,* noted that "although the Administration indicates that their AMERICA 2000 strategy is open and inclusive enough for all students to be accommodated, UCPA Governmental Activities staff are concerned that the proposed activities are not appropriate for students with disabilities and . . . could ultimately result in the exclusion of students with disabilities from education reform initiatives."

Inclusion *must* begin during the school years, Colleen Wieck stresses:

> We want the integration of children with disabilities at the earliest possible time, because we want those children prepared for the future.
>
> We have to be sure that their schooling is relevant to their adult life. We have to move on from paper compliance with 94–142 and with IEPs to what is actually happening to the child as a student and as a person. And that means that we want school curricula that enhance their ability to live and work as independently as possible as adults.

Adds John D. Kemp, UCPA national executive director, "The next generation of persons with disabilities should have every right to succeed or fail, rights our fellow able-bodied citizens take for granted." Achieving that "right" was behind the long struggle of people in the disability movement, which culminated in the passage of a long-needed law in 1990.

The Americans with Disabilities Act

When President Bush signed the Americans with Disabilities Act (ADA) on July 26, 1990, he said, "Let the shameful walls of exclusion come tumbling down." The U.S. Senate's leading proponent of the law, Senator Tom Harkin, declared that "With the passage of the ADA, we as a society make a pledge that every child with disabilities will have the opportunity to maximize his or her potential to live proud, productive, and prosperous lives in the mainstream of our society." Representative Steny Hoyer, who took the lead on behalf of the legislation in the House of Representatives, called ADA "the most significant civil rights legislation since the Civil Rights Act of 1964." It has also been termed "the twentieth-century equivalent of the Emancipation Proclamation."

ADA was passed by overwhelming votes in both the House and Senate. According to Harkin, the purpose of the act is "to provide clear, strong, consistent, enforceable standards addressing all forms of discrimination against individuals on the basis of disability," whether stemming from prejudice, thoughtlessness, or indifference. It prohibits such discrimination in employment, public service, transportation, public accommodations, and telecommunications.

The prohibitions are to be phased in at various dates, with some provisions in effect in 1992. This offers immediate hope that the schools' transition planning will increasingly result in positive outcomes, that young people who acquire job or career skills during their school years will find employment "out there" for which they are qualified.

Ed Roberts, president of the World Institute on Disability, has hailed ADA as "by far the best act we've passed relating to disability. It gives people like me a kind of empowerment: I'm not going to let anyone discriminate against me. I have a lot of talent, I have a lot of things to contribute, I don't want to live on welfare, I'd like to earn my own living and pay taxes. We're talking a lot more now not about what society owes us, but about our responsibility to society."

The proof of that "empowerment," however, will only be seen some years down the road, in statistics showing that a greater percentage of people with disabilities are employed, in the experiences of men and women with disabilities living and socializing in the community, in the increase in ramps and curb cuts and elevators and wider doorways making life in the community more accessible to people with impairments.

Needed: "Curb Cuts in People's Minds"

If the experience of families with a child who is disabled with the "Magna Carta" of PL 94-142 is any criterion, however, community inclusion won't just happen, any more than has classroom inclusion, without people determined to make it happen. The prejudice and discrimination against people with disabilities that existed the day before the Americans with Disabilities Act became law didn't simply disappear the moment the law was signed.

Much has changed since the Education for All Handicapped Children Act became law in 1975; but a lot hasn't. In the process of making many things happen, parent advocates have learned a lot too. About reaching "hearts and minds," for example, a process in which laws on the books play a catalytic role.

"Legislation pushes things along," says Marge Goldberg, PACER co-director. "But the attitudes that made them necessary in the first place are hard to change. First we get the law; the law doesn't change things overnight, but after a while the pressure of the law changes awareness and then it does change attitudes." Patricia Smith adds:

It's an attitudinal change that needs to happen, for children with disabilities in the schools as well as adults out in the world. I think of the implementation of IDEA's educational mandates and ADA's prohibition of discrimination like the mandate that every sidewalk curb in this country is supposed to be cut for access by people in wheelchairs by 1996.

Well, I think you need curb cuts in people's minds so that new or different ideas have easier access. Perhaps by the year 2000 kids will have all the opportunities they're supposed to have, but parents will still have to be vigilant. Because our task of educating society is never-ending.

That doesn't seem very long from Florene Poyadue's perspective as an African-American: "Ten years is certainly not a long enough time to effect the mental changes, the attitude changes. Look how long we've been struggling as people of color to get that kind of attitude change.

"People forget that just twenty-five years ago *we* were South Africa in *this* country, and it took us a hundred years just to get from slavery to South Africa, *after* the Emancipation Proclamation. Now it's been twenty-five years from our being South Africa, but people are still having a hard time with this attitude change."

Paula Goldberg is somewhat more optimistic about how quickly the changes will take place, feeling that "in the forseeable future the situation of children with disabilities *will* change and improve. Society's attitudes will also change, as more people with disabilities are included in more aspects of our daily lives and become more visible, more a part of everyday activities."

Some practical steps have to be taken first, if children with special needs are to take that future step from the school to the community, she points out. "We have not yet begun to make the same sort of 'quiet revolution' in the adult service system that was accomplished with the enactment of PL 94-142 for children in school. There is nothing comparable to help adults out in the community."

Martha Ziegler not only agrees but feels such a system might be modeled after existing community services for older people, with some improvements—perhaps a one-stop center where men and women with disabilities could find hot meals, recreation programs, daycare services, medical attention, and job-finding or other counseling as needed.

"Hang In There"

If you're a new parent of a child with a disability, or a young parent, or an older parent faced with new and unanticipated problems, it won't be easy to focus on such fifteen-or-twenty-years-away problems and solutions. You are likely to be totally involved with the here and now, perhaps finding it difficult to cope with that gloom-and-doom prognosis from "someone who should know, if anyone does."

If so, take some comfort from Ed Roberts. A quadriplegic who uses a wheelchair and a ventilator, he is the respected president of the World Institute for Disability and a leader in the disability community worldwide.

> If I had one piece of advice for parents it would be this: Be very leery of what doctors and health care people and other professionals tell you about your kid. Because somehow so many of them tend to be extremely pessimistic, to overemphasize the negative effects of the disability, whatever it is.
>
> Take, for instance, a child born with Down syndrome. You can't know for at least a year how much of a problem it will be. But some may tell you, "Get rid of the kid. Put him away in an institution." Or of someone with a physical disability: "He's helpless and hopeless." No one can predict that.
>
> What is most important is that you make your kid feel good about himself or herself. You have to give your child confidence, the feeling that he or she is an OK kid, that having a disability is not the worst thing in life, that they *can* have higher expectations for themselves.
>
> And you have to feel that confidence, too. You have to believe—and help your child believe—that no matter how severe the disability, your child will one day be able to live independently, live and work and be a useful contributing member of society."

For parents who may find that hard to believe, one final word from Martha Ziegler, parent advocate, parent leader, and mother of a grown daughter with autism who moved out of her mother's house and into a group home at age twenty-eight. "Hang in there," Martha says, "even on your worst days. There's much more hope for your child than you can possibly believe. I know."

21

"It's Okay, All the Ways I Feel"
The Rights of Parents

One last area must be addressed: parents not as parents but as people.

It is all too common for parents to be so totally caught up in the daily pressures and priorities of meeting the needs of a child with a disability that they forget that they themselves are human beings with needs. If it were possible to combine and encapsulate the experiences of the many parents who have offered to share them, it would perhaps be this final counsel:

The parent who does not remember to be human does not always help the child to become more so. More than any other parents, you need to stay in touch with yourself and constantly, whenever necessary, to reaffirm your humanness by the exercise of these shared human rights:

The Right to Cry

The first right of any parent who learns that his or her child has been born with a permanent disability or has become disabled is to grieve, to mourn, to feel sorry for herself or himself, to agonize over the question, Why me? Instead of the joy and celebration you expected during all those months of waiting, you find yourself caught up in a period of mourning for the child, in fact for two children: the child you have and the "perfect child" you lost. And sometimes the pain becomes unbearable.

It helps to let it out, say those who have been through it, to cry, yell, scream, not to hold in all the fear and hurt and anxiety. It is nothing to hide or to be ashamed of: you are not the only one who hurts. Talk to those others. They can tell you: this too will pass.

It is OK to grieve. There is a time for grief, and it is necessary. And I would say that the agony passes: as one gives up the dreams and accepts the reality of the child, whatever it is, one gradually begins to enjoy each gain the child makes and take pleasure in whatever he can do. That's the world of acceptance. It's not a bad world, necessarily. It's just that getting there is so very hard.

Know that we really all hurt at first, and it didn't seem like things would ever be the same, and in a way they're not. But after ten years, I laugh at jokes, I still jog, I go to movies. Our lives went on.

But I do still cry sometimes, not always. And I still wish my daughter could walk and go to school without special help (so does she!). But it's okay, the way I feel, all the ways I feel.

The Right to Be Angry and Not Be Ashamed of It

Understand, with a part of you, that life is not always fair and that no one hands out guarantees for a perfect life or perfect children. But understand with another part of you that that is no excuse for what happened to you. You have a right to blame God, to demand to know why He has forsaken you, and even, at times, to hate the child: for being born imperfect, for changing your life, for destroying your dream.

You need to know that the anger will also pass, and that it is not your own exclusive anger, but one that thousands, tens of thousands of others have felt, feel, will feel.

After all of the counseling, no one ever bothered to tell me that the anger, rage, and frustration, unfortunately directed at times toward the child, were normal. I was not a rotten person, or going off my rocker, but a human being, reacting to a loss in a very human way.

Though anger is acceptable, understand that you must not allow it to possess and destroy you. And you will discover other parents who accept your anger because they have shared it; or simply people close to you, who will also listen and accept your feelings because they accept you.

One thing I found that helped me was that when friends said, "I know what you're going through," in that real caring, sympathy voice, I would stare at them with my Irish eyes and say, "No you don't, but I'll tell you what and how I feel right now." And after I did this, I felt better. And believe it or not, my friends appreciated it, because then they *did* have some kind of idea of where my thoughts and pain and anger were coming from. It helped.

The Right Not to Feel Guilty

The first thing to understand is that having a child with a disability is nobody's fault. It just happens. It is pointless to waste precious time and to torture yourself by looking back on your pregnancy, the delivery, whether there were any known disabilities in the child's ancestry, whether or not you wanted the child, trying to find out how you sinned. That kind of child can happen to the purest, best, nicest, right-thinkingest family in the world. Don't torture yourself by continuing to look for signs that it is God's judgment: what kind of God would disable a baby to get back at *you?*

Don't feel that you're being punished by God for some reason or other by having a handicapped child. I've considered that myself, but it happens, or could happen, to anyone. It's a terrible mistake by Nature, which I wish could never be possible; but unfortunately it does happen and did happen and you have to be strong and deal with it.

And it is just as wasteful to feel guilty about the way, all the ways, you feel. It is normal, it is OK to feel depressed about what has happened to your life or about the baby's future, or even to have "bad feelings" and hostile thoughts about the child. Only the most angelic of parents never ever has had them.

They are only a problem, they only become "bad," if you can't get past them and over them, because then they can become paralyzing. It can get worse; you can go around and around inside your skull: you can feel ashamed of feeling guilty about feeling hostile. If talking with your spouse (who may have those feelings, too), your friends, or your family doesn't help, seek out a professional: your doctor, a counselor, a therapist. Most parents, you may be surprised to learn, have need of such help at one point or other in their lives.

Once you get over feeling guilty about having brought an "imperfect" child—a "spoiled" human being—into the world, you are on your way to accepting the child for who he or she is and helping others to accept the child too, as is. Perhaps this will help you to get on accepting: why should anyone else if you don't?

To other parents who have just learned their child is handicapped, I would say: Even though this isn't the "normal" child you expected, this child has real value in this world.

The Right to Feel You're Doing the Best You Can

You must tell yourself that you are coping with an enormously difficult situation the best way you know how. You have the right not to feel, and not to let professionals or friends or family make you feel, that the child's problems or difficulties are the result of your failure or inadequacy. You are entitled not to beat yourself sick over what you're *not* doing.

I used to have a big guilt feeling whenever I was not giving therapy to my son. If I was doing something for myself, or doing housework, I felt I should be working with my son instead. Now I realize it's not just the minutes of actual physical exercise: my son's therapy is the total way I care for him.

You have the right to feel good about your efforts: only you know how much.

We are doing all we can for Kelly. We try not to miss any avenue of help, and knowing several years from now that we tried everything possible for her, we ourselves will feel good about any future decisions.

You have every right to feel confident that you can look back at some future time and know in your heart that no one could have done more.

I may not always have been right in doing what is best for my child, but it was *my* best, and I can live with myself, and I don't have trouble sleeping at night.

The Right to Make Your Own Decisions

Only the family can decide what is best for the child and the family, but in the beginning, parents often have so little faith in their own competence and judgment that they automatically accept the "decisions" of the experts: therapists, physicians, health care professionals, educators, or others. It becomes a habit: accepting as "decisions" what are in fact no more than recommendations.

With added experience and growing competence, every parent needs to recognize that she or he has the right to listen to, and benefit from, the best professional and other counsel and guidance available and then *not* accept it, if it doesn't seem right for the child, *that* child.

When your child is having OT [occupational therapy], PT, and speech therapy, plus a nursery school teacher and all the doctors you take her to, you have a great many people giving you advice. Your head swims for a while, because you try to do what everyone says, until you realize that it is *your* child, and you know what's best for her, and what your family can handle. I do for my child what I feel she needs and weed out all the rest.

There comes, gradually or suddenly, the realization that when it comes to *your* child, you too are an expert, perhaps the most expert of all.

I have learned that I must be in charge of everything. I have sometimes chosen to disregard the advice of professionals; I am a "professional" too, a mother. I take everyone's opinions, remarks—good or bad—into consideration, and then I make the decision, taking all of Sean into account.

The Right to Respect

You deserve respect for your feelings, your opinions, your priorities, for you as a person.

It is easy for some to overlook parents' feelings, to be heroes in someone else's situation:

The professionals would say, "As you can tell, I have no children, but you should do this, this, and this." I always felt when they said things like that that they needed personal experience before handing out advice.

If professionals can't really put themselves into any parent's shoes or understand the kind of life you lead, if their advice comes across as easy to say and hard to do, you have the right to demand that they pay attention to your opinions, not wave them aside.

You have the right to insist that educators take into account *your* priorities for your child, even when you emphasize survival strategies and socialization rather than alphabetization.

Whether you have a Ph.D. or never finished high school, you have the right to demand that professionals respect you as a co-worker and a peer in a joint effort, helping the child.

No offense to any professional who may happen to read this, but I resent most professionals I've run into treating parents as nonprofessionals and incompetent idiots. This attitude has bothered me very much all the years I've had to be associated with special ed. I think professionals should realize that parents are intelligent human beings too.

The Right to Get Help

Parents have the right to receive help without being ashamed to ask for it. No family that has a child with special needs can manage entirely by itself, especially if there are other children. There is always too much to do: no way to care for the child with the disability and still prepare meals, do the laundry, clean the house, carpool, shop, spend time with the other children—the full daily routine plus. So whenever people ask whether they can be helpful, *always* say yes.

You'll lose 90 percent of your friends and relatives that way, the ones who were just being polite and thought that *you'd* be too polite to accept. But the ones who actually do what they've just offered to do and then (praise be!) offer again, will become your lifelong friends (even if they are already your life-long relatives).

But don't feel that you must wait for somone to offer. Don't wait to "burn out" because you didn't want to "impose" on people who shouldn't have waited for you to ask.

I am caged between home, work, doctors, and special schools. I need volunteer services—to help drive my daughter to school, to babysit on occasion: I can't even take her shopping, as she can't sit in a carriage. I am still in need of help. Volunteers, where are you?

Ask for the help you need, not just from friends and relatives. Look for other parents with whom to exchange babysitting, carpooling, shopping. Look for agencies that may be able to provide respite care, daytime assistance, mother's helpers. Build a support network: some will be "too busy," but you'd be surprised how many people *will* help, if asked.

If someone I knew had a disabled child, I would cook for them, run errands, offer rides, babysit (very important), clean their house, etc. etc. These are the things that mean the most

to us. People for the most part are wonderful, and I will always
be grateful for that.

The Right to Have and Be a Family

You are entitled to all the joys of family life. Having a child with
a disability does not have to mean being less of a family, or no
family at all.

I am well aware that the stress of a handicapped child can cause
many marriages to fall apart; in our case, I think that it was
love of John that kept us together.

No one else can offer family members what they can offer
each other. It is natural that the major responsibility for keeping
the family together generally falls on the mother, but it ought not
to be a one-woman show. The burden of care for a child with
special needs becomes considerably lighter in families in which
husband and siblings share it, and all family members join in
teaching the child that he or she is part of a family and must
respect the rights of others.

Parents can strengthen the family by refusing to give up family
celebrations, parties, picnics, trips, and all the other joys that
families customarily share; by reassuring the other children that
spending so much time with the one child does not mean loving
the others less, and proving it by making special times for the
others, when the quality of the time together compensates for the
lesser quantity; and by finding special times for each other.

It's *hard* to take care of a severely handicapped child, and
there are days when you just wish you could give up. But in
addition, you have to make time for yourself and your spouse;
and you can't neglect your other children either. It's a lot of
work and extra time, but I can say that you *can* become a
closer, stronger family, as we have.

The Right to Go on Living

You have the right to be a human being, the right to keep as many as possible of the interests and involvements you both had before the child and the disability came along to change your life.

You have the right to walk away from the child once in a while; the right to get away from everything, alone or with your spouse or a friend, for a few minutes, a day, even a week: no parent can live forever in total togetherness with any child—disabled or not—without beginning to feel more like a prisoner than a parent.

You have the right to pay attention to your own health and well-being, mental and physical, to spend some part of each day caring for *yourself*, the right to organize some part of your life—even if only a small part—selfishly, to your own satisfaction and not necessarily anyone else's. You have never needed opportunities for relaxation and a little pleasure as much as you do now, precisely when the opportunities are fewer. You are entitled to these small and momentary distractions, however much you may worry about what's happening to your child, however much you may feel that you can't afford the time or the money, however much you may feel that your family or friends or neighbors may misinterpret what you're doing.

You have the right not always to be a parent, the right to become a student, to become an activist, to enjoy a hobby, to have an interest or a dozen interests that do *not* include the child, yet in no way detract from your love and concern for the child: there is nothing so healing, so energizing, as such an occasional *other* concern.

You can accept that you must continue doing whatever is necessary and possible to provide for your child's well-being, but you must also realize that you can be most helpful if you do not allow yourself to "burn out," if you also have a life of your own.

You can accept that you must continue to meet your child's special needs, but understand that you also have the right not to define your life entirely by them.

The Right to Be Human, and Only Human

I am lucky to have a pediatrician I can be honest with. If I get to feeling that I just can't stand my child one more minute, or feel that I could be abusive, or I wish that I could give up my responsibilities to my child and just leave, I can talk to the doctor about it, and he helps me to understand that I am not superhuman.

I also find that being honest with my child at difficult times helps me cope, and it appears to help him understand why I lose my sanity at times. I try to let my child know when I have had a bad day, and that I might be a little less tolerant than usual, and when I need to be left alone. You would be surprised how much a child can understand. By the same token, I try to detect when my child needs more warmth and understanding, when *he* has had a bad day.

I think I've tried too hard sometimes to be Supermom, which is harder on you in the long run. I'm beginning to start doing things for myself again.

I really don't fill my brain or my life with thoughts of Down syndrome. I go along and live my life and accept the joys as they come. I am happy. I am not glad the kids are retarded; one has nothing to do with the other. I get bothered when people marvel at me because I am coping with my "burden" so well. To me it's not a burden; it's my life.

I do for my kids whatever it is they need, and it becomes our way and our life-style. I am not Supermom, I am not an angel, I am not blessed by heaven with the patience and love to be a great mother to two handicapped kids. I am not perfect. I am just me.

The Right to Laugh

You have the right to laugh, even if you thought you never would again.

You have the right to have—or to develop, or to cultivate—

a sense of humor, especially for those moments when it hurts too much to cry. Nobody can continue to cope with the daily routine of caring for a child with special needs without a sense of humor.

You deserve to joke, to fool around, and sometimes even to be silly—alone, with the disabled child, with others in the family, or with close friends—without feeling guilty about it: life can become terribly grim with everyone walking around on tiptoes, as though it were forever a house in mourning. Laughing, even with a child in the room who has a severe disability, is not a criminal act, not a faux pas, not something to feel ashamed of. Nothing in man's law or God's says you have to spend every minute remembering, or in tears.

You even have the right to enjoy life again, really to enjoy life. Once you reacquire the knack—oh yes, every parent loses it for a time—you are likely to find, as others before you have, that the enjoyable moments have a greater worth and intensity than they ever used to have. Because such joys are fewer, you enjoy each one more: that's the compensation you get.

The Right to Believe in Miracles

You have the right to believe in miracles and to make them happen, just as these other parents do, each in a different way:

> We are just thankful our daughter is with us now. She could have given up at birth, but she's a real fighter, and she's going to try her hardest to fight her disability and be as normal a child as she can possibly be. All I can say to any parent is, please never give up hope for your child.

> We would hope to say "Hang in there" to any parents who are discouraged. A handicap, after all, means only that things will be harder, but not impossible to do. *Never* give up, and *never* allow your child to give up.

> The week of January 15 my five-year-old son Jason said his first complete sentence. It was, "Mama, pretty lights on the wall." I still have some Christmas lights up in my house; maybe

they will be up for a whole year, especially now. Just when you reach the end of your rope, they will do something like this to you.

I think it is important to take one step at a time. . . . I would say to take each day as it comes. . . . Take one day at a time! And when times get real tough, make it through hour by hour! There are plenty of good times to make you forget the bad. . . . Don't worry about ten or twenty years from now, and what will happen to your child then. . . . Try to deal with today, and not look too far into the future.

You'll learn not to take anything for granted. The smallest accomplishments for a normal child can be major steps for yours. . . . When a person has any kind of handicapping condition, the simplest things in life are considered major triumphs. . . . Besides the joys all parents experience (albeit at times delayed), we feel intensified happiness at our daughter's accomplishments, as she truly works out small tasks which come naturally to most infants. . . . I feel the one thing we have really learned is to appreciate the small things in life that we took for granted with our son: Christina's first step at age two, her first jump at age three years and nine months. There are many many more.

When some doctors are pessimistic and make statements like "Your child will never speak or walk," we ignore them. If you listened to all that negative talk, what would be the use of trying?
We don't live in a dream world or believe Timmy will be "normal" one day, but we have to help him do as much as possible. He wasn't supposed to speak, but he can say "dada," "hi!" and "mama." And therapists have told us he will probably walk some day.

Never let *anyone* make sweeping predictions about your child's future. He or she may never turn out "normal," but if you're willing to work real hard, *anything* is fixable. Your goal may have to be 100 percent effort for 2 percent progress, but it *will* pay off. Do your homework and then go for it.

If you believe in your child and help in his or her struggle, you *will* get some kind of reward. Even if that might be just three seconds standing alone . . . Never believe anyone who says your child will never walk, talk, go to school, and so forth. Don't give up hope, even though it is sometimes hard, hard, hard. . . . Tough times never last. Tough people do.

We were told that our daughter was brain-damaged and were advised not to search for help such as therapy, etc; that she would only progress on her own. She cried about fifteen hours a day, disrupted our family life for two years—mother in mourning. Institutionalization was suggested at three months and again at eight months. We rejected the idea, because she was our child. Instead we set up an exercise program ourselves and discovered she was very bright and vocal. She is nine now, and in regular classes, with special education services.

What would I tell parents? To arm yourself with information, to live one day at a time, and to believe in miracles.

The one right that distinguishes you, and bonds you to others like you, like all these other parents of children with disabilities, is the right not to give up. The right never to give up: the right to believe in miracles, great and small, and the right to make them happen if you can.

I do my best to live in the present. The past is gone, and so be it. The biggest problem is that relatives and some others are always expecting a great miracle: that Chris will walk and talk. This drives me up a wall. Chris has so *many* miracles that don't seem to count for them. He is alive, he communicates, he eats and enjoys it, he loves and hugs and kisses, and he laughs and smiles and is happy.

He has so much to give. He has so much love, so much personality. I tune in to him. I listen with my ears, eyes, head, and heart. When he cries, I tune in and am able to understand. He is terrific and I tell him so. That's what life is about: coping and making the best out of the life we have. My son is doing that.

I don't need him to walk and talk, but I absolutely have to have him smile and give me a kiss. He does! We have had a *different* kind of miracle.

A Word to Professionals

This is a book in which parents of children with disabilities advise other parents about how to get help. But from it you can also learn a great deal about the way parents feel, about their children, about themselves, about you.

The longer you've been working with children who have special needs, the more likely that you've had the experience of dealing with parents whose skepticism—if not outright hostility—came through even while they were asking for help. It is all too easy to dismiss such instances with a pat formula, to diagnose such attitudes as either parental over-anxiety or guilt over having had a "spoiled" child. In some cases that may be true; but some of the accounts in this book (the many families who were told by physicians to "put the vegetable away," for instance) may persuade you to ask yourself whether you have the right to assume that every parent feels such guilt.

What parents have said in this book may make you wonder, the next time an obviously "hostile" parent walks into your office or faces you from the other side of your desk, whether this is one of those parents who has had so disturbing an experience with a health care professional somewhere along the line that it continues to color all his or her subsequent attitudes toward *all* professionals, until some professional (perhaps you) can recolor them the color of trust.

You may have reservations about the comments: that they do not truly reflect the feelings of the parents *you* see. That is quite possible, though you should also consider that parents may be less forthcoming in your office than they have been on these pages. We were not attempting a scientific research study; we simply asked as many parents as we could contact* to tell us about their experiences, and how they would advise other parents to go about seeking help. And well over 600 families selected themselves and chose to answer.

Demographically and geographically they *are* a diverse cross section: (1) in terms of their children's disabilities—moderate and severe, mental and/or physical, single and multiple, relatively high-incidence and rare syndrome—and (2) in terms of family situation: many were divorced or separated, but there were also families that described the way they had been drawn more closely together because of the child, single-child families, families with two or more children with a disability, adoptive families, adoptive families who chose two or more children with special needs.

Most who answered or whom we talked to were mothers—as expected—but there was a good representation of fathers. We heard about babies born to teenagers, and to mothers in their late thirties and forties. We heard from or spoke to urban, suburban, and rural families, families able to send their children to expensive private schools and therapy centers, and families basically dependent on Medicaid for health care.

Your profession will determine the specific kind of help for which parents seek you out. But many make it clear that they would also be grateful for whatever additional help you can give them in "working the system." Helpful, for starters, would be a list of parent and disability and advocacy agencies, and names of individuals (with phone numbers) who might be able to provide supportive services or other assistance. You could help connect parents with other parents in the same situation. Offer the names of two or three books you've either read or heard other parents recommend, for additional information or guidance after they leave your office. Though the *child* is your patient, there is one other very important thing the parents want from you: positive reinforcement for *them,* for the parents.

No matter how negative the prognosis for the child, parents need to feel that there is something they can do, with your help, to make things *better.* No matter what your honest professional opinion may be, no matter how reluctant you may be to raise false hopes, what many parents are saying is that you help them to survive and to cope by not destroying their faith that "miracles" *can* sometimes be made to happen.

—Dr. Sol Gordon

*See Appendix C.

Appendix A

Some Helpful Reading . . .

Biklen, Douglas. *Let Our Children Go*. Syracuse: Human Policy Press, 1974. Still an excellent organizing manual.

Buscaglia, Leo, ed. *The Disabled and Their Parents*. New York: Holt, Rinehart and Winston, 1983.

Darling, Rosalyn B., and Jon. *Children Who Are Different*. St. Louis: C.V. Mosby Company, 1982.

Des Jardins, Charlotte. *How to Get Services by Being Assertive*. Chicago: Chicago Coordinating Council for Handicapped Children, 1990.

Featherstone, Helen. *A Difference in the Family*. New York: Basic Books, 1980.

Gordon, Sol and Judith. *Raising a Child Conservatively in a Sexually Permissive World*. New York: Simon & Schuster, 1982.

Griffith, D. M., Quinsey, V. L., and Hingsburger, D. *Changing Inappropriate Sexual Behavior: A Community-Based Approach for Persons with Developmental Disabilities.* Baltimore: Paul H. Brookes, 1989.

Kushner, Harold S. *When Bad Things Happen to Good People.* New York: Avon, 1983.

Meyer, D. J., Vadasy, P., and Fewell, R. *Living with a Brother or Sister with Special Needs.* Seattle: University of Washington Press, 1985.

Pressman, Harvey, ed. *Making an Exceptional Difference: Enhancing the Impact of Microcomputer Technology on Children with Disabilities.* Boston: Exceptional Parent Press, 1987.

Shields, C. V. *Strategies: A Practical Guide for Dealing with Professionals and Human Service Systems.* Richmond Hill, Ontario: Human Services Press, 1987.

Simons, Robin. *After the Tears: Parents Talk about Raising a Child with a Disability.* New York: Harcourt Brace Jovanovich, 1987.

Turnbull, A. P. and H. R. *Parents Speak Out: Then and Now.* Columbus, OH: Charles Merrill, 1985.

. . . and Some Helpful Resources

Bibliography of Selected Resources on Cultural Diversity for Parents and Professionals Working with Young Children Who Have, or Are at Risk for, Disabilities (Available from PACER, Minneapolis, MN 55417-1055).

Directory of National Information Sources on Disability (Clearinghouse on Disability Information, Office of Special Education and Rehabilitative Services (OSERS), U.S. Department of Education, Washington, DC).

Disability, Sexuality, and Abuse: An Annotated Bibliography (Paul H. Brookes, Baltimore, MD 1991). More than 1,100 entries.

Guide to Selected National Genetic Organizations (National Center for Education in Maternal and Child Health, Washington, DC 1991). Lists more than 150 agencies and support groups concerned with genetic disorders and birth defects.

Parent Resource Directory for Parents and Professionals Caring for Children with Chronic Illness or Disabilities, Christopher Schmitt, ed. (Association for the Care of Children's Health, Bethesda, MD 1991). Names, addresses, and phone numbers of U.S. and Canadian parent/counselors with their expertise on specific disabilities.

Reader's Guide for Parents of Children with Mental, Physical, or Emotional Disabilities, compiled by Cory Moore (Woodbine House, Rockville, MD 1990). Comprehensive listing of books, articles, films, videos.

Selected Readings for Parents of Handicapped Children: A Bibliography (National Library Service for the Blind and Physically Handicapped, Library of Congress, Washington, DC 20542).

Self-Help Sourcebook, Edward J. Madara and Abigail Meese, eds. (American Self-Help Clearinghouse, Saint Clares-Riverside Medical Center, Denville, NJ 1990). Includes support groups for parents of children with specific disabilities, plus some useful (800) telephone numbers.

Two sources for free guides and information packets on children with disabilities are:

National Information Center for Children and Youth with Disabilities (NICHCY), P.O. Box 1492, Washington, DC 20013; (800) 999-5599. Available items include Spanish-language materials.

National Rehabilitation Information Center (NARIC), 8455 Colesville Road, Suite 935, Silver Spring, MD 20910-3319; (800) 346-2742.

Not just a magazine—virtually a parent support network:
Exceptional Parent, 1170 Commonwealth Avenue, 3rd floor, Boston, MA 02134-4646. Published eight times a year.

Appendix B

Federal Agencies and National Disability Organizations

In addition to the organizations cited in the chapters dealing with specific aspects of parent/family concern, the federal agencies, clearinghouses, national disability organizations, and parent groups provide information and/or assistance to families and professionals concerned with children who have disabilities. Some groups are more accessible than others, however; parents should be warned that sometimes persistence may be required.

The following listing has been provided by the National Information Center for Children and Youth with Disabilities (NICHCY), P.O. Box 1492, Washington, DC, 20013-1492; (800) 999-5599 and (703) 893-6061.

NICHCY provides free information to assist families, educators, caregivers, advocates, and others in helping children and youth with disabilities become participating members of the community. NICHCY operates as a national clearinghouse through the Clearinghouse Program authorized in IDEA, the 1990 amendments to the original PL 94-142, the Education of Handicapped Children Act.

NICHCY provides personal responses to specific questions, referrals to other organizations, prepared information packets, publications on current issues, and technical assistance to parent and professional groups. NICHCY maintains databases with current information on disability topics, including periodical articles and books; and on organizations concerned with disability issues, including parent groups, professional associations, and state, regional, and national organizations.

Clearinghouses

ERIC Clearinghouse on Handicapped. & Gifted Children
Council for Exceptional Children (CEC)
1920 Association Drive
Reston, VA 22091-1589
(703) 620-3660

Higher Education and Adult Training for People with Handicaps (HEATH)
One Dupont Circle NW, Suite 800
Washington, D.C. 20036-1193
(202) 939-9320; (800) 544-3284
(Voice/TDD)

National Clearinghouse for Professions in Special Education
1800 Diagonal Rd., Suite 320
Alexandria, VA 22314
(703) 519-3800

National Health Information Center
P.O. Box 1133
Washington, D.C. 20013-1133
(301) 565-4167; (800) 336-4797

National Information Center on Deafness (NICD)
800 Florida Ave. NE
Washington, D.C. 20002
(202) 651-5051 (Voice); (202) 651-5052 (TDD)

National Maternal and Child Health Clearinghouse
38th and R Sts. NW
Washington, D.C. 20057
(202) 625-8410

National Rehabilitation Information Center (NARIC)
8455 Colesville Rd., Suite 935
Silver Spring, MD 20910-3319
(301) 588-9284; (800) 346-2742
(Voice/TDD)

Organizations

American Council of Rural Special Education (ACRES)
Western Washington University
Miller Hall 359
Bellingham, WA 98225
(206) 676-3576

American Foundation for the Blind (AFB)
15 West 16th St.
New York, NY 10011
(212) 620-2000; 800-232-5463

American Occupational Therapy Assn. (AOTA)
P.O. Box 1725, 1383 Piccard Drive
Rockville, MD 20850
(301) 948-9626

American Physical Therapy Association (APTA)
1111 North Fairfax St.
Alexandria, VA 22314
(703) 684-2782

American Speech-Language-Hearing Assn. (ASHA)
10801 Rockville Pike
Rockville, MD 20852
(301) 897-5700 (Voice/TDD); (800) 638-8255

Association for the Advancement of Rehabilitation Technology (RESNA)
1101 Connecticut Ave. NW, Suite 700
Washington, D.C. 20036
(202) 857-1199

Association for the Care of Children's Health (ACCH)
7910 Woodmont Ave., Suite 300
Bethesda, MD 20814
(301) 654-6549

Association for Persons with Severe Handicaps (TASH)
7010 Roosevelt Way NE

Seattle, WA 98115
(206) 523-8446

The Arc (formerly Association for Retarded Citizens of the U.S.)
2501 Ave. J
Arlington, TX 76006
(817) 261-6003

Autism Society of America (formerly NSAC)
8601 Georgia Ave., Suite 503
Silver Spring, MD 20901
(301) 565-0433

Council for Exceptional Children (CEC)
1920 Association Drive
Reston, VA 22091
(703) 620-3660

Epilepsy Foundation of America (EFA)
4351 Garden City Drive, Suite 406
Landover, MD 20785
(301) 459-3700; (800) 332-1000

Head Start (Project)
Administration for Children, Youth and Families
Office of Human Development Services
U.S. Dept. of Health & Human Services
P.O. Box 1182
Washington, D.C. 20013
(202) 245-0572; (800) 245-0572

Independent Living Res. Utilization Proj. (ILRU)
The Institute for Rehabilitation and Research

3400 Bissonnet, Suite 101
Houston, TX 77005
(713) 666-6244

International Rett Syndrome Association
8511 Rose Marie Drive
Fort Washington, MD 20744
(301) 248-7031

Learning Disability Association of
America (LDA) (formerly
ACLD)
4156 Library Rd.
Pittsburgh, PA 15234
(412) 341-1515; (412) 341-8077

March of Dimes Birth Defects
Foundation
1275 Mamaroneck Ave.
White Plains, NY 10605
(914) 428-7100

Muscular Dystrophy Association
(MDA)
3561 East Sunrise Drive
Tucson, AZ 85718
(602) 529-2000

National Alliance for the Mentally
Ill (NAMI)
2101 Wilson Blvd., Suite 302
Arlington, VA 22201
(703) 524-7600; (800) 950-NAMI

National Down Syndrome Congress
gress
1800 Dempster St.
Park Ridge, IL 60068-1146
(312) 823-7550; (800) 232-NDSC

National Down Syndrome Society
666 Broadway
New York, NY 10012
(212) 460-9330; (800) 221-4602

National Easter Seal Society
70 East Lake St.
Chicago, IL 60601
(312) 726-6200; (312) 726-4258
(TDD); (800) 221-6827

National Head Injury Foundation,
Inc.
333 Turnpike Rd.
Southborough, MA 01772
(508) 485-9950; (800) 444-6443

National Library Service for the
Blind & Physically Handicapped
The Library of Congress
Washington, D.C. 20542
(202) 707-5100

National Spinal Cord Injury Association
sociation
600 West Cummings Park, Suite
2000
Woburn, MA 01801
(617) 935-2722; (800) 962-9629

Orton Dyslexia Society
724 York Rd.
Baltimore, MD 21204
(410) 296-0232; (800) 222-3123

Sibling Information Network
CT University Affiliated Program
991 Main St., Suite 3A
East Hartford, CT 06108
(203) 282-7050

Sick Kids (need) Involved People (SKIP)
990 2nd Ave., 2nd Floor
New York, NY 10022
(212) 421-9160; (212) 421-9161

Special Olympics
1350 New York Ave. NW, Suite 500
Washington, D.C. 20005-4709
(202) 628-3630

Spina Bifida Association of America
1700 Rockville Pike, Suite 540
Rockville, MD 20852
(301) 770-7222; (800) 621-3141

Technical Assistance to Parent Programs (TAPP) Network
Federation for Children with Special Needs

95 Berkeley St., Suite 104
Boston, MA 02116
(617) 482-2915; (800) 331-0688

Trace Research & Development Center on Communication, Control, and Computer Access for Handicapped Individuals
S-151 Waisman Ctr., 1500 Highland Ave.
University of Wisconsin-Madison
Madison, WI 53705-2280
(608) 262-6966

United Cerebral Palsy Associations, Inc.
1522 K St., NW, Suite 1112
Washington, D.C. 20005
(202) 842-1266; (800) 872-5827

Parent Networks, Coalitions, and Groups

In the following listings, some parent groups may appear more than once, since many assist parents and families in more than one way—providing information, advocacy and advocacy training, mutual support, or a combination of the above.

The first listing is provided by the National Parent Network on Disabilities (NPND), 1600 Prince Street, Suite 115, Alexandria, VA 22314; (703) 684-6763. NPND is a nonprofit organization dedicated to improving the lives of persons with disabilities. NPND's mission is to speak as the collective voice representing the perspectives, needs, and interests of parents and family members of persons of all ages with a disability, regardless of the type of disability.

The founders of the network were the federally funded Parent Training and Information (PTI) Centers located in all fifty states and Puerto Rico; to that number have been added other parent coalitions. A second category of membership is Parent Groups, some of which serve specific disabilities, while others serve parent-helping-parent groups. NPND's third category of membership is Affiliated Organizations. They comprise supportive national and international organizations that serve the needs of parents and families.

Parent Coalitions

Marie-Anne Aghazadian
302-366-0152
Parent Information Center of Delaware
700 Barksdale Rd., Suite 6
Newark, DE 19711

Sharon Bishop
405-681-9710
Pro-Oklahoma UCP of Oklahoma
1917 S. Harvard Ave.
Oklahoma City, OK 73128

Carol R. Blades
205-478-1208
Special Education Action Committee, Inc.
P.O. Box 161274
Mobile, AL 36616-2274

Debbie Braud
Project Prompt U.C.P. of Greater New Orleans
1500 Edwards Ave., Suite O
Harahan, LA 70123

Doris Braxton
313-245-3978
Parent Information Center—Special Education

Detroit Public Schools
2601 Ellery (Bunche School)
Detroit, MI 48207

Marsha Buck
907-586-6806
SEPTER SE Regional Resource Center
210 Ferrytown #200
Juneau, AK 99801

Richard Burden
219-234-7101
IN*SOURCE, Indiana Resource Center for Families with Special Needs
833 Northside Blvd., Bldg. #1
South Bend, IN 46617

Sharon Burleson
304-624-1436
West Virginia Parent Training and Information Center
Schroat Professional Building
Suite 2-I
229 Washington Ave.
Clarksburg, WV 26301

Margaret M. Burley
614-431-1307
Ohio Coalition for the Education of Handicapped Children
933 High St., Suite 106
Worthington, OH 43085

Molly Cole
203-667-5288
The Family Center
Department of Social Work, Newington Children's Hospital
181 E. Cedar St.
Newington, CT 06111

Connie Curtin
802-655-4016
Vermont Information and Training
Network
Champlain Mill #37
Winooski, VT 05404

Diana Cuthbertson
201-654-7726
Statewide Parent Advocacy Network
516 North Ave. East
Westfield, NJ 07090

Christine Davis
215-546-1166
Parents Union for Public Schools
in Philadelphia
311 South Juniper St. #602
Philadelphia, PA 19107

Terri Dawson
307-684-2277
Wyoming Parent Information Center
270 Fort St.
Buffalo, WY 82384

Charlotte Des Jardins
312-939-3513
Coordinating Council for Handicapped Children (CCHC)
20 E. Jackson Blvd. Room 900
Chicago, IL 60604

Kathryn Erickson
701-852-9426
Pathfinder Parent Training & Information Center
1600 2nd Ave., SW
Minot, ND 58701

Janice Foreman
409-866-4726
Partnerships for Assisting Texans
with Handicaps (PATH)
6465 Calder, Suite 202
Beaumont, TX 77707

Martha Gentili
206-565-2266
Washington PAVE
6316 South 12th
Tacoma, WA 98465

Patty Gerdel
913-273-6343
Families Together, Inc.
1023 SW Gage Blvd.
Topeka, KS 66604

Marth E. Gilgen
208-342-5884
Idaho Parents Unlimited, Inc.
4696 Overland Rd. #478
Boise, ID 83705

Paula Goldberg
612-827-2966
PACER Center
4826 Chicago Ave. South
Minneapolis, MN 55417-1055

Deborah Guimont
207-582-2504
Maine Parent Federation Inc.
(SPIN)

P.O. Box 2067
Augusta, ME 04338-2067

Connie Hawkins
704-892-1321
Exceptional Children's Assistance
Center
P.O. Box 16
Davidson, NC 28036

Deidra Hayden
703-836-2953
Parent Educational Advocacy
Training Center
228 South Pitt St., Room 300
Alexandria, VA 22314

Cathy Heizman
513-381-2400
Child Advocacy Center, SOC Information Center
106 Wellington Place
Cincinnati, OH 45219

Dara Howe
615-327-0294
Support & Training for Exceptional Parents
1805 Hayes St., Suite 100
Nashville, TN 37203

Janet Jacoby
813-623-4088
Family Network on Disabilities
1211 Tech Blvd., Suite 105
Tampa, FL 33619

Bonnie Johnson
501-221-1330
Arkansas Disability Coalition
10002 W. Markham, Suite B7
Little Rock, AR 72205

Eric Joice
609-392-4900
Epilepsy Foundation of N.J.
206 W. State St.
Trenton, NJ 08608

Kathy Kelker
406-657-2055
Parents Let's Unite for Kids, PLUK
EMC/IHS, 1500 North 30th
Billings, MT 59101-0298

Joan Kilburn
415-499-3877
MATRIX—A Parent Network &
Resource Center
P.O. Box 6541
San Rafael, CA 94903

Carla Lawson
515-576-5870
Iowa Pilot Parents
33 N. 12th St., P.O. Box 1151
Fort Dodge, IA 50501

Colleen Lee
803-734-3547
Parents Reaching Out to Parents of
South Carolina, Inc.
2712 Middleburg Drive
Suite 102
Columbia, SC 29240

Paulette Logsdon
502-589-5717
Kentucky Special Parents Involvement Network (KY-SPIN)
318 West Kentucky St.
Louisville, KY 40203

Randi Suzanne Malach
505-867-3396
EPICS Parent Project

P.O. Box 788
Bernalillo, NM 87004

Judy Martz & Barbara Buswell
719-531-9400
PEAK Parent Center, Inc.
6055 Lehman Drive, #101
Colorado Springs, CO 80918

Cheron J. Mayhall
503-373-7477
Oregon COPE Project, Inc.
999 Locust St. NE, Box B
Salem, OR 97303-5299

Cory Moore
301-379-0900
Parents' Place of Maryland, Inc.
7257 Parkway Drive, Suite 210
Hanover, MD 21076

Nancy Nelson
605-335-8844
South Dakota Parent Connection,
Inc.
P.O. Box 84813
Sioux Falls, SD 57118-4813

Betty Palmer
614-453-2806
P.A.L.S. (Parents & Loyal Sup-
porters)
1214 Selsam Ave.
Zanesville, OH 43701

Jani Pittman
805-834-2272
Bakersfield Association for Retarded Citizens
2240 South Union Ave.
Bakersfield, CA 93307

Helen W. Post
801-272-1051
Utah Parent Center
2290 East 4500 South #110
Salt Lake City, UT 84117

Florene Poyadue
408-288-5010
Parents Helping Parents
535 Race St., Suite 140
San Jose, CA 95126

Sue Pratt
517-485-4084
CAUSE
313 S. Washington Square #040
Lansing, MI 48933

Nancy Prescott
203-739-3089
Connecticut   Parent   Advocacy
Center
5 Church Lane, P.O. Box 579
East Lyme, CT 06333

Anne Presley
601-922-3210
Mississippi Parent Advocacy Center
332 New Market Drive
Jackson, MS 39209

Judith Raskin
603-224-7005
Parent Information Center
P.O. Box 1422
Concord, NH 03302-1422

Ann Robinson
312-922-0317
Designs for Change

220 S. State St. #1900
Chicago, IL 60604

Charlene Rogerson
702-735-2922
Nevada Technology Center
2880 East Flamingo Rd. #A
Las Vegas, NV 89121

Elaine Schab-Bragg
Parent to Parent Support
2230 8th Ave.
Seattle, WA 98121

Karen T. Schlesinger
212-677-4650
Resource for Children with Special
  Needs
200 Park Ave. South #816
New York, NY 10003

Jeanette Seaman
215-434-8076
Lehigh County Family Driven/
  Family Support Service
1036 N. Godfrey St.
Allentown, PA 18103

Carmen Selles
809-763-4665
Asociation de Padres Pro Bienestar
  de Niños Impedidos de Puerto
  Rico
P.O. Box 21301
Rio Piedras, PR 00928-1301

Edith Sharp
313-557-5070
Parents Are Experts UCP of Metro
  District
17000 West 8 Mile Road, Suite
  380
Southfield, MI 48075

Jean Sigler
404-346-0525
Nebraska Parents Information &
  Training Center
3610 Dodge St., Suite 225
Omaha, NE 68131

Mary Slaughter
602-468-3001
Pilot Parent Partnerships
2150 E. Highland Ave. #105
Phoenix, AZ 85016

Pat Smith
404-761-3150
ARC of Georgia
1851 Ram Runway, #104
College Park, GA 30337

Deborah Stamm
414-272-4500
Parent Education Project (PEP)
  United Cerebral Palsy of SE
  Wisconsin
2320 W. Wells St. #502
Milwaukee, WI 53203

Doreen Pam Steneberg
415-644-2555
Disability Rights Education and
  Defense
2212 6th St.
Berkeley, CA 94710

Joan M. Tellefsen
714-533-8275
Team of Advocates for Special
  Kids, Inc.
100 W. Cerritos Ave.
Anaheim, CA 92805-6546

Louise M. Thieme
717-845-9722
Parent Education Network
333 East 7th Ave.
York, PA 17404

Marianne Toombs
417-882-7434
Missouri Parents Act (MPACT)
1722 W. South Glenstone #125
Springfield, MO 65804

Sallie Van Curen
505-842-9045
Parents Reaching Out to Help (PRO)
1127 University Blvd., NE
Albuquerque, NM 87102

Sally M. Wade
813-974-5001
Florida Diagnostic and Learning Resources System
3500 East Fletcher Ave. #225
Tampa, FL 33612

Joan M. Watkins
716-885-1004
Parent Network Center of Western NY
1443 Main St.
Buffalo, NY 14209

Jenny Weaver
907-735-2228
Parents as Resources Engaged in Networking and Training Statewide
Box 733
Pelican, AK 99832

Martha Ziegler
617-482-2915
Federation for Children with Special Needs, Inc.
95 Berkeley St., Suite 104
Boston, MA 02116

Parent Groups

Gail Allen
717-336-7222
Association for Children's Mental Health
170 S. Coolidge Rd.
Woodbrook Village
E. Lansing, MI 48823

Patty Appleton
601-982-4003
Mississippi Families as Allies
5135 Galaxie Drive, Suite 302-C
Jackson, MS 39206

Nancy Arbuckle
713-520-9471
Family to Family Network
4101 Greenbriar, Suite 307
Houston, TX 77098

Linda Barth
303-797-1699
Mile High Down Syndrome
P.O. Box 620847
Littleton, CO 80162

Sandy Bertelson
701-225-1550
Family Education Enhancement Team
Dickenson Public Schools
P.O. Box 1047, 444 4th St. W.
Dickenson, ND 58601

Susan Christensen
402-390-0417
Special Education Community Club
816 South 94th St.
Omaha, NE 68114

Joanne Claytor
714-787-6500
Family Outreach Team
1960 Chicago Ave., Suite E-1
Riverside, CA 92507

Kim Crews
907-263-9285
Special Education Parent Resource Center
Whaley Center
2220 Nichols St.
Anchorage, AK 99508

Joyce Dolcourt
801-364-7060
Freeman-Sheldon Parent Support Group
509 E. Northmont Way
Salt Lake City, UT 84103

Jana Dransfield
214-368-4772
Hydrocephalus Association of N. Texas
P.O. Box 670552
Dallas, TX 75225

Julie Gordon
414-336-5333
Mothers United for Moral Support, Inc
150 Custer Court
Green Bay, WI 54301

Anna Gordy
215-221-5640
Independent Concerned Parents
2412 N. 30th St.
Philadelphia, PA 19132

John Hill
504-896-9268
Children's Hospital
The Education & Support Program
200 Henry Clay Ave.
New Orleans, LA 70118

Gail Hilliard Nelson
202-529-7600
Lt. Joseph P. Kennedy Institute
801 Buchanan St. NE
Washington, DC 20017

Kathy Hunter
301-248-7031
International Rett Syndrome Association
8511 Rose Marie Drive
Fort Washington, MD 20744

Paul Jochim
708-310-8876
Rett Syndrome, Chicago Area Support Group
1325 Chatsworth
Hoffman Estate, IL 60194

Shelley Kaplan
404-238-4568
The Smart Exchange
P.O. Box 724704
Atlanta, GA 30339

Fran Levinson
718-436-7979
Share Center—U.C.P.

160 Lawrence Ave.
Brooklyn, NY 11230

Beverly McConnell
313-256-3684
Family Support Network of Michigan
Exec. Plaza, 9th Floor
N. Tower, 1200 Sixth St.
Detroit, MI 48226

Jacki McCormack
612-778-1414
Pilot Parents in Ramsey County
425 Etna St., #35
St. Paul, MN 55106

Cindy Nixon
704-333-7107
SUN Network (St. Marks Unique
  Needs Net)
601 N. Graham St.
Charlotte, NC 28202-1400

The Parent Council to Recognize,
  Accept, Commit, Embrace, the
  Right to Live at Home
42 Cedar Lane #A16
Ossining, NY 10562

Cindy Politch
617-266-4520
Greater Boston Association for
  Retarded Citizens, Inc.
1249 Boylston St.
Boston, MA 02215

Alice Porembski
603-882-6333
Pilot Parents Program
32 D. W. Hwy, Harris Pond #22
Merrimack, NH 03054

Betty Romero
318-491-2040
Community-Based Services Project
4240 Legion
Lake Charles, LA 70601

Sue Smith
404-756-0187
Georgia Parent Support Network
1559 Brewer Blvd., SW
Atlanta, GA 30310

Joan Stoddard
714-979-0729
Family Support Network
3010 W. Harvard St. #D
Santa Ana, CA 92704

Georgie Stoner
216-633-2055
Family Information Network
90 W. Overdale Drive
Tallmadge, OH 44278

Karen Taycher
702-870-7050
Nevada Association for the Handicapped
6200 W. Oakey Blvd.
Las Vegas, NV 89102-1142

Pat Tomka
203-792-3540
Western Connecticut Association
  for the Handicapped & Retarded, Inc. (WeCARE)
11 Lake Ave. Extension
Danbury, CT 06811

Karen Turnbull Herz
517-831-5245
Special Kids, Special Families

611 N. State Rd.
Stanton, MI 48888

Beth Vietze
317-653-2454
Family Support Project
620 Tennessee St.
Greencastle, IN 46135

Affiliated Members

Mary Beth Bruder
914-285-7052
New York Medical College
Rm. 425, MRI, Cedarwood Hall
Vahalla, NY 10595-1689

Lori Burrus
717-274-5122
New Directions for Progress Family Support Services
502 Walnut St.
Lebanon, PA 17042

Timothy Coltman
516-265-3001
Suffolk Child Development Center
Landing Meadow Rd.
Smithtown, NY 11787

Karen Faison & Naomi Karp
703-241-8868
Family and Integration Resources
2823 N. Yucatan St.
Arlington, VA 22213

Beverly Farquhar
207-883-2117
National Association of School Nurses, Inc.

P.O. Box 1300
Scarborough, ME 04074

Tom Goodwin
202-797-0818
State of the Art, Inc.
1736 Columbia Rd., NW, #110
Washington, DC 20009

Ellen K. Hunt
805-683-2145
Family First
P.O. Box 5273
Santa Barbara, CA 93150

William E. Jones
301-588-8252
American Association of University Affiliated Programs (AAUAP)
8630 Fenton St., Suite 410
Silver Spring, MD 20910

Peggy LeBlanc
504-896-9286
National MCH Resource Center at Children's Hospital
200 Henry Clay
New Orleans, LA 70118

Joel Levy
212-563-7474
Young Adult Institute
460 West 34th St.
New York, NY 10001-2382

Liz Lindley
206-523-8446
TASH-The Association for Persons with Severe Handicaps
7010 Roosevelt Ave.
Seattle, WA 98115

Donald Meyer
206-368-4911
Sibling Support Project Children's
Hospital
4800 Sand Point Way NE, CL-09
Seattle, WA 98105

Beatriz Mitchell
Protection and Advocacy System
1720
Louisiana Blvd. NE #204
Albuquerque, NM 87110-7069

Nancy Okinow
612-624-3939
National Center for Youth with
Disabilities,
University of Minnesota
Box 721—UMHC
Harvard St. at E. River Rd.
Minneapolis, MN 55455

Julie Racino & Steven Taylor
315-443-3851
Center on Human Policy
200 Huntington Hall
Syracuse, NY 13244-2340

Jim Santos
202-628-3630
Special Olympics International
1350 New York Ave., NW #500
Washington, DC 20005

Michael Sharp
919-966-2841
Family Support Network,
University of NC
CB# 7340, UNC-CH
Chapel Hill, NC 27599

Jan Sterling
800-766-0800
Sterling Medical Marketing
37200 Central Court
Newark, CA 94560

Cathy Steward
313-768-4569
Proj. Inform—Genesee Intermediate School Dist.
2413 W. Maple Ave.
Flint, MI 48507

H.R. Turnbull
913-864-7600
Beach Center on Families & Dis-
ability
The Institute on Life Span Studies
BCR, 3111 Haworth
University of Kansas
Lawrence, KS 66045

Joan Weiss
202-331-0942
Alliance of Genetic Support
Groups
1101 22nd St. NW #800
Washington, DC 20037

Barbara Wilcox
812-855-6508
Institute for the Study of Developmental Disabilities
Indiana University
2853 E. Tenth St.
Bloomington, IN 47405

Martha Williams
603-394-7040
Center for Resource Management
2 Highland Rd.
South Hampton, NH 03827

Parent-to-Parent Programs

This list contains contact information obtained through a national survey of parent-to-parent programs conducted by the Beach Center on Families and Disability at The University of Kansas, 3111 Haworth Hall, University of Kansas, Lawrence, KS 66045; (913) 864-7607. A national directory, describing services provided, available materials, program demographics, and families and disabilities served by each program, will be available by June 1993.

Alabama

Parent-Paraprofessional Early Intervention Project
Auburn University
1234 Haley Center
Auburn, AL 36849
(205) 826-5943

Cleft Lip & Palate Support Group of Birmingham
4707 Chablis Way
Birmingham, AL 35244
(205) 987-7913

Parent Network
2046 Beltline Hwy., Suite 4
Decatur, AL 35601
(205) 355-6192

Alabama Deaf Blind Multihandicapped Assn.
P.O. Box 480204
Linden, AL 36748
(205) 295-8013

Special Ed. Action Committee
P.O. Box 161724
Mobile, AL 36616-2274
(205) 478-1208

Arkansas

Parent to Parent
2130 College Ave.
Conway, AR 72032
(501) 327-3317

Northwest Arkansas Parent to Parent
969 Rush Drive
Fayetteville, AR 72701
(501) 521-5696

Parent to Parent
Union Station Square, Ste. 412
Little Rock, AR 72201
(501) 375-4464

Arizona

Arizona Pilot Parents
P.O. Box 697
Ganado, AZ 86505
(602) 755-3411

Pilot Parent Partnership
2746 Holiday Drive
Lake Havasu City, AZ 86403
(602) 855-1915

Pilot Parent Partnerships
2150 E. Highland, Suite 105
Phoenix, AZ 85016
(602) 468-3001

SHARING—Down   Syndrome
   Parent Support Group
2451 W. Paradise Lane
Phoenix, AZ 85023
(602) 275-1426

Graham County Pilot Parent Partnership
P.O. Box 353
Thatcher, AZ 85552
(602) 428-4731

Pilot Parents
P.O. Box 707
Whiteriver, AZ 85941
(602) 338-4325

California

FOCUS—Pilot Parents
P.O. Box 3697
Chico, CA 95927
(916) 891-5865

Parent Referral Network
P.O. Box 109
Eureka, CA 95502
(707) 445-8841

Exceptional Parents Unlimited
Fresno ARC
420 N. Broadway
Fresno, CA 93701
(209) 442-0265

First Step
15444 Regalado
Hacienda Heights, CA 91745
(818) 855-3891

Cleft Parent Guild
7120 Franklin Ave.
Los Angeles, CA 90046
(213) 874-3300

Down Syndrome Parents' Group
6350 Laurel Canyon Blvd., #429
N. Hollywood, CA 91606
(818) 761-0044

COPE Project—UCP of Alameda-
   Contra Costa Counties
1970 Broadway
Suite 605
Oakland, CA 94612
(415) 832-7430
(415) 939-8000

DES Action
1615 Broadway
Oakland, CA 94612
(415) 465-4011

Parent to Parent Infant Support
   Group
Children's Hosp. of Orange Co.
P.O. Box 5700
Orange, CA 92613
(714) 997-3000

PROUD
P.O. Box 5822
Orange, CA 92613-5822
(714) 974-6419

Touchstone
378 Cambridge Ave., Suite K
Palo Alto, CA 94306
(415) 328-4495

Special Care Parents
P.O. Box 22322
Sacramento, CA 95822
(916) 395-2338

Parent to Parent Program of San
Diego County
Exceptional Family Resource Center
3914 Murphy Canyon Rd., Suite A205
San Diego, CA 92123
(619) 268-8252

Bay Area Cleft Palate Awareness
Coalition
2360 Clay St., Ground Floor
San Francisco, CA 94115
(415) 923-3306

Parents Helping Parents, Inc.
535 Race St., Suite 220
San Jose, CA 95126
(408) 288-5010

Matrix: Parent Network and Resource Center
P.O. Box 6541
San Rafael, CA 94903
(415) 499-3877

Family Support Network
1800 N. Bush St., Suite 201
Santa Ana, CA 92706
(714) 836-5511

Circle of Hope
1015 Cedar St.
Santa Cruz, CA 95060
(408) 335-7404

Valley Parents Support Group
P.O. Box 5973-272
Sherman Oaks, CA 91413
(818) 902-1616

Direct Link for the Disabled, Inc.
P.O. Box 1036
Solvang, CA 93463
(805) 688-1603

AVENUES
P.O. Box 5192
Sonora, CA 95370
(209) 928-3688

California Association for Parents
of Visually Impaired
440 Winston Way
Upland, CA 91786
(714) 946-5682

Colorado

SKIP of Colorado, Inc.
930 S. Kittredge Way
Aurora, CO 80017
(303) 368-8733

Sturge-Weber Foundation
P.O. Box 460931
Aurora, CO 80046
(800) 627-5482

Child Language Center
University of Colorado
CB-409, Dept. CD-55

Boulder, CO 80302
(303) 492-5375

Colorado Cleft Palate Association
8080 Kincross Drive
Boulder, CO 80301
(303) 530-3067

PEAK Integration Project
6055 Lehman Drive, #101
Colorado Springs, CO 80918
(719) 531-9400

Bridges
7475 Dakin, Suite 635
Denver, CO 80221
(303) 428-0310

Little People of America
7117 E. Euclid Drive
Englewood, CO 80111
(303) 740-8555

Effective Parents Project, Inc.
1227 N. 23rd St., Suite 104
Grand Junction, CO 81501
(303) 241-4068

Parents Reaching Out
710 Kipling, #303
Lakewood, CO 80215
(303) 238-0240

Mile High Down Syndrome Association
P.O. Box 620847
Littleton, CO 80162
(303) 797-1699

Parent-Professional Partnership
1077 Laurie Circle
Meeker, CO 81641
(303) 878-3491

Parents as Partners in Special Education
11130 Harris Way
Thornton, CO 80233
(303) 452-5958

Connecticut

Cornelia deLange Syndrome Foundation
60 Dyer Ave.
Collinsville, CT 06022
(800) 223-8355

Connecticut Association for Handicapped & Retarded, Inc.
11 Lake Ave. Extension
Danbury, CT 06811
(203) 792-3540

Connecticut Cleft Lip & Palate Parent Group, Inc.
10 Starr Place
East Hampton, CT 06424
(203) 267-4816

Parent   Resource   Network—
HARC
170 Douglas St.
Hartford, CT 06114-2499
(203) 525-1213

Yale-New Haven Hospital PATH
Carolyn Caprino
20 York St.
New Haven, CT 06504
(203) 488-9640

Oxford Special Ed. Support
10 White Gate Rd.
Oxford, CT 06483
(203) 426-7649

Connecticut Traumatic Brain Injury Association
1800 Silas Deane Hwy., Suite 224
Rocky Hill, CT 06067
(203) 721-8111

Parent Line
630 Oakwood Ave., Suite 221
W. Hartford, CT 06110
(203) 953-8929

Parent Sharing
P.O. Box 254
West Simsbury, CT 06092
(203) 282-0280

Delaware

Parent Information Center of Delaware, Inc.
700 Barksdale Rd., Suite 6
Newark, DE 19711
(302) 366-0152

Florida

Neo-Care (NICU)
P.O. Box 160683
Altamonte Springs, FL 32716
(407) 263-4317

Gold Coast Down Syndrome Organization
3735 N.W. 52nd St.
Boca Raton, FL 33496
(407) 994-6710

Parent to Parent of Pinellas Co.
1998 Sun Tree Blvd.
Clearwater, FL 34623
(813) 462-9687

Parent to Parent
P.O. Box 1774
Cocoa, FL 32923
(407) 459-1788

Parent-to-Parent of Walton Co.
Rte. 5, Box 185
Defuniak Springs, FL 32433
(904) 892-2803

Parent to Parent of Broward Co.
421 S. W. 20th St.
Ft. Lauderdale, FL 33315
(305) 523-0373

Parent to Parent-St. Lucie Co.
1901 S. 11th St.
Ft. Pierce, FL 34950
(407) 468-5389

NICU Parent Support Group
JHM Health Center
Box J-296
Gainesville, FL 32610
(904) 392-6427

Parent to Parent of Alachua Co.
4805 S.W. 45th St.
Gainesville, FL 32608
(904) 378-1827

Central Florida Parent to Parent
1709 Onondaga Drive
Geneva, FL 32732
(407) 349-5018

Parent to Parent of Polk Co.
4440 Spring Lane
Lakeland, FL 33811
(813) 646-8058

FAME (Families at Mayport are Exceptional)
PAO, P.O. Box 205

NAVSTA
Mayport, FL 32228
(904) 246-5226

IVH Parents
P.O. Box 56-1111
Miami, FL 33156
(305) 232-0381

Parent to Parent of Miami
9151 SW 6th St.
Miami, FL 33174
(305) 223-7379

Parent to Parent of Miami, Inc.
12310 SW 92nd Terrace
Miami, FL 33186
(305) 274-3501

Parent to Parent—Hispanic
9151 SW 6th St.
Miami, FL 33174
(305) 223-7379

Special Parents
409 Dixie Rd.
Milton, FL 32570
(904) 432-4513

Parent to Parent of Collier County
4875 6th Ave., SW
Naples, FL 33999
(813) 455-1522

VIPs (Veteran Intensive Care Parents)
P.O. Box 2700
Pensacola, FL 32513-2700
(904) 474-7656

Charlotte Co. Parent to Parent
23213 Oleon Blvd.
Port Charlotte, FL 33980
(813) 629-2808

Parent to Parent of Martin Co.
P.O. Box 162
Port Salerno, FL 34992-0162

Parent to Parent of St. Lucie County
422 N.W. Concord Drive
Port St. Lucie, FL 34983
(407) 878-3284

Parent to Parent of Palm Beach County
1201 Australian Ave.
Riviera Beach, FL 33404
(407) 863-3310

FACE of Sarasota, Inc.
P.O. Box 1424
Sarasota, FL 34230
(813) 349-5484

Parent to Parent of Nanatee—Sarasota, Inc.
350 Braden Ave.
Sarasota, FL 34243
(813) 747-2270

Parent to Parent of Hernando County
7158 Toledo Rd.
Spring Hill, FL 34606
(904) 683-6602

Big Bend EH/SED Parent to Parent
319 Fairfield Ave.
Tallahassee, FL 32301
(904) 539-5099

Parent/Infant Program
500 N. Appleyard Drive
Tallahassee, FL 32304
(904) 487-7515

Hillsboro Parent to Parent
8905 Oren Ave.
Tampa, FL 33614-1830
(813) 289-8967

Parent Education Network
1211 Tech Blvd., Suite 105
Tampa, FL 33619
(813) 623-4088
(800) TALK-PEN

Parent to Parent of Florida
3500 E. Fletcher Ave., Suite 225
Tampa, FL 33612
(813) 974-5001

Georgia

Parent to Parent of Georgia, Inc.
2939 Flowers Rd. S., Suite 131
Atlanta, GA 30341
(404) 451-5484
(800) 229-2038

Preemie Parents Support Group
P.O. Box 71953
Marietta, GA 30007-1953
(404) 973-3295

Cobb County Parent to Parent
1595 Hawthorne St.
Smyrna, GA 30080
(404) 435-2484

Hawaii

Family Support Services
1319 Punahou St., Bingham 211
Honolulu, HI 96826
(808) 973-8511

Hawaii Down Syndrome Congress
419 Keoniana St., #804
Honolulu, HI 96815
(808) 949-1999

IMPACT
49 Ihea Place
Pukalani, HI 96788
(808) 572-7225

Idaho

Parents Reaching Out to Parents
2195 Ironwood Court
Coeur d'Alene, ID 83814
(208) 667-6409

Parent to Parent of Idaho Falls
201 H St.
Idaho Falls, ID 83402
(208) 522-3532

Parent to Parent
2714 8th Ave.
Lewiston, ID 83501
(208) 746-8599

Idaho Autism Association
2470 Warren Ave.
Twin Falls, ID 83301
(208) 734-7279

Parent to Parent
Rte. 3, Box 6554
Twin Falls, ID 83301
(208) 733-3191

Illinois

Archway Services for Children
1108 W. Willow
Carbondale, IL 62959
(618) 549-4442

Developmental Svcs. Center
1304 W. Bradley
Champaign, IL 61820
(217) 356-9176

Chicago Family Support Pilot Project
20 E. Jackson Blvd., Room 900
Chicago, IL 60604
(312) 939-3513

Illinois Next Steps—Parents Reaching Parents
100 W. Randolph, Suite 8-100
Chicago, IL 60601
(800) 233-3425
(312) 814-4042

Keshet: Jewish Parents of Children with Special Needs
3525 W. Peterson, T-17
Chicago, IL 60645
(312) 588-0551

S. Metropolitan Assn. for Low-Incidence Handicapped
800 Governor's Hwy.
Flossmoor, IL 60422
(708) 333-7812

National Association for Down's Syndrome
P.O. Box 4542
Oak Brook, IL 60522-4542
(708) 864-8061

Indiana

New Horizons
P.O. Box 98
Batesville, IN 47006
(812) 934-4528

Connection for Special Kids
Rte. 2, Box 256
Berne, IN 46711
(219) 589-3543

NEO FIGHT
4363 Idlewild Lane
Carmel, IN 46032
(317) 843-0850

Down Syndrome Support Association of Central Indiana
10792 Downing St.
Carmel, IN 46032
(317) 574-9757

Clark County Parents of Special Children—New Hope Preschool
9208 Hwy. 62
Charlestown, IN 47111
(812) 256-5101

Passages for Preschool
P.O. Box 1005
Columbia City, IN 46725
(219) 244-7688

Disabilities Services, Inc.
P.O. Box 808
Crawfordsville, IN 47933
(317) 362-4020

Michiana Chapter—National Sudden Infant Death Syndrome Foundation
418 Constitution Avenue
Elkhart, IN 43526
(219) 533-0266
(219) 523-2371

Cleft Lip & Palate Support Group
1609 California Avenue
Fort Wayne, IN 46805
(219) 426-1258

Down Syndrome Association of
    NW Indiana
2927 Jewett Ave.
Highland, IN 46322
(219) 838-3656

HEAR Indiana
5316 Carrolton Ave., A-5
Indianapolis, IN 46220
(317) 926-3015

Indiana Parent Info. Network
2107 E. 65th St.
Indianapolis, IN 46220
(317) 232-2291

MDA Support Group of Central
    Indiana
2110 E. 65th St.
Indianapolis, IN 46220
(317) 257-6598

Parents Support Network—Hem-
    ophilia of Indiana
1100 Burdsal Pkwy.
Indianapolis, IN 46208
(317) 924-6208

TOUCH Wabash Center
2000 Greenbush St.
Lafayette, IN 47904
(317) 423-5531

Everybody Counts
6701 Broadway, Suite B
Merrillville, IN 46410
(219) 769-5055

Parents with Dreams
Rte. 6, Box 210
Scottsburg, IN 47170
(812) 752-6811

ROOTS-WINGS Parent Involve-
    ment Program
Rte. 3, Box 9
Scottsburg, IN 47170
(812) 752-4892

Down Syndrome Family Support
P.O. Box 6579
South Bend, IN 46660
(219) 289-4831

NICU Parent Support Group
Memorial Hospital of South Bend
615 N. Michigan St.
South Bend, IN 46601
(219) 287-2293

Knox County Advocates for Spe-
    cial Kids
1806 Indiana Ave.
Vincennes, IN 47591
(812) 882-0375

Iowa

Autism Society of the Quad Cities
P.O. Box 472
Bettendorf, IA 52722-0472
(319) 386-6359

Family Educator Connection Pro-
    gram
3706 Cedar Heights Drive
Cedar Falls, IA 50613
(319) 273-8250

Gladys Zobac
2101 O Ave. NW
Cedar Rapids, IA 52405
(319) 396-0210

Pilot Parents—ARC Linn Co.
136 36th Street Drive, SE, Suite
A5
Cedar Rapids, IA 52403
(319) 365-0487

Union County Pilot Parents
P.O. Box 57
Creston, IA 50801
(515) 782-2917

Parent Educator Connection
MPRRC, Drake University
Des Moines, IA 50311
(515) 271-3936

Special Care Parents
1922 E. 12th St.
Des Moines, IA 50316
(515) 255-5943

Iowa Pilot Parents
Iowa Exceptional Parent Center
33 No. 12th St., P.O. Box 1151
Fort Dodge, IA 50501
(800) 383-4777
(515) 576-5870

Parent to Parent
133 Lillian
Ottumwa, IA 52501
(515) 682-6467

Epilepsy Support Group
426 Sherrylynn Blvd.
Pleasant Hill, IA 50317
(515) 263-0370

Parent-Educator Connection
102 S. Main, AEA 4
Sioux Center, IA 51250
(712) 722-1931

NICU Parent to Parent Support
Group
2505 S. Lyon
Sioux City, IA 51106
(712) 276-7845

Siouxland Head Injury Assn.
1423 Court
Sioux City, IA 51105
(712) 255-2447

Parent to Parent Support Group
2320 S. Olive
Sioux City, IA 51106
(712) 274-2838

Kansas

Autism Society of Kansas
2512 N. 75th St.
Kansas City, KS 66109
(913) 299-2027

Salina Area Parent to Parent Program
Saline County Health Dept.
300 W. Ash, Room 107
Salina, KS 67401
(913) 827-9376

Family to Family
9401 Nall, Suite 100
Shawnee Mission, KS 66207
(913) 648-4772
(800) 783-1356

Rubinstein-Taybi Syndrome (RTS
Parent Group)
414 E. Kansas
Smith Center, KS 66967
(913) 282-6237

Families Together
P.O. Box 86153
Topeka, KS 66686
(913) 273-6343

Pilot Parents
Topeka ARC
2701 Randolph St.
Topeka, KS 66611
(913) 232-0597

Connecting Point
P.O. Box 1120
Wichita, KS 67201
(316) 943-3356

Sedgick County Down Syndrome
Parents—ARC
P.O. Box 1120
Wichita, KS 67201
(316) 943-1191

Kentucky

PUSH Infant and Preschool Program
P.O. Box 781
Frankfort, KY 40602
(502) 875-4403

Parent Outreach, Council for Retarded Citizens
1146 S. Third St.
Louisville, KY 40203
(502) 584-1239

Louisiana

Neonatal Intensive Care Unit—
Parents, Inc.
3146 Lake Forest Park Ave.
Baton Rouge, LA 70816
(504) 293-3562

Parent Conference on Special Education
Louisiana Dept. of Education
P.O. Box 94064
Baton Rouge, LA 70804-9064
(504) 342-3636

Louisiana Rett Syndrome Foundation
Rt. 8, Box 1737
Sailfish Drive
Lake Charles, LA 70605
(318) 474-5727

Parent to Parent of Louisiana Education and Support Program
200 Henry Clay Ave.
New Orleans, LA 70118
(504) 896-9274
(504) 896-9268

Concerned Parents for Students
1022 Gulf Lane
Sulphur, LA 70663
(318) 528-2191

Maine

Maine Parent Federation—SPIN
P.O. Box 2067
Augusta, ME 04338-2067
(207) 582-2504

Parent to Parent
United Cerebral Palsy of North-
eastern Maine, Inc.
103 Texas Ave.
Bangor, ME 04401
(207) 941-2885

Parents Helping Parents
5 Paul St.
Brunswick, ME 04011
(207) 725-6365

Mid-Coast Children's Services
11 Maple St.
Rockland, ME 04841
(207) 594-8474

York County Parent Awareness
475 Main St.
Sanford, ME 04073
(207) 324-2337

Maryland

Learning Disabilities Association
320 Maryland National Bank
Building
Baltimore, MD 21202
(301) 265-6193

Maryland Family Support Network
for Children with Special Needs
c/o Maryland Infants and Toddlers
Program
118 North Howard St., Suite 608
Baltimore, MD 21201
(800) 535-0182

National Federation of the Blind
Parents of Blind Children Division
1800 Johnson St.

Baltimore, MD 21230
(301) 659-9314

Parent to Parent Network
160 Funke Rd.
Glen Burnie, MD 21146
(301) 222-7187

Epilepsy Foundation of America
4351 Garden City Drive
Landover, MD 20785
(301) 459-3700

Montgomery County ARC
11600 Nebel St.
Rockville, MD 20852
(301) 984-5792

Massachusetts

Greater Boston Parent to Parent
1249 Boylston St.
Boston, MA 02215
(617) 266-4520

Parent to Parent of Birth Defects
Service
Children's Hospital, Fegan 10
300 Longwood Ave.
Boston, MA 02115
(617) 735-7037

SPIN Project
Federation for Children with Special Needs
95 Berkeley St.
Boston, MA 02116
(617) 482-2915

South Shore Parent to Parent
South Shore ARC
250 Elm St.

Hanover, MA 02339
(617) 335-3023

Parents First Call Program
P.O. Box 632
Holden, MA 01520
(508) 835-3950
(617) 893-1355

Lenox Parent Advisory Council
10 Sherwood Drive
Lenox, MA 02140

Parent to Parent
247 Smith St.
New Bedford, MA 02740
(508) 966-8551

National Tay-Sachs Parent Peer
  Group
385 Elliot St.
Newton, MA 02164
(617) 964-5508

New Horizons
388 Columbus Ave. Extension
Pittsfield, MA 01201
(413) 499-4537

Raynham Parent Advisory Council
687 Pleasant St.
Raynham, MA 02767
(508) 822-1598

Parents Helping Parents
55 Blue Rock Rd.
South Yarmouth, MA 02664
(508) 398-3866

Wachusett Area Parent Advisory
  Council
11 Laurel Ave.

Sterling, MA 01564
(508) 422-8322

Massachusetts Down Syndrome
  Congress
124 Greenwood Lane
Waltham, MA 02154
(617) 742-4440

HOLD—Helping Our Learning
  Disabled
10 Waycross St.
Worcester, MA 01603
(508) 752-2906

Michigan

Hand and Hand
P.O. Box 658
Bay City, MI 48707
(517) 892-4533

Parent to Parent
ARC Oakland County
690 E. Maple
Birmingham, MI 48009
(313) 646-4522

Southeast Michigan Parents of Premature Infants
1680 Washington
Birmingham, MI 48009
(313) 258-6753

Peer Support Project—Parents
  Are Agreeable
622 N. Seventh St.
Gladstone, MI 49837
(906) 428-3135

Down Syndrome Association of
  W. Michigan
P.O. Box 8703

Kentwood, MI 49518
(616) 874-6008

Parent Network Program
Michigan Protection and Advocacy
Service
109 W. Michigan Ave., Suite 900
Lansing, MI 48933-1709
(517) 487-1755

Peer Support Project
530 W. Ionia St., Suite C
Lansing, MI 48933
(517) 487-9260

Peer Support Project
7039 Gra-Al Shores
Rapid River, MI 49878
(906) 474-6666

Parents of Children with Special
Needs
1105 S. Clinton Ave.
St. Johns, MI 48879
(517) 224-4383

MPS Research Funding Center
3260 Old Farm Lane
Walled Lake, MI 48390
(313) 363-4412

Minnesota

Pilot Parents—Kanabec Co.
Rt. 1, Box 290
Braham, MN 55006
(612) 396-2115

Lakes Area Pilot Parents
P.O. Box 327
Brainerd, MN 56401
(218) 828-4463

Pilot Parents—Minnesota
201 Ordean Building
Duluth, MN 55804
(218) 726-4745

Hemifacial Microsomia—Golden-
har Syndrome Family Support
Network
2724 Minnesota Ave.
Duluth, MN 55802
(218) 722-7376

Pilot Parents of NE Minnesota
201 Ordean Building
Duluth, MN 55802
(218) 726-4725

Pilot Parents of Martin Co. Area
P.O. Box 635
Fairmont, MN 56031
(507) 238-1979

Pilot Parents of Rainy River Region
P.O. Box 790
International Falls, MN 56649
(218) 283-9773

People to People: One-to-One
Support
514 N. Cedar
Owatonna, MN 55060
(507) 451-0576

Midstate Pilot Parents
P.O. Box 1536
St. Cloud, MN 56302
(612) 253-6844

Pilot Parents in Ramsey Co.
425 Etna St., #35
St. Paul, MN 55106
(612) 778-0788

Pilot Parents of Northeast Minnesota
1201 S. 8 1/2 St.
P. O. Box 7066
Virginia, MN 55792
(218) 749-8273

Pilot Parents of South Minnesota
P.O. Box 266
Waseca, MN 56093
(507) 685-4558

Turner's Syndrome Society of the United States
768-214 Twelve Oaks Center
15500 Wayzata Blvd.
Wayzata, MN 55391-1416
(612) 475-9944

Missouri

Missouri Head Injury Association
3632-BW Truman Blvd.
Jefferson City, MO 65109
(314) 893-2444

Pilot Parents Program
P.O. Box 10984
Springfield, MO 65808
(417) 883-2593

Montana

Parents, Let's Unite for Kids
EMC/IHS, 1500 N. 30th St.
Billings, MT 59101-0298
(406) 657-2055

Region II Child and Family Services—Home-Based Services
600 Sixth St., NW

Great Falls, MT 59403
(406) 452-9531

Osteogenesis Imperfecta Foundation Peer Contact Network
P.O. Box 768
Manhattan, MT 59741-0768
(406) 284-6038

Parents of Children with Special Needs
School of Education
University of Montana
Missoula, MT 59812
(406) 542-1330
(406) 243-5344

Nebraska

Exceptional Parents Night Out—Parent Support Group
1025 N. Sheridan
Grand Island, NE 68803
(308) 381-5925
(308) 382-3933

PALLS—Preschool Activities for Language & Learning Skills
ESU #9, P.O. Box 2047
Hastings, NE 68901
(402) 463-5611

Pilot Parents
114 W. Sixth St.
Lexington, NE 68850
(308) 324-4428/3828

League of Human Dignity
Independent Living Center
1701 P St.
Lincoln, NE 68507
(402) 471-7871

Parents Encouraging Parents
Nebraska Dept. of Education
301 Centennial Mall, S.
Lincoln, NE 68509
(402) 471-2471

Pilot Parent Coordinator
215 Centennial Mall S., #410
Lincoln, NE 68508
(402) 477-6925

Pilot Parents Program
Greater Omaha ARC
3610 Dodge St.
Omaha, NE 68131
(402) 346-5220

Parent to Parent
826 Arlene Ave.
Papillion, NE 68046
(402) 592-2719

Nevada

N-STEP—Nevada Specially
  Trained Effective Parents
6200 W. Oakey
Las Vegas, NV 89102
(702) 870-7050

PACEER HUGS
University of Nevada-Reno Col-
  lege of Education
Room 201
Mail Stop 278
Reno, NV 89557
(702) 784-4921

New Hampshire

New Hampshire Special Families
  United
P.O. Box 1141

Concord, NH 03302-1141
(800) 356-8881 (Concord area)
(603) 224-2022

Treacher Collins Family Network
P.O. Box 5
Concord, NH 03302-0005
(603) 226-4371

Upper Valley Support Group
P.O. Box 622
Hanover, NH 03755
(603) 448-6311

Parents Supporting Parents
48 Old County Rd.
Plaiston, NH 03865
(603) 646-7884

New Jersey

Cleft Lip & Palate Support Group
Children's Hospital of Philadelphia
501 Douglas Drive
Cherry Hill, NJ 08034
(609) 482-6554

Family Support Services Program
New Jersey Association of the
  Deaf-Blind
28 Kennedy Blvd.
E. Brunswick, NJ 08816
(908) 249-4433

Parent Partners
P.O. Box 494
Hewitt, NJ 07421
(201) 728-8744

Down Syndrome Parent to Parent
ARC of Essex County
7 Regent St.

Livingston, NJ 07039
(201) 535-1181

Association for Children with Russell Silver Syndrome
22 Hoyt St.
Madison, NJ 07940
(201) 377-4531

Parents Encouraging Parents (PEP)
ARC—Morris Chapter
P.O. Box 123
Morris Plains, NJ 07950
(201) 765-9661

New Mexico

Parents Reaching Out—Alamogordo
P.O. Box 3631, BRS-A
Alamogordo, NM 88311
(505) 437-9290

Parents for Behaviorally Different Children
7732 Hermanson Place, N.E.
Albuquerque, NM 87110
(505) 296-5317

Parents of Preterm Infants Network (PPIN)
University of New Mexico Hospital
Dept. of Pediatrics
Albuquerque, NM 87131
(505) 277-3946

PRO—Parent to Parent Network
1127 University, NE
Albuquerque, NM 87102
(800) 524-5176
(505) 842-9045

PRO—Parent Support Network
4106 Winchester
Las Cruces, NM 88001
(505) 522-5669

New York

Parent-Friend: One to One
845 Central Ave.
Albany, NY 12206
(518) 438-8785

Newborn & Family Support Services Network
North Central Bronx Hospital
Social Work Department
3424 Kossuth Ave.
Bronx, NY 10467
(212) 519-4796

New York League for Early Learning, Inc.
7420 Fourth Ave.
Brooklyn, NY 11209
(718) 745-6006

Headway for Brain Injured, Inc.
55 Melroy Ave.
Lackawanna, NY 14201
(716) 822-2261

Levittown Hydrocephalus Support Group
Satellite Information Center
59 Market Lane
Levittown, NY 11756
(516) 735-3247

The Jewish Guild for the Blind
Downstate Resource Network
15 West 65th St.

New York, NY 10023
(212) 769-6327

Parents of Special Children, Inc.
P.O. Box 5357
Oswego, NY 13126
(315) 343-6480

Parent Assistance Committee on Down Syndrome
208 Lafayette Ave.
Peekskill, NY 10566
(914) 739-4085

St. Charles Early Intervention Program
501 Myrtle Ave.
Port Jefferson, NY 11777
(516) 331-6400

Parents Available to Help (PATH)
Special Care Nursery
Vassar Hospital
Poughkeepsie, NY 12601
(914) 454-8500

Parent to Parent
239 Champion Ave.
Webster, NY 14580
(716) 265-3778

Parents for Parents, Inc.
P.O. Box 121
Yorktown Heights, NY 10598
(914) 962-3326

North Carolina

Parent to Parent
Appalachian State University
Boons, NC 28608
(704) 262-2182

Family Support Network of North Carolina
CB #7340, University of North Carolina
Chapel Hill, NC 27599
(800) 852-0042
(919) 966-2841

North Carolina Family Parent Group
Oral, Facial, & Communicative Disorders Program
UNC School of Dentistry
Chapel Hill, NC 27514
(919) 966-2275

Sharing Parent, Inc.
P.O. Box 561986
Charlotte, NC 28256-1986
(704) 548-8011

Cape Fear Association of Parents Helping Parents
3403 Melrose Rd.
Fayetteville, NC 28304
(919) 486-1605

Parent to Parent Support
1200 N. Elm St.
Greensboro, NC 27401
(919) 379-4373

Parents Supporting Parents
Irons Bldg., ECU Campus
Greenville, NC 27858
(919) 757-4494

Catawba Co. Mental Health
Early Childhood Intervention Services
Rt. 3, Box 339

Hickory, NC 28602
(704) 328-5361

Tri-County Local Unit of Autism
Society of North Carolina
Rt. 3, Box 339
Hickory, NC 28602
(704) 328-5361
(704) 256-5242

HOPE—Helping Other Parents
Through Empathy
300 Enola Rd.
Morganton, NC 28655
(704) 433-2877

Parents Helping Parents
2717 Neuse Blvd.
New Bern, NC 28562
(919) 633-0242
(919) 633-0775

Parent to Parent
Phone Friends
P.O. Box 411
Smithfield, NC 27577
(919) 934-5121

The Tuberous Sclerosis Connection
North Carolina Tuberous Sclerosis
Association
1005 Indianhead Circle
Snow Hill, NC 28580
(800) 622-6872
(919) 747-8592

Parents Supporting Parents
1501 Dock St.
Wilmington, NC 28401
(919) 762-1744

Parents Together
4505 Shattalon Drive
Winston-Salem, NC 27106
(919) 924-5301

North Dakota

Family First: Education for Empowerment
P.O. Box 1883
Jamestown, ND 58402
(701) 252-2847

Ohio

Parent to Parent Support
814 West St.
Caldwell, OH 43724
(614) 732-5188

Family First
1821 Summit Rd., G-30
Cincinnati, OH 45237
(513) 821-3533

Ohio Protection & Advocacy
8625 Denallen Drive
Cincinnati, OH 45255
(513) 474-2385

Parent Listeners—Down Syndrome Association of Greater
Cincinnati
1821 Summit Rd., Suite G-20
Cincinnati, OH 45237
(513) 761-5400

Parent Connection—Cleveland
Regional Perinatal Network
11001 Cedar Ave.
Cleveland, OH 44106
(216) 844-3391

Family First
2917 Sherwood Rd.
Columbus, OH 43209
(614) 338-1719

Family First
360 S. Third St., Suite 101
Columbus, OH 43215
(614) 228-4333

National Head Injury Foundation
Ohio Association
751 Northwest Blvd.
Columbus, OH 43212
(800) 686-9563
(614) 424-6968

Family First—Region II
16 Vassar Drive
Dayton, OH 45406
(513) 275-0990

UCP Family First
722 Valley St.
Dayton, OH 45404
(513) 222-2113

Special Needs Information Center
P.O. Box 87
Girard, OH 44420
(216) 545-2837

Miami Valley Down Syndrome Association
1444 Beaver Creek Lane
Kettering, OH 45429-3704
(513) 294-1240

National Tuberous Sclerosis Association (NTSA)
State Rep. Coordinator
3006 Plum Creek Parkway

Medina, OH 44256
(301) 459-9888

Families in Touch
Mental Health Association of Licking County
65 Messimer Drive
Newark, OH 43055
(614) 522-1351

Human Growth Foundation
N.E. Ohio Chapter
1393 Dill Rd.
S. Euclid, OH 44121
(216) 381-0797

Family Network
90 W. Overdale Ave.
Tallmadge, OH 44278
(216) 633-2055

Family First of NW Ohio
United Health Services
151 N. Michigan, Suite 200
Toledo, OH 43624
(419) 242-9587

Oklahoma

Family Support Project
7427 E. 67th Place
Tulsa, OK 74133
(918) 744-1000

Oregon

Lane County Direction Service
250 Silver Lane, #10
Eugene, OR 97404
(503) 461-2212

Parent Network Program
45 W. Broadway
Eugene, OR 97401
(503) 343-5256

Caring Parents
2825 Barnett Rd.
Medford, OR 97504
(503) 773-6281, Ext. 4569

NICU Parent Support Group—
Rogue Valley Medical Center
2825 Barnett Rd.
Medford, OR 97504
(503) 770-4233

Parents Supporting Parents
6901 SW Eighth Ave.
Portland, OR 97219
(503) 244-6719

Pilot Parent Program—Tri County
718 W. Burnside, #316
Portland, OR 97212
(503) 223-7279

Pennsylvania

Family Outreach
836 E. 15th St.
Chester, PA 19013
(215) 872-6313

Brain Injury Support Groups:
  Heading On
595 W. State St.
Doylestown, PA 18901
(215) 345-2636

Parent Support Center
252 Waterford St.
Edinboro, PA 16412
(814) 734-5610

Westmoreland County Parent to
  Parent
1228 Brinkerton Rd.
Greensburg, PA 15601
(412) 832-1063

S. June Smith Center—Down's
  Syndrome Support Group
115 Armstrong Lane
Lancaster, PA 17603
(717) 872-9294

Hemifacial Microsomia—Golden-
  har Syndrome Family Support
  Network
6 Country Lane Way
Philadelphia, PA 19115
(215) 677-4787

Intensive Caring Unlimited
910 Bent Lane
Philadelphia, PA 19118
(215) 233-4723

Parent Specialist Education Program
2350 W. Westmoreland St.
Philadelphia, PA 19140
(215) 229-4550

Parent to Parent
1001 Brighton Rd.
Pittsburgh, PA 15233
(412) 322-6008

Mary Anne Ohlinger
P.O. Box 322
Temple, PA 19560

National Foundation for Peroneal
  Muscular Atrophy
Crozer Mills Enterprise Ctr.

600 Upland Ave.
Upland, PA 19105
(215) 499-7486

N. Central Pennsylvania Head Injury Network
777 Rural Ave.
Williamsport, PA 17701
(717) 321-2660

Rhode Island

Down Syndrome Society of R.I.
99 Bald Hill Rd.
Cranston, RI 02920
(401) 463-5751

Parent Support Network
855 Waterman Ave.
Suite D
East Providence, RI 02914
(401) 431-1240

Parent Training Program—Special Education Program Services Unit
22 Hayes St.
Providence, RI 02908
(401) 277-3505

PRO—Parents Reaching Out
Division of Family Health
Department of Health
75 Davis St.
Providence, RI 02863
(401) 277-2312

Central Region Early Intervention
3445 Post Rd.
P.O. Box 7789
Warwick, RI 02887-7789
(401) 739-2700

South Carolina

Family Support Program
Easter Seal Center
325 Calhoun
Charleston, SC 29401
(803) 723-7224

Nat'l Information Clearinghouse for Infants with Disabilities & Life Threatening Conditions
CDD
Benson Building, 1st Fl.
Columbia, SC 29208
(800) 922-9234, Ext. 201

Nat'l Information System for Vietnam Vets & Their Children
CDD
Benson Building, 1st Fl.
Columbia, SC 29208
(800) 922-9234, Ext. 401

South Dakota

Parent to Parent, Inc.
3936 S. Western Ave.
Sioux Falls, SD 57105
(605) 334-3119

Tennessee

Project ECHO-ETSU Center for Early Childhood
P.O. Box 15, 520-A
Johnson City, TN 37614-0002
(615) 929-5662

Parents & PostOp
801-A Teaberry Lane
Knoxville, TN 37919
(615) 691-2418

Wee Care
6019 Walnut Grove
Memphis, TN 38119
(901) 766-5023

Parents of Special Children
P.O. Box 3192
Murfreesboro, TN 37133
(615) 849-1225

Parents Reaching Out
203 Burlington
Nashville, TN 37215
(615) 297-8129

Texas

Pilot Parent
ARC—Austin
2818 San Gabriel
Austin, TX 78705-3598
(512) 476-7044

Parent Care of Austin
1603 E. 38 1/2 St.
Austin, TX 78722
(512) 472-8351

Down Syndrome Guild
4335 Rickover
Dallas, TX 75244
(214) 239-8771

Project KIDS
Dallas Ind. School District
12532 Nuestra
Dallas, TX 75130
(214) 490-8701, Ext. 5210

Tarrant Co. Society for Hearing
   Impaired Infants & Youth
4520 Diamond Loch North

Forth Worth, TX 76180-8877
(817) 498-8251

Parent to Parent
3201 Ridgeview Lane
Irving, TX 75062
(214) 255-7815

Partners Resource Network
12602 Moss Hollow Court
Live Oak, TX 78233
(512) 599-0719

Developmental Education
Birth to Two (DEBT)
1628 19th St.
Lubbock, TX 79413
(806) 766-1172

Parent Case Management Prog.
3001 S. Jackson
San Angelo, TX 76904
(915) 949-9535

Craniofacial Anomaly Support Association
3501 Oakhorne Drive
San Antonio, TX 78247
(512) 496-0270

Parent Helpline
P.O. Box 7330, Station A
San Antonio, TX 78285
(512) 228-2222

Utah

Graduate Parents—Primary Children's Medical Center
100 N. Medical Drive
Salt Lake City, UT 84113-1100
(801) 588-3899

Parent to Parent Program
2290 E. 4500 South, Suite 110
Salt Lake City, UT 84117
(801) 272-1051

Parent to Parent—Univ. of Utah
Hospital c/o NBICU
50 N. Medical Dr., Room 2368
Salt Lake City, UT 84132
(801) 581-2098

Family Support Network of Utah
10672 S. Rembrandt Lane
Sandy, UT 84070

Vermont

Vermont Interdisciplinary Team
for Intensive Special Education
Center for Developmental Disability
University of Vermont
Burlington, VT 05405-0160
(802) 656-4031

Parent to Parent of Vermont
1 Main St.
69 Champlain Mill
Winooski, VT 05404
(802) 655-5290

Virginia

SW Virginia Parent to Parent
Drawer II
Big Stone Gap, VA 24219
(703) 523-0682

Craniofacial Anomalies Clinic
UVA Medical Center
P.O. Box 376

Charlottesville, VA 22908
(804) 924-5801

Human Growth Foundation
7777 Leesburg Pike, Suite 202S
P.O. Box 3090
Falls Church, VA 22043
(703) 883-1773

Harrisonburg-Rockingham Parent
to Parent
1251 Smithland Rd.
Harrisonburg, VA 22801
(703) 433-5821

Parents of Preemies
2822 Chasbarb Court
Herndon, VA 22071
(703) 860-9356

Twin Co.—Galax Parent to Parent
P.O. Box 931
Hillsville, VA 24343
(703) 236-2122

Parent to Parent of Southside Virginia
2008 Wakefield St.
Petersburg, VA 23508
(804) 862-9940

Parent to Parent—Virginia
301 W. Franklin St.
P.O. Box 3020
Richmond, VA 23284
(804) 225-3876

Parent to Parent of Greater Richmond
Family-Children's Service of Richmond
1518 Willow Lawn Drive

Richmond, VA 23230
(804) 282-4255

Parent to Parent—Parent Support
Group
2110 Avenel Ave.
Roanoke, VA 24015
(703) 774-3636

Parent to Parent—Roanoke Valley
3020 Mansfield St.
Roanoke, VA 24012
(703) 366-3551

Parents of Children with Down
Syndrome Parent Outreach
451 Orchard St.
Vienna, VA 22180
(703) 281-1211

Washington

Parent to Parent Support
425 Park Ridge Rd.
Bellingham, WA 98225
(206) 679-8919

Parent to Parent Support Group
3243 N. Perry Ave.
Bremerton, WA 98310
(206) 377-3473

Parent to Parent Support Prog.
P.O. Box 602
Everett, WA 98206
(206) 258-2459

Parent to Parent
P.O. Box 276
Leavenworth, WA 98807
(509) 663-6001

Parent to Parent Support Program
for Thurston Co.
4228 Amber Court, SE
Olympia, WA 98501
(206) 352-1656

Parent to Parent Support Program
1009 Georgiana St.
Port Angeles, WA 98362
(206) 457-8355

Parent to Parent Support Program
2230 Eighth Ave.
Seattle, WA 98121
(206) 461-7834

Cleft Connection
110 Prefontaine Place South, Suite
500
Seattle, WA 98104
(206) 296-4610

Family Empowerment Project
12208 Pacific Highway, SW
Tacoma, WA 98499
(206) 588-1741

Pierce Co. Parent to Parent
12208 Pacific Highway, SW
Tacoma, WA 98499
(206) 588-1741

West Virginia

Autism Services Center
Pritchard Building, Suite 907
605 Ninth St.
P.O. Box 507
Huntington, WV 25710-0507
(304) 525-8014

West Virginia Head Injury Foundation
P.O. Box 574
Institute, WV 25112-0574
(304) 766-4892

Wisconsin

Pilot Parents
Route 2
P.O. Box 434
Ashland, WI 54806
(715) 682-6647

Brown County ARC
P.O. Box 12770
Green Bay, WI 54307-2770
(414) 498-2599

D.E.A.F.
P.O. Box 1825
Green Bay, WI 54305-5825
(414) 437-7531

Mothers United for Moral Support
150 Custer Court
Green Bay, WI 54301
(414) 336-5333

Wee-Life Parents
4215 Rodney Drive
Lodi, WI 53555
(608) 592-4648

Dane County AMI
101 E. Mifflin St.
Madison, WI 53703
(608) 262-4400

Cleft Lip & Palate Helpline
2808 E. Newton Ave.
Milwaukee, WI 53211
(414) 962-1053

Parent to Parent-ARC
818 Sixth St.
Racine, WI 53403
(414) 634-6303

Wyoming

National Fragile X Association
P.O. Box 1759
Worland, WY 82401
(307) 347-9465

Assistive Technology Resource Centers

This list of resource centers throughout the United States was supplied by the Alliance for Technology Access, 1128 Solano Avenue, Albany, CA 94706-1888; (510) 528-0747; Fax (510) 528-0746. For additional information on any of the aspects of assistive or augmentative communication technology discussed in Chapter 13, contact the center in your state. Note that some may be contacted not only by telephone but by AppleLink and by fax.

Alabama

Birmingham Alliance for Technology Access Center
Birmingham Independent Living Center
3421 5th Ave. South
Birmingham, AL 35222
205/251-2223 or 251-0863
Judy Roy
AppleLink: BILC

Technology Assistance for Special Consumers
P.O. Box 443
Huntsville, AL 35804
205/532-5996
Pamela Harnden
AppleLink: TASC
Fax #: 205/532-5994

Alaska

Alaska Center for Adaptive Technology
700 Katlian, Suite B
Sitka, AK 99835
907/747-6962;   800/478-6962 (AK)
Mark Jacobina
AppleLink: ACAT

Arkansas

Technology Resource Center
c/o Arkansas Easter Seal Society
2801 Lee Ave.
Little Rock, AR 72205
501/663-8331
Ginny Heiple
AppleLink: TRC

California

Computer Access Center
2425 16th St., Room 23
Santa Monica, CA 90405
310/450-8827
Donna Dutton
AppleLink: CAC.SM

DCCG-Technology Resources for People with Disabilities
2547 8th St., 12-A
Berkeley, CA 94710
510/841-3224
Lisa Wahl
AppleLink: DCCG
Fax #: 510/841-7956

Special Awareness Computer Center
Rehabilitation Center
2975 North Sycamore Dr.
Simi Valley, CA 93065
805/582-1881
Suzanne Feit
AppleLink: SACC

Special Technology Center
590 Castro St.
Mountain View, CA 94041
415/961-6789
Lisa Cohn
AppleLink: STC
Fax #: 415/961-6775

Team of Advocates for Special Kids
100 W. Cerritos
Anaheim, CA 92805
714/533-TASK

Sharon Nieves
AppleLink: TASK

Colorado

AccessAbility Resource Center
1056 East 19th Ave., B-410
Denver, CO 80218-1088
303/861-6250
Ann Grady
AppleLink: AARC

Florida

Computer CITE
15 E. New Hampshire St.
Orlando, FL 32804
407/898-2483
Carol Adams
AppleLink: CITE
Fax #: 407/895-5255

Georgia

Tech-Able
1040 Irwin Bridge Rd.
Conyers, GA 30207
404/922-6768
Lynn S. Chiu
AppleLink: TECHABLE
Fax #: 404/922-9813

Hawaii

Aloha Special Technology Access
Center
1750 Kalakaua Ave. #1008
Honolulu, HI 96826
808/955-4464
Eric Arveson
AppleLink: ALOHASTAC

Illinois

Northern Illinois Center for Adaptive Technology
3615 Louisiana Rd.
Rockford, IL 61108
815/229-2163
David Grass
AppleLink: ILCAT

Technical Aids & Assistance for the Disabled Center
1950 West Roosevelt
Chicago, IL 60608
312/421-3373
Margaret Pfrommer
AppleLink: TAAD

Kansas

Technology Resources for Special People
3023 Canterbury
Salina, KS 67401
913/827-0301
Dawn Merriman
AppleLink: TRSP

Kentucky

Blue Grass Technology Center for People with Disabilities
894 Georgetown St.
Lexington, KY 40511
606/255-9951
Jean Isaacs
AppleLink: BLUEGRASS

Disabled Citizens Computer Center
Louisville Free Public Library

4th and York Sts.
Louisville, KY 40203
502/561-8637
Mary Ellen Harned
AppleLink: DCCC
Fax #: 502/561-8657

SpeciaLink
36 W. 5th St.
Covington, KY 41011
606/491-2464
Walter & Elaine Hackett
AppleLink: SPECIALINK

Louisiana

CATER-Center for Adaptive Technology and Educational Resources
1636 Toledano St., Suite 311
New Orleans, LA 70115-4598
504/899-8375;   800/75-CATER (LA)
Sandra Cunningham
AppleLink: CATER

Maine

Maine Parent Federation
P.O. Box 2067
Augusta, ME 04338-2067
207/582-2504
Margaret Squires
AppleLink: MPF

Maryland

Learning Independence Through Computers, Inc.
28 E. Ostend St., Suite 140
Baltimore, MD 21230
410/659-5462

Mary Salkever
AppleLink: LINC
Fax #: 410/539-2087

Massachusetts

Massachusetts Special Technology Access Center
12 Mudge Way, 1–6
Bedford, MA 01730
617/275-2446
Mary Zupkus
AppleLink: MASTAC

Michigan

Living & Learning Resource Centre
Physically Impaired Association of Mich.
601 W. Maple St.
Lansing, MI 48906
517/487-0883; 800/833-1996 (MI)
Donna Heiner
AppleLink: LLRCPIAM
Fax #: 517/371-5898

Minnesota

PACER Center, Inc.
4826 Chicago Ave. South
Minneapolis, MN 55417-1055
612/827-2966 (voice or TDD)
Judy Simon
AppleLink: PACER.CTR

Missouri

Technology Access Center
12110 Clayton Rd.
St. Louis, MO 63131
314/569-8404 or 8100

Nancy Lacey
AppleLink: TACSTL
Fax #: 314/993-5937

Montana

Parents, Let's Unite for Kids
1500 N. 30th St.
Billings, MT 59101-0298
406/657-2055
Katharin Kelker
AppleLink: PLUK

Nevada

Nevada Technology Center
2880 East Flamingo Rd., Suite A
Las Vegas, NV 89121
702/735-2922
Bruce McAnnany
AppleLink: NTC

New Jersey

The Center for Enabling Technology
9 Whippany Rd.
P.O. Box 272
Whippany, NJ 07981
201/428-1455
Cathy Tamburello
AppleLink: CET

Computer Center for People with disAbilities
c/o Family Resource Associates, Inc.
35 Haddon Ave.
Shrewsbury, NJ 07702
201/747-5310
Joanne Castellano
AppleLink: CCDA

New York

Techspress
Resource Center for Independent Living
409 Columbia St.
Utica, NY 13502
315/797-4642 (voice or TDD)
Russ Holland
AppleLink: TECHSPRESS
Fax #: 315/797-4747

North Carolina

Carolina Computer Access Center
Metro School
700 East Second St.
Charlotte, NC 28202
704/342-3004
Judy Timms
AppleLink: CCAC
Fax #: 704/342-3004

North Dakota

Pathfinder Parent Training and Information Center
ATA Computer Resource Center
1600 2nd Ave. SW
Minot, ND 58701
701/852-9426; 701/852-9436
Kathryn Erickson
AppleLink: Pathfinder
Fax #: 701/838-9324

Ohio

Technology Resource Center, Inc.: Enabling People with Disabilities
2140 Arbor Blvd.
Dayton, OH 45439-1510

513/294-8086
Pat Cashdollar / Terry Trzaska
AppleLink: CARS

Oregon

Oregon Outback Technology Access Center
P.O. Box 2916
La Grande, OR 97850
503/962-7258
Julie Farnam / Steve Clements
AppleLink: OUTBACK

Tennessee

East Tennessee Special Technology Access Center, Inc.
5719 Kingston Pike
Knoxville, TN 37919
615/584-4465
Lois Symington
AppleLink: EASTTN

Technology Access Center of Middle Tennessee
Fountain Square, Suite 126
2222 Metro Center Blvd.
Nashville, TN 37228
615/248-6733
Bob Kibler
AppleLink: TAC
Fax #: 615/259-2536

West Tennessee Special Technology Resource Center
Lambuth College
Carney Johnston Hall
401 Maple St., P.O. Box 3683

Jackson, TN 38303
901/424-9089 or 90
Margaret Doumitt
AppleLink: WESTTN
Fax #: 901/424-9090

Texas

SHIP Resource Center
University United Methodist Church
5084 DeZavala Rd.
San Antonio, TX 78249
512/699-1137
Jackye Guzley
AppleLink: SHIP
Fax #: 512/696-7723

Utah

Computer Center for Citizens with Disabilities
401 Twelfth Ave., Suite 114
Salt Lake City, UT 84103
801/321-5770
Craig Boogaard
AppleLink: CCCD

Virginia

Tidewater Center for Technology Access
Special Education Annex
273 N. Witchduck Rd.
Virginia Beach, VA 23462
804/473-5106
Cindy Storm
AppleLink: TCTA

Washington

Seattle Technology Alliance for
Resources and Training
257 100th Ave. NE
Bellevue, WA 98004
206/637-9848
Grant Lord
AppleLink: START
Fax #: 206/450-0767

West Virginia

Project G.L.U.E.
c/o Children's Therapy Clinic
2345 Chesterfield Ave.
Charleston, WV 25304
304/342-6501
Margaret McGarrity
AppleLink: GLUE

Self-Help Clearinghouses in the United States and Canada

The following list was provided by the American Self-Help Clearinghouse, St. Clares-Riverside Medical Center, Denville, NJ 07834; (201) 625-7101; TDD (201) 625-9053. Staff and volunteers provide current information and contacts for any national self-help groups that deal with the caller's particular concern. If no appropriate national group exists, information can often be provided on model groups operating in other parts of the country, or individuals attempting to start such networks. For "Ideas for Starting a Self-Help Group," send a self-addressed stamped envelope. The Self-Sourcebook ($10) provides information and contacts for more than 600 national and model groups.

Self-Help Clearinghouses in the United States

California* 1-800-222-LINK (in CA only); for verification, call (213) 825-1799
Connecticut (203) 789-7645
Illinois* 1-800-322-M.A.S.H. (in IL); recently closed—call (708) 328-0470 for update
Iowa 1-800-383-4777 (in Iowa); (515) 576-5870

Kansas 1-800-445-0116 (in KS); (316) 689-3843
Massachusetts (413) 545-2313
Michigan* 1-800-752-5858 (in MI); (517) 484-7373
Minnesota (612) 224-1133
Missouri, Kansas City (816) 561-HELP
Nebraska (402) 476-9668
New Jersey 1-800-FOR-M.A.S.H. (in NJ); (201) 625-9565
NY—Brooklyn (718) 875-1420

NY—Long Island
(516) 348-3030
NY—Westchester*
(914) 347-3620
NY State—(call Westchester for referral only to other local clearinghouses in the State)
NC—Mecklenberg area
(704) 331-9500
Ohio—Dayton area
(513) 225-3004
Oregon—Portland area
(503) 222-5555
PA—Pittsburgh area
(412) 261-5363
PA—Scranton area
(717) 961-1234
Rhode Island (401) 277-2231
SC—Midlands area
(803) 791-9227
TN—Knoxville area
(615) 584-6736
Texas* (512) 454-3706
Greater Washington, DC
(703) 941-LINK
*maintains listings of additional local clearinghouses operating within that state.

for national U.S. listings and directories:
American Self-Help Clearinghouse (201) 625-7101;
TDD 625-9053;
National Self-Help Clearinghouse
(212) 642-2944.

Self-Help Clearinghouses in Canada

Calgary (403) 262-1117
Halifax (902) 422-5831
Saskatchewan (306) 652-7817
Toronto (416) 487-4512
Vancouver (604) 731-7781
Winnipeg (204) 589-5500 or
633-5955

National newsletter, *Initiative*
(613) 728-1865 (C.C.S.D. in Ottawa)

Other Helpful Organizations

Alliance of Genetic Support Groups (genetic illnesses), in U.S. 1-800-336-GENE
National Organization for Rare Disorders, in U.S.
1-800-999-N.O.R.D.
O.D.P.H.P. National Health Information Clearinghouse, in U.S. 1-800-336-4797

Appendix C

Further Acknowledgments

Our gratitude goes to the many organizations and publications that helped to get our questionnaire into the hands of parents nationwide. With thanks to the others as well, those who made us aware of their assistance, either directly or through participating parents, include the following:

- Alexander Graham Bell Association for the Deaf
- American Council for the Blind and *The Braille Forum*
- American Foundation for the Blind
- Association for Children and Adults with Learning Disabilities and *ACLD Newsbriefs*
- Association for Children with Down Syndrome, Long Island, New York
- Associations for Retarded Citizens in *California: Alameda County New Jersey: Somerset, Sussex, and Union Counties New York: Westchester County Pennsylvania: Bucks County*
- The Barclay School, Atlanta, Georgia
- Children's Specialized Hospital, Mountainside, New Jersey

- Disabled American Veterans, National Amputation Chapter No. 76, Whitestone, New York, and *The Amp*
- Epilepsy Foundation of America
- Epilepsy Foundation of New Jersey
- *Gaucher's Disease Registry Newsletter*
- International Association of Parents of the Deaf and *The Endeavor*
- Jefferson Township (New Jersey) Public Schools
- Louisiana Center for Cerebral Palsy and Developmental Disabilities, New Orleans
- National Association of Parents of the Visually Impaired
- National Association of Private Residential Facilities for the Mentally Retarded and *Links*
- National Federation of the Blind Parents' Group and *Future Reflections*
- National Network of Parent Coalitions
- National Society for Children and Adults with Autism
- New York Association for the Learning Disabled and *The News*
- New York Institute for the Education of the Blind
- Newton (Massachusetts) Public Schools
- Northern State College Department of Special Education and Communications Disorders, Aberdeen, South Dakota, and *People with Special Needs/Down Syndrome Report*
- Overlook Hospital, Summit, New Jersey
- Parent Advocates for the Visually Impaired of Colorado
- Parent Information Center, Concord, New Hampshire
- Parents of Handicapped Children, Camden, New Jersey
- Parents' Support Group, Haskell, New Jersey
- Shawnee Mission (Kansas) Medical Center
- South Metropolitan Association for Low-Incidence Handicapped, Harvey, Illinois
- Spaulding for Children, Westfield, New Jersey
- Spina Bifida Association of America
- Summit (New Jersey) Hearing School
- TASK: Team of Advocates for Special Kids, Orange, California
- Union County (New Jersey) Association for Children with Learning Disabilities
- United Cerebral Palsy chapters: California: Contra Costa/Alameda, The North Bay and San Mateo/Santa Clara; Maine; New Jersey: Union County; New York: New York City
- Webster Avenue Family Resource Center, Rochester, New York
- *The Matilda Ziegler Magazine for the Blind*

Index